Labor-Religion Prophet: The Times and Life of Harry F. Ward

AIS Retrospections Series

The Humanistic Teachings of Earl S. Johnson, Earl S. Johnson, edited by John D. Haas

AIS Forum Series

The Optimum Utilization of Knowledge: Making Knowledge Serve Human Betterment, edited by Kenneth E. Boulding and Lawrence Senesh

Barriers to Integrity: Modern Modes of Knowledge Utilization, Donna H. Kerr

About the Book and Author

Labor-Religion Prophet:
The Times and Life of Harry F. Ward

Eugene P. Link

As first national chairman of the American Civil Liberties Union, the first professor of Christian ethics at both Boston University and Union Theological Seminary, and a pioneer of dialogs between religion and Marxism, Harry F. Ward led a life marked with many milestones. An advocate of the working-class and the underprivileged, Ward avoided the doctrinaire approach often associated with the institutional church, choosing to emphasize the compatible humanitarian concerns shared by both labor and religion. *The Social Creed of the Churches*, which he wrote in 1907, was the first significant religious document written in the United States to confront industrialism; that treatise and the trade unions established the basis and provided the atmosphere for the reforms of the New Deal.

In this, the first biography of Harry F. Ward, Eugene Link stresses a social historical approach. He draws extensively from the Ward family archives to paint a rich portrait of the most prominent and controversial proponent of the social applications of Christianity in the early twentieth century.

Eugene P. Link is professor emeritus of history at State University of New York, Plattsburgh. Dr. Link began his association with Harry Ward as a student at Union Theological Seminary in the 1930s; when Dr. Link married, Harry Ward performed the ceremony. In the course of his career, Dr. Link has served as a Fulbright Lecturer in India, as dean of social sciences for SUNY-New Paltz, and as chairman of the sociology department for the University of Denver.

Labor-Religion Prophet: The Times and Life of Harry F. Ward

Eugene P. Link

With a foreword by Corliss Lamont and illustrations by Lynd Ward

Westview Press / Boulder, Colorado

Academy of Independent Scholars Retrospections Series

Copyright © 1984 by Westview Press, Inc.

Published in 1984 in the United States of America by
Westview Press, Inc.
5500 Central Avenue
Boulder, Colorado 80301
Frederick A. Praeger, President and Publisher

Library of Congress Cataloging in Publication Data
Link, Eugene P., 1907–
  Labor-religion prophet.
  (Academy of Independent Scholars retrospections series)
  Bibliography: p.
  Includes index.
  1. Ward, Harry F. (Harry Frederick), 1873–1966. 2. Church and labor—United States—History. 3. Church and social problems—United States—History. 4. Sociology, Christian—United States—History. I. Title. II. Series.
HD6338.2.U5L55   1983   261.8′34562′0924   83-17108
ISBN 0-86531-621-X

Printed and bound in the United States of America

To the students of Harry F. Ward,
in and out of the Church,
who have joined his Wild Pilgrimage
in search of the more sustaining community.

Contents

Figures

Foreword

In the continuing and increasingly intense struggles during the twentieth century for civil liberties, democracy, social justice, and international peace, Dr. Harry F. Ward (1873–1966) stands out as one of America's most militant and effective individuals. Living until ninety-three, he remained active to the end, like his great fellow nonagenarians, John Dewey, Alexander Meiklejohn, and Bertrand Russell.

Dr. Ward early made a name for himself as an eloquent minister in the church, stressing that the clergy should be actively concerned with social and economic issues. So it was that he was one of the founders in 1907 of the Methodist Federation for Social Service (later Social Action). When in 1953 the House Un-American Activities Committee smeared Dr. Ward as a Communist conspirator, he answered by stating: "My judgments and actions concerning political and economic issues are derived from the basic ethical principles of the religion of Jesus, of which I am a minister and teacher." Dr. Ward's position enabled him to cooperate fruitfully with naturalistic Humanists like myself and many others fighting for the Good Society.

Thus in 1920 he became the stalwart chairman of the Board of Directors of the American Civil Liberties Union, a post he held until 1940. He resigned at that time in protest over the ACLU's disgraceful Communist purge resolution, which led directly to the expulsion of Elizabeth Gurley Flynn because she was a member of the Communist party (the expulsion was rescinded posthumously in 1976). From the time I became a director of the ACLU in 1932, I worked closely with Dr. Ward and later dedicated to his memory *The Trial of Elizabeth Gurley Flynn by the A.C.L.U.*, a book that I edited. It was always a pleasure and a privilege to be associated with him.

For some seven decades Harry Ward unceasingly worked for the building of a better world. From 1934 to 1940 he was chairman of the American League for Peace and Democracy and later became an outspoken opponent of the unforgivable American aggression in Vietnam. At the same time he wrote influential books presenting his mature views on economics and politics, including *The Bible and Social Living* (1916), *Our Economic Morality* (1930), and *Democracy and Social Change* (1940). He also published three volumes about the Soviet Union, where he had traveled extensively. The best known of these is *In Place of Profit* (1933). Meanwhile Dr. Ward produced numberless pamphlets as well as articles for such progressive journals as the *Christian Century* and the *Churchman*.

As some acquaintance with Dr. Ward's various writings makes clear, he gradually came to believe not only that the capitalist system was a failure in an economic sense but also that its crude and often cruel functioning violated the ethics of Jesus by elevating personal monetary profit as a person's chief aim instead of brotherly love and the welfare of the community. In 1950 he stated:

> The most urgent moral imperative of our times is the need to accomplish the transition from capitalism to socialist society now under way in a considerable portion of the earth without another world war. This imperative derives its urgency from the discovery and use of more and more powerful weapons of mass killing and total destruction, including the destruction of the basic moral values which mankind has so painfully gained. This situation means that judgment day has come for all governments, economic systems and religions.

In this statement Dr. Ward had in mind the entire world, so much of which he knew at firsthand through his travels to Europe, Soviet Russia, India, China, and Japan. He considered himself both a good American and a world citizen.

We must not forget that Dr. Ward was a forceful teacher both as a minister at church occasions and as an established professor of Social Service at Boston University, 1913–1918, and professor of Christian Ethics at Union Theological Seminary, 1918–1941.

He was a somewhat slender and frail-looking man—reminding me of Gandhi—yet a clear and dynamic speaker. At his ninetieth-birthday celebration in Carnegie Hall he spoke for a whole hour.

Dr. Ward's signal success in providing leadership and inspiration to American dissidents was fully attested by the extreme hostility towards him of the Federal Bureau of Investigation (FBI). The Ward dossier, recently obtained by the Methodist Federation for Social Action under the Freedom of Information act, shows that FBI Director J. Edgar Hoover in 1943 placed Ward's name on a list for "custodial detention" as a security risk in case of a national emergency and kept it there for the rest of his life.

Harry Ward's enormous influence through his public life was of course supplemented by the person-to-person inspiration that he gave. He and I exchanged visits occasionally, with me going to see him at his simple home across the Hudson in Palisades, New Jersey. There we talked freely and intimately. Richard Morford, executive director emeritus of the National Council of American-Soviet Friendship, describes the atmosphere: "To enjoy luncheon in the alcove with Mrs. Ward pouring tea and Dr. Ward serving the bread which he himself regularly baked. To walk in the garden, when spring spading was in progress, when early summer brought the roses into their glory, and when, in the fall, Dr. Ward tenderly prepared all the plants for the winter rest. To sit before the fireplace listening to stories of earlier adventures."

Professor Link's biography of Harry F. Ward is particularly relevant during these unhappy times when Reaganism is proving an even worse threat to social justice in the United States than was McCarthyism and in addition is menacing the entire world. This book, reviving the memory of one of America's truly great crusaders, will serve to stimulate and strengthen those who are resisting and striving to overcome the evil policies and deeds of our federal government.

Corliss Lamont

Preface

The weight of this sad time
we must obey;
Speak what we feel, and not
what we ought to say.
—William Shakespeare
(King Lear)

Harry Frederick Ward was a compelling figure in the first fifty years of this century and in the overall history of our country. Most readers probably have not heard of him for historical reasons. He cannot be labeled with ease and because he was carelessly labeled, he became a historical casualty. The intent of this book is to present Ward's socially perceptive, analytical mind, his ideas, his centrality of purpose, his courage, and his contribution to American life and culture as they emerged in a society that, for the most part, was unprepared to consider him with rationality. I also hope to fill gaps in our church and social history that will help the reader understand the goals of many laboring and religious persons in the first half of the twentieth century.

Ward's central concern was for people—working people on farms, in factories, and in mines, although he did not exclude others whose rights were violated. Because he chose to defend workers and minorities, he became the victim of unmerciful attacks, virulent curses combined with attempts to ignore, belittle, or misrepresent his words and actions. These were the easiest ways to dispose of a controversial, prophetic figure.

Of course, Ward was not alone in suffering during the Dies and McCarthy cold-war periods, from which we have not yet recovered. His distinctiveness came from the directness and clarity of his ideas, ideas that will have to be dealt with in the dilemma that is sure to come—the division of the world's goods among all of the world's people.

Whereas most minor heroes of the Labor-Religion tradition lie buried in the leaves of history, there has been a renaissance in the study of political economy that has brought forth books describing the greater leaders and movements for social change in the first half of the nineteen hundreds. Ward's students were involved in direct ways in so many of these movements. Frank Adams's *Unearthing Seeds of Fire* (263),* about the Highlander Folk School, was published in 1975. The school's founder and guide was Myles Horton, who has acknowledged Ward as the source of much of his inspiration. Thomas Krueger, historian at the University of Illinois, has written of the work of James Dombrowski and the Southern Conference for Human Welfare in *And Promises to Keep* (288). Dombrowski was Ward's student at Union Theological Seminary and his graduate assistant. Frank Adams is now working on a biography of Dombrowski. A less adequate book, but one marking the new trend in research of and recognition for writers in the "people," or the "antiestablishment" tradition, is Tony Dunbar's *Against the Grain* (276). As these investigations accumulate, the almost inseparable relationship between Religion and Labor will emerge. Spirit and bread, faith and work actually cannot be divided. Scholars in the disciplines of sociology and the history of religion have recognized this fact and have noted the tendency of sociologists to associate directly or indirectly with the labor movement as a religious as well as a scientific activity. Many seminarians, in like fashion, have found a basis for their religious convictions in supporting the arduous efforts of working people to achieve a sense of personhood. Pope John Paul II has internationalized this view in his encyclical on human work.

The historians who have dealt with this interaction between Labor and Religion have distinguished the differences between the "moral majority," with its pious absolutes seeking personal salvation, and the deeper religious experience woven into the more profound processes of history. In the latter purview, incarnate

---

*Throughout this book, numbers in parentheses refer to listings in the Bibliography.

deity (the people) chiseled orderly, ethical social experience on tablets of stone for a Hammurabic or an Asokan code, or a Ten Commandments. We can also note how many useless decalogues dealing with priestly pedantry were forerunners of the great ethical Mosaic Code dealing almost exclusively with human relations; yet it survived oblivion. Neither timeless nor changeless, such codes must be adapted to new situations. In 1907, in the United States, the Social Creed of the Churches emerged, and the spokesperson was Harry Frederick Ward.

This person was an unusual embodiment of the Labor-Religion interaction: He combined the two social forces into one process, one drive in his life. He was not simply another "social gospel" preacher who bifurcated work and faith, as most church and social historians have categorized him. Rather his unusual philosophy made him a human being with broad concerns and extensive fields of influence.

This book traces the conditions that fostered the Social Creed (a taproot of the Religion-Labor dialogue) and the influence of Ward on its origin and subsequent development. Several historians believe this to be the groundwork for the New Deal. If the labor unions of the nation pressured for the principles in the New Deal legislation, and of course they did, they were encouraged by many church people and the Student Christian Movement in the colleges and universities, which had been inspired by Ward's writings on how to implement the creed. In the name of Christian Ethics, these groups, indirectly at times, came to the aid of the trade unions by setting up a favorable climate of opinion. The unions could not have succeeded alone.

Equally important, and perhaps more so, was that portion of the Labor-Religion coalition in which Ward played a dramatic role as chairman of the board during the first two decades of the American Civil Liberties Union (ACLU). Mary Van Kleeck, director of Women in Industry, U.S. Department of Labor and one-time president of the International Conference on Social Work, always referred to Ward as "the *first president* of the ACLU." She felt so strongly about his leadership role—he was definitely more than chairman to her. Ward, the first professor of Social Service at the Boston School of Theology and afterwards the first professor of Christian Ethics at Union Theological Seminary, felt that violations of the civil rights of laborers were most destructive to the body politic. If allowed to go unchallenged, such repression would inevitably, he thought, spread upward to destroy democratic procedures in education and government generally. The New York City office of the American Civil Liberties Union was, in a pragmatic sense, Ward's church.

Ward's involvement with the League Against War and Fascism, his experimentalism in fashioning a new society in this country called New America, and his exploration of the first proletarian government in the world—the Union of Soviet Socialist Republics—are also described in this book. The League, which appears to be the first and last united front in U.S. history, brought out Ward's skills as an organizer and his practice of involving working people and their organizations as well as religionists of every persuasion.

In attempting to discover Ward's impact on history, one would quickly think of the Theology of Liberation, which is widely current in the Western world. Because this body, largely of the Catholic faith, is concerned with civil rights, revolutions, and Marxism just as Ward was, one might wonder about the differences between it and the Social Christianity of Ward—certainly, both bond religion and labor. This book makes suggestions on why the two movements have not as yet joined forces fully.

Ward's family of "procreation" as well as "orientation" seems to demonstrate his unity of purpose and action. The family was a microcosm of society: Labor, production, recreation, even income was a sharing, communistic, Christian experience. It dominated Ward's vision and hope for all human beings. The family constellation and its interrelations are discussed throughout the book. In present-day historiography, family contexts are often omitted, minimized, or treated only tangentially. Personal behavior and public activity are to be kept in opposite pockets. This antipodal approach is rigidly preserved in the Soviet Union. The two superpowers for once seem to find an agreement in separating the personal life from citizenship roles. Any thought that as a person is in his *home*, so is he, seems unacceptable. Also unacceptable is Buddha's caveat that as a person is in his *work*, so is he. However, I have used the family context of "the social self" because it is logical and it is loyal to the pragmatic philosophy of Ward. His lifelong friend George A. Coe wrote, "It is impossible to be alone with God," and his contemporary John Dewey shared that sense of social responsibility when he wrote, "There is no such thing as a 'private act.'" Personal interviews and family papers were made fully available to me; the Ward family made no attempt to hide anything or to censor anything.

The ideology reflected in this book, the reader may suspect by now, is conditioned by the philosophic pragmatism of George Herbert Mead. It is called variously these days "symbolic interactionism," "Meadism," or "social behaviorism." Mead and Ward, who were friends in Chicago, agreed that this approach tends to remove the mystical or heroic interpretation of a biographee. "Setting" and "process" are concepts important to this methodology, hence the subtitle *The Times and Life of Harry F. Ward*.

The primary source for the biography was the Ward papers in the library of Union Theological Seminary in New York City and Ward's published writings. The extensive family letters were in file folders, for the most part, each labeled to indicate major activities and organizations (viz., "Federation," "ACLU," "New America," "UCCD," "roses," "birthdays," and so on) in which Ward and his family were involved. A selected bibliography of secondary sources and manuscript collections, a list of personal interviews, and a definitive bibliography of Ward's writings (assembled with the help of a bibliography compiled by Herbert Aptheker in 1968) are at the end of the book. Some citations are in the text of the book itself, and small parenthetical numbers refer to sources in the bibliography. My intention has been to avoid an appearance of pedantry to a layman, a trade unionist, or a member of the clergy who glances at this book and at the same time to give the social historian some guidance to the sources. Unless otherwise noted, all quotations from Harry Ward came from writings in his papers or private interviews with him and members of his family.

Harry Ward deserves to be known among a wide spectrum of people—those whose roots are deep in religious conviction, those whose identity with workers and producers of the world is close, those who believe in collective action and cooperation to achieve more social justice, and those who affirm Carlyle's "eternal yea" that life, not death, is the better act of faith.

*   *   *

In looking back over a life of teaching and research I must thank again and again the staffs of the libraries of America. The War and Peace Collection of Stanford University, the Peace Collection at Swarthmore College, the American Civil Liberties Union collection at Princeton University, and the Thomas Amlie and William Gorham Rice papers in the State Historical Society of Wisconsin Library were all made available to me by courteous and helpful librarians. The seminary libraries of Yale (George A. Coe papers), Harvard Divinity, Boston School of Theology, and Drew Seminary (Madison, New Jersey; the complete files of the *Social Questions Bulletin*) deserve special thanks.

Also, in an exceptional way, I am indebted to Union Theological Seminary Library where I studied the Ward papers for many months and to my own State University Library at Plattsburgh. Here the librarians retrieved books, papers, and filmstrips through interlibrary loans, provided a private carrel for me, and were unstinting with time and energy.

The State University Research Foundation of New York provided me with three grants. The Harry F. Ward Memorial Fund held by the Methodist Federation for Social Action assisted me with typing and Xerox costs. George McClain, director of the Federation, has provided steady encouragement for my work.

My history colleagues Douglas Skopp and George Pasti read several chapters for me. Their comments helped clarify topics in their fields of expertise. Principal readers of the entire manuscript, Lee H. Ball and Arnold Johnson, both of whom were students of Ward and familiar with his life and thought, also helped me enormously. Shirley Kent Gorton (formerly Mrs. Rockwell Kent) also made insightful comments on several chapters. The descendants of Harry Ward—his two sons, their wives, and his granddaughters—have been generously supportive. Gordon and Margaret Ward read the manuscript, made several editorial suggestions, and made family stories more accurate. Lynd and May McNeer Ward read the manuscript and were candid and enlightening in their interviews recalling the memories of "Dad." May counseled, "You must describe 'Dad' as you found him to be. It is your book—not ours or any of your readers." This advice was appreciated. The author accepts the responsibility for any errors and for the interpretation of the facts as he has come to understand them.

The Academy of Independent Scholars of the University of Colorado at Boulder provided specific, effective aid in getting the book published. The academy has the meritorious purpose of supporting retired scholars who wish to continue writing and being published. The old academic oyster bound in a hard shell, constrained in flaccidity and opaqueness, often hides a pearl of great surprise when writing as he pleases. I hope this book will in some fashion fulfill that promise.

The original wood engravings used in this book were done by Lynd Ward. All but two of them first appeared in his impressive novel *Wild Pilgrimage*, published in 1932. The eighty-nine engravings that carried the message of that book were dedicated "to my father, who sees these things with a clearer eye." Lynd Ward's engravings and murals have become widely known in the art world; recent awards and honors continue to attest to Mr. Ward's talent and work. The permission given by the Ward family to use these engravings is deeply appreciated.

And finally, my wife of forty-five years, Beulah Meyer Link, has been a steadfast friend and useful sharp critic during all the stages of the book. For my Fidelio, these lines:

Florestan: My Leonora, what you have done for me.
Leonora: It is nothing, dearest Florestan.

As Florestan knew it was, in fact, everything, so do I.

Eugene P. Link

The Prophet. (Photo by Nanda Ward.)

1
Preparatory Years

> *The Gospel of Christ knows no religion but social,*
> *no holiness but social holiness.*
> —John Wesley (1739)

"Hardy Country" in England begins to the east of 5 Queens Row, Turnham Green, District of Brentford, County of Middlesex, where Harry Ward, Jr., was born into a Methodist home on October 15, 1873. This boy grew up to become one of the most, if not the most, controversial clergyman in American history. On but two shoulders he carried three heavy burdens: a sharp challenge to the growing military-industrial complex with its profit motivation; a wide-ranging defense of labor and its organizations; and a Christian Ethics stance that saw the first two issues as resolved in the Soviet Union, the world's first socialist state.

With the exception of receiving his name from his staunchly "free church" father, who had ancestors from Ireland, neither the ethnic influences of his mother's French people nor those of the Irish had much to do with the conditioning of Harry or his siblings. It appears that the textures of the more-immediate social situation were of greater importance.

His father was a businessman at 272 High Road in nearby Chiswick. "Harry Ward, Butcher and Provisions Merchant" read the sign over the shop. The business was so thriving and successful that he had to hire "shop assistants." In addition to his business, Harry, Sr., was a Methodist lay preacher, widely acclaimed according to a citation in an album given to Harry, Jr., on his departure to the United States in 1890.

A letter preserved in the Ward papers at Union Seminary (11)*

---

*As noted in the Preface, reference numbers in parentheses refer to listings in the Bibliography.

2

reveals more of the dedicated Wesleyan Methodism of the home. In a letter Harry, Sr., wrote to his son in 1891 he described the death of his wife, Florence Jeffrey Ward, only forty-two years old, who had left the Church of England after her marriage to become a devout Methodist. His father explained that on the day of her death, it was "so foggy it made her breathing difficult." In fact, it was "so foggy [he] couldn't display [his] Christmas goods" in his store windows. She suffered dreadfully as the end came nearer, prayed to die, and sang a Wesleyan hymn, "All Ye That Pass By," with her husband and the minister. Then she whispered, "I have seen the gates of Heaven." Some of her relatives came "but none to say a word of comfort." She was a "rebel."

In addition to the forceful religious atmosphere that dominated the home, the father's business activities influenced the son so much that he wrote of these later. The thriving business required all the energies of Harry's father and long hours from the shop assistants—fourteen hours a day. The workers at one time organized a protest and Harry, Sr., sprinkled soapy water and flour on them from an upstairs window. They were refused the twelve-hour day, and the workers continued to label their shopkeeper a "sweater." It is significant that among the papers Harry, Jr., preserved was a flier that berated his father's working conditions. Perhaps it affected his conscience so much that he joined a union and spent a lifetime opposing "sweating" and exploitation.

Harry's help in the shop began early. He recalled that at age fifteen he drove to Covent Garden to get vegetables or down to the docks on the Thames River to get cheese. Handling the horses that pulled the dray became one of his early skills, and the aggressiveness of other drivers forced the boy to fight like a modern taxi driver for a place in line to pick up provisions for his father's shop. In addition to sides of beef, wheels of cheese, and vegetables, young Ward hauled live Belgian hares and pigs, which had to be slaughtered on arrival by one of the hired men. The suffering and slow dying of the animals distressed the lad so much that he was given a small gun to deliver a coup de grace to the half-dead creatures. Many have said that in later life he combined this tender-harsh behavior. Once he shot himself in the hand, resulting in a serious wound. Could his drayman's experiences of competition for recognition have resulted in his becoming somewhat of a daredevil? His taking risks in driving horses resulted in his father keeping him home for a time. This thread of risk taking in the social fabric of rebels appears repeatedly in Ward's life.

Some rebellious act at the end of his fifteenth year probably was the reason for his father sending him to a boys' school. Like many such English schools of the nineteenth century, it was a stern institution with harsh physical conditions, including bad food. The experience had several effects. It might explain his later resentment for social classes, because the school was for sons of tradesmen who were not permitted in the upper-class "public school," where clothing, speech, and manners were different and more prestigious. A rheumatic heart condition developed, which he lived with for many years. A positive outcome of this illness, however, was young Ward's being sent to live with aunts in the more salubrious climate of Lyndhurst. This woodland area, called New Forest, was abundant with oaks, beeches, beautiful scenery, and a variety of wildlife. Ward spoke often of this pleasant sojourn in Lyndhurst, the place that aroused his life-long love of flowers, trees, and the out-of-doors. The Test River, renowned for its trout fishing, was nearby, and Ward developed an expertise used throughout his life to provide food on extended hikes into the wilderness. A final compliment to this sojourn came years later when he honored the memory of the area by naming a son "Lynd."

When Harry Ward was seventeen years old, he emigrated to the United States. A desire for a university education was responsible for his leaving England, for as a tradesman's son he could not enter an institution worthy of his manifest alertness and ability. England with its class system had never accepted the Jeffersonian philosophy of the *inalienable* rights of men and women as expressed in the Declaration of Independence. "Equality" and "rights" tend to be hollow nouns by which to swear in every corner of the globe, even in countries where discrimination is outlawed. In America the founding fathers and the nation's historical experience have brought the nouns a little more into action, into people's blood and marrow, so that in a greater degree than elsewhere social class is minimized. Ward came, as millions of others had, to gain an inalienable right to learn and know. This opportunity impressed him profoundly in later life as he dealt with the need for drastic social change worldwide and at home with blacks, foreign born, women, and other minorities.

The people of the Methodist Chapel of young Harry Ward's village presented the seventeen-year-old lad with a photograph album of close friends and important local people. The inscription read "to H. Ward, Jun. who has for some time been a local preacher in the Wesleyan connexion and has assisted the work in the mission band and as a deputy class leader."

Fortunately, Ward had an uncle living in Utah who could help him just as his aunts had at Lyndhurst. In May 1891, Harry arrived at 316 South Main Street, the home of Hugh Ward in Salt Lake City, and soon found himself driving horses again! It was a welcome chore because of his skill and love for animals. For a few months he lived with another uncle, an Idaho farmer. These experiences made a deep imprint on him. He loved the ruggedness of the work and climate, and the courage of the western people, especially the cowboys, filled him with such admiration that in later years he presented copies of Zane Grey stories to his children as gifts.

The youthful Ward did other types of work to earn a living. He continued lay preaching in Utah with what was called "street work," rather like the Salvation Army, preaching on street corners. This was the beginning of his constant wish to reach out to those who seldom, if ever, entered the church. His mission went beyond Wesley's central desire to convert "the lost." By effort, he hoped to awaken the smug "Christians" in their snug sanctuaries to the condition of their less-favored human beings. It is interesting, too, that he was for a time secretary to the Mormon Board of Education, without being a Mormon, and a chaplain at the local army post.

Harry Ward began to fulfill his American dream when he entered the University of Southern California in Los Angeles in 1893. There he met a teacher, George Albert Coe, who profoundly affected his life. Coe left at the end of the year—it is said because of student hooliganism—to teach at Northwestern University.

The story persists in the Ward family that the entire freshman class actually was expelled for pranks committed during classes and that Ward himself was caught in that action. In any case, the great respect Ward had for his philosopher-teacher caused him to follow Coe to Northwestern, a university founded by a Methodist physician, John Evans. The influence of this pioneer is reflected in the name Evanston, Illinois, as well as in the lofty Mount Evans in Colorado near which he founded the University of Denver.

The confluence of a Wesleyan social-holiness background and the pragmatic mind of George Coe molded Harry Ward's thought in a profound way. In fact, the social passion of the Wesleys interacting with what Coe called the "scientific method" gave rise in the two young men (Coe was only a few years older than Ward) to a continuing process of mutual exploration of theories and appropriate actions to be taken. One author has written that Ward's Evangelical Methodism caused him to accept the perfectibility of human nature, but that is a little erroneous. The Methodists gave Ward John Wesley's concern for the poor and the slave and the faith that human effort could bring about change. However, when this drive merged with the pragmatism of the Chicago environs of which Coe was a part, the immutable instincts and the concept of a fixed human nature began to disappear in favor of the more-dynamic theory of the "social self arising in experience."

This milieu for Ward's thought and action surrounded him on all sides. In later life it would help him avoid the Niebuhrian impasse of original sin or the human-nature view, which supports the dualistic position of the Social Gospel—that individual salvation and social ethics are two different entities. The Coe-Ward interaction is of central concern in this book because it represents not only a dynamic social view but also an optimistic and rational religious drive.

Another professor at Northwestern, John Henry Gray, made an extraordinary impression on Ward and was later to become an intimate friend of the Ward family. He was called "Uncle John" by the children, as Coe was called "Uncle George." Ward majored in philosophy under Gray and minored in political science under Coe. Gray brought a third emphasis into Ward's life, namely a sharp criticism of capitalism and its rowdy individualism. The student was now hearing of Karl Marx.

Gray believed that unions must flourish and eventually must share in the management of all enterprises in order to be countervailing regulators of industry. It was Gray who suggested that his student read *The Social Aspects of Christianity* (277) by Richard Ely, a well-known professor of Economics at the University of Wisconsin. Ely believed that Christianity was largely of this world, and its task was to build the kingdom of righteousness on earth. The Second Commandment declared that to love one's neighbors was tantamount to loving God. The book, with the elaborations and additions of Gray, became a critique of an unjust economic order and its corrupting profit motive. It made Ward seriously consider for the first time what subjects should be taught in a school of theology—less theology, more economics and social science.

Other skills that came out of his college experience were to serve Ward as he began to formulate the central purposes of his life. He became interested in, and was successful at, forensics. In a debate with Pomona College in 1893, Ward presented the case for education not being a qualification for voting. His argument was an early expression of "learning by doing," in which he said that one learns to vote by voting, not necessarily by reading and writing. The process of voting led one into learning just as surely as formal education did. (The argument was most useful in Third World countries after World War II when independence and democracy essentially forced voting upon millions of illiterate people.) In other words, action was an expression of freedom and it preceded learning. John Dewey later carefully explained and defended this theory in his book *Democracy and Education* (1916).

At Northwestern the intercollegiate debate that drew large crowds was the one between Northwestern and Michigan. The governor of Michigan presided one year, and the next year Adlai Stevenson, Sr., vice-president of the United States, introduced "Harry Ward of Los Angeles, California" as the third speaker for the negative on the issue of building the Panama Canal. Northwestern won and the third speaker received the highest ratings of the evening on both "argument" and "delivery."

Figure 1.1 *Harry F. Ward as a debater, Northwestern University, 1897. Daisy's "dear heart." (Ward family photo collection.)*

Special achievement was acknowledged for his oratory by the Northern Oratorical League. This led to invitations to deliver lectures for which he received a little money. The president of Northwestern, Henry Wade Rogers, also recommended Ward as a fluent speaker. Ward's topics included some figures he had greatly admired, such as "The Hero of Khartoum," sometimes known as General George ("Chinese") Gordon, an idealistic fighter and martyr for the triumph of the British Empire. He seems a strange hero for this young orator soon to become a sharp critic of imperialism, yet Gordon and Rudyard Kipling were at that time in Ward's pantheon for their rugged courage in the face of great odds, for their dreams of better days, and—in Gordon's case—for sacrificing his life for his beliefs. Ward named the older of his sons after Gordon. Antonio Maceo, another hero about whom young Ward lectured, was quite different from the two Englishmen. Maceo is still an honored revolutionary in modern Cuba, acclaimed for his struggle between 1868 and 1870 to give blacks equal rights and to win independence from Spain. Ward's hero worship was a maturing process. Throughout, he admired persons with clear purpose and fortitude. In some respects he absorbed the virtues and life-styles of people whom he admired and praised.

Cricket and tennis were his favorite sports at Northwestern, and other student activities rounded off his education. In his junior year he was president of the student YMCA, and in his senior year his abilities in philosophy were so outstanding George Coe offered him remuneration to read and grade logic papers.

John Gray noted the Harvard Club of Chicago was offering a one-year scholarship in 1897 and urged his student to apply. Gray, Coe, and Northwestern's President Rogers lent their written support, bringing the opportunity to earn a Master's degree to the young man.

The year in Philosophy at Harvard was a crowning one. Like philosopher George Herbert Mead, who became a philosopher at the University of Chicago ten years earlier, Ward absorbed the thinking of William James and deliberated the works of Josiah Royce. Like Mead he became a student friend of the James family, although not a babysitter for the children as Mead had been. One A paper was "A Synopsis of Herbert Spencer's Data on

Figure 1.2 *Harry F. Ward as captain of the tennis team at Northwestern University, 1897. (Ward family photo collection.)*

Ethics" written in 1897. Later he wrote "A Synopsis of T. H. Green's Prologomena with Comments" and "The Authority of Society over the Individual." This latter paper included the arresting sentence, "The only voice to be obeyed is the voice of the ideal of individual realization." One can sense a mind developing and inquiring.

It seems there are cycles every thirty, fifty, or seventy years when young scholars, particularly philosophers, tend to wear long hair, a moustache, or beard. Possibly they wish to avoid quick identification or to hurry the maturation process. Whatever the cause, young philosopher Ward had a moustache and long hair during the fall and winter of 1897. In spring he wrote to Daisy Kendall, his Northwestern girl friend, that he had cut off the moustache so that he could "feel like a white man," a jarring phrase from an individual who resisted all forms of racism.

Ward's activities during the impressive year at Harvard included writing love letters to Daisy—in which he often enclosed a well-written romantic poem—sports, and diligent study. His grades were four A's and one B+ in Philosophy and an A in Government.

In the spring of 1897, Daisy Kendall[1] had agreed to meet Harry Ward for a set or two on a Northwestern University tennis court. This was their first date. Her family were Methodists in Kansas City, Missouri, where her father became wealthy in the manufacturing of shoes. Her suitor, however, was poor, almost indigent, needing extra money to fulfill his marriage plans.

Daisy and Harry graduated in 1897 and she went back home. The courtship was carried on with letters between Kansas City and Harvard. These were pleasant, old-fashioned letters, free from the excessive, unrealistic romanticism of that time and certainly free of the equally unrealistic eroticism of the present. Amazingly, none of their letters used pious clichés. Harry would use "if the Gods permit" and both closed at first with "Sincerely," then "Ever," then "Ever yours," and finally with "Love."

Besides tennis, they discovered a mutual joy in fresh, brisk air, the sea and sky, the sun, mountains, and hills—all the earth's plants and creatures. Before pollution was rampant, they agreed there was "no lewdness in a stream, no poison in sparkling water." They played checkers and dominoes together all their lives, with Harry insisting that "she usually won." Others have said Daisy had a talent for games and puzzles. They played card games called "Trees," "Wild Flowers," "Roses" (a flower Harry specialized in growing), "Authors," "Musicians of Different Nations," and "Symphonies." Their children joined in as they became old enough.

Neither cared for opera. Harry thought it was a show-off place for the idle rich and a lot of upper-class nonsense without social significance. When radio came into the home Harry followed baseball and heavyweight boxing; Daisy chided him gently for his interest in "cruel fisticuffs." Both opposed profanity because it was wrong to curse a fellow human being. Gambling, too, was dismissed, not because of Methodist command, but because "it took from the common good without labor." Alcohol of any kind was taboo because it ruined the robust good health they both cherished.

Daisy was five-foot-two in her favorite low-heeled shoes, had large blue eyes, medium-brown hair, and a round "muffin" face, to use the classification of a personality psychologist. A little chubby at marriage, her tendency to become more so brought from her mate occasional serious comments and urges to exercise. Harry was five-foot-nine with, in medical terms, "a high forehead, blue eyes, large nose, regular mouth, small chin, chestnut hair, fair complexion and a long face," or as the psychologist tagged the other half of the human race, a "horse face."

To earn money in order to marry, Harry turned to his pen, which had helped him to write clearly for debates and for his essays and orations. This time he wrote poetry in a Kipling manner. One of his efforts called "The Awkward Squad" praised the students who refused to be lured into the college social set. "The War Cry of Greed" was an antiwar poem he signed as "Hotspur." This was probably to indicate he had no fear of stirring up lions. It is not certain whether he was able to sell these controversial poems, although he was remarkably successful with adventure stories, which he sold to *The Black Cat* magazine.[2] He also sold "Duck Shooting in Comfort" to *Outing* for the April 1899 issue. More lectures on General "Chinese" Gordon added to the prospective marital fund, which finally reached a sufficient size for a wedding in 1899.

Shortly after the wedding, Daisy received an exhilarating letter from Bishop John Vincent about a speech her new husband made at a national meeting of Methodists in St. Louis. Another prominent Methodist, Jesse B. Young, also heard the speech and wrote a letter to Daisy's father praising the discourse abundantly.

Harry, or Hal as Daisy called him privately, cherished her in so many ways. Their interaction was an ideal example of complementary action. For example, "I can manage horses, but not machines," said Hotspur Ward. So Daisy did all the car driving. Neither would he try to repair the car. It chugged along for years with repairs and driving done by the woman at the wheel.

Two years after Harry Ward and Daisy Kendall were married they spent a three-month delayed honeymoon in England, Scotland, Ireland, and Switzerland. His diary, careful and detailed, gives information and impressions of his English boyhood. Much of the tour was by bicycle through the south and west of England, over to Ireland by boat, then to Scotland and North England and on to Switzerland, returning by way of Norwich and Cambridge. The new bride thought the adventure a bit of an endurance contest, especially after she fell from her bicycle on one of the Blackdown Hills.

Several entries mention Ward relatives scattered over counties from Greater London to Somerset, the two aunts in Lyndhurst, Aunt Tilly's inn in Burley, Sandy-Down ("grandfather's old home"), Boldse Church and its graves of great-grandfather and wife, and Cadman "where grandfather lived." At Salisbury, he noted visiting with great Aunt Matilda, the "last of her generation of Wards."

Impressions and observations were illustrated by photographs, and reports were made on the weather and on the varieties of flowers and trees in the lush English countryside. At some places Harry felt he had to exhibit to his spouse his skills in fishing for trout and hunting rabbits. No doubt can be raised that he was an outdoor man who loved nature in its limitless facets or that this love originated in his native England, long before he came to America.

Notes

1. Daisy's given name was Harriet Mae Kendall. Her father had insisted on the name, but her mother disliked it and called her "Daisy," which prevailed.

2. Contributors to this magazine had national reputations. Albert Biglow Paine, Jack London, and W. M. Stannard are examples. *The Black Cat* sold for five cents a copy.

2
The Little Minister in Vibrant Chicago

> *There is only one religion, though*
> *there are a hundred versions of it.*
> —G. B. Shaw

> *Sup sorrow with the poor.*
> —Canon S. A. Barnett,
> Founder of Toynbee Hall

Jane Addams once called Harry Ward "my little minister." He earned this salutation as he was being molded by the bold city of Chicago at the turn of the century. Chicago was described by Carl Sandburg as having "big shoulders," whose "painted girls lure the farm boys under the street lights."[1] However, a long list of persons in Chicago—philosophers, novelists, poets, architects, painters, and thinkers like Darrow, Debs, and Ward—were concerned with reform and social change. They were revolting against the oppression of mind and body by an expanding, urban industrialism.

Charles Merriam's refreshing views on political science and Albion Small's new "sociology" were University-of-Chicago products. The Settlement House movement, aimed at relieving the suffering and deprivation of those caught in slums, began at Oxford University in England, where students and faculty organized Toynbee Hall to aid the poor in East London. The social ferment spread as far away as Tokyo and was the inspiration for the second settlement house in the United States, Jane Addams's Hull House of Chicago.[2]

George Herbert Mead, also of the University of Chicago, was asserting that because human nature is malleable "it ought to be possible" to reform and change all aspects of society. Since there was no "human nature" for a scapegoat, nor was "original sin" available for the church, government had no justification by science to allow slums and poverty or to incarcerate and kill. Religion that preached hell for a sinning "self" gave way to the disturbing thought that all of us are collectively responsible for the individual "social self" that can be "saved" only by society approximating something nearer to the Kingdom of God on earth. While Theodore Dreiser in his *An American Tragedy* of 1925 had sought to detail the social nature of Clyde Griffiths, the lad of the slums who was created by society to commit murder, Jane Addams had tried to prevent this tragedy by more-enlightened social services. It was a time of volcanic eruption in our history and its dust drifted beyond the nation's borders, bringing ideas that questioned absolutes of all varieties about human nature, its instincts, and its rigid institutional expressions. All this and more was in the air that the young Ward breathed.

The "little minister" turned down an offer of his professor friend, John Gray, to teach economics at Northwestern. He accepted instead the offer to become the second head resident of the Northwestern Settlement House in 1898. The house was founded in 1891, the third one after the Neighborhood Guild on the Lower East Side of New York City on this continent. Hull House was the second. The creative Scot, Patrick Geddes, had started a similar institution at Edinburgh University and called it University House. Some in Chicago wanted to call theirs by that name also; others wanted it to be Kingsley House in honor of Charles Kingsley, one of the founders of this tremendous movement, but Northwestern Settlement House prevailed.

Why did Ward join the settlement movement? Since he never attended a theological seminary he was not qualified to take a church minister's position; taking Methodist "Conference Studies" while he managed the settlement house would lead to his certification as a minister. Another reason was his interest in and concern for expanding the walls of the church to include the surrounding community. He hoped to awaken the church to a new day. He was beginning to think of the Social Gospel as one—beginning to question the dichotomy of the gospel into an evangelical personal salvation on the one hand and the Social Gospel on the other. There was but one gospel—the social. The settlement house was therefore a kind of church for him.

A prominent shirt manufacturer in Chicago, noting this ideal of Ward's, sponsored with the aid of the Chicago City Mission Society what one might call a street church. The community, however, seemed too diverse, with its mixture of impoverished Poles, Germans, and Scandinavians, to effect any kind of unity. Women and children tended to come but not the men. This troubled Ward, especially when he discovered one of the chief reasons: The workmen objected to corporation heads giving money for pie-in-the-sky religion instead of giving it for better wages and working conditions. To involve labor in the church no celestial-aspirin theology would suffice. Young Ward made meaningful involvement with labor a cardinal principle for the church for the rest of his years.

Within one block of the Chicago Settlement House (University of Chicago) of Mary McDowell, Ward and Daisy watched Graham Taylor's efforts to get wary workers into his church. Preaching from a springboard wagon in the slum streets, each Sunday he moved closer to his church door. Then, on a rainy day, he invited his followers in. Despite all Taylor's sympathy and effort the ploy really did not work, and as Taylor himself wrote, "Jesus remained in the streets."

The Wards tried to get more Northwestern students to give time and effort to the settlement by inspiring them to follow the ideals of Wesley, Kingsley, and Maurice, as well as the "unto the least" pleas of Ruskin. It was difficult to keep the students' Kingsley Club active, and Ward himself became president to give stronger leadership. He formed "a good baseball team" and developed a settlement news sheet called "The Neighbor." Daisy, as secretary of the Home Culture Club, kept accurate membership rolls and distributed information. She did so well that both Elizabeth Cady Stanton and Frances E. Willard stopped by to give lectures to her club.

Trouble arose. A touch of anarchist philosophy seemed to have influenced some of the council members of the Northwestern Settlement House. Like the Students for a Democratic Society in the sixties, they wanted no entrenched leaders, no head resident; rather they held that the institution would function best by house meetings. A head, as a fount of authority, would be fatal, for how could one person know all important matters first hand?

The critics maintained that the council, not an individual, must administrate and take charge of finances.

Ward became a victim of this view and was summarily dismissed as head resident on May 29, 1890. In a reply to the council's action, he noted the unfairness of such a sudden decision supported only by charges of misunderstandings and implications of his unsuitability to carry on settlement work.

Needless to say, the two Wards were stunned. At once they went to their faculty friends, George Coe and John Gray, and got their immediate support. Then Ward wrote the reasons, as he saw them, for the abrupt action. First, as the head resident of Northwestern Settlement House, he bore the responsibility for smooth operations but was in fact constantly bypassed or overridden by people outside the house. Secondly, a member of his staff was "fired" by these "outsiders" without his knowledge. Thirdly, special interests were interfering to push him out. Fourthly, Mrs. Harold McCormick (of the famous McCormicks of Chicago) would not give money to the boys' work program until the "mess things were in was corrected." Ward had wished to rectify all this and felt he could have, as it was one of the few times in his life he had wealth and power like the McCormicks' defending him. What really hurt the young couple was that "uncharitable and unfellowship" action put a "stigma of dismissal" on the two so early in their lives.

The stigma had little effect, however, because the young man had been serving as a lay preacher in the Wabash Avenue Methodist Church from 1900 to 1902 and now was qualified to become a fully accredited minister. Ward was certified to preach in 1902 by the Rock River Conference, where he retained his membership throughout the rest of his life.

The first Methodist churches he served were the Wabash Avenue (1900–1902) and the Forty-Seventh Street (1902–1904) in the Chicago slums. He practiced the open-air style of preaching on the streets—in America called "field preaching"—after the example of Graham Taylor and the distinctive Methodist tradition of Charles and John Wesley and George Whitfield.

The Wards' home was here in "the reeking odors of the garbage dumps, the dirt and squalor surrounding this church"—they were not commuting do-gooders dodging reality. A businessman in the Forty-Seventh Street church, Mr. W. H. Burn, became irritated and wrote to say things were not going well and there was criticism. "After your first Sunday I was plainly given to understand that the appointment was not satisfactory," he wrote (11), adding that he had offered Ward some suggestions, but criticisms persisted. More time should be spent mingling with the parish people instead of with outsiders; another criticism, the insistence that Ward should have been personally acquainted at all times with church financial affairs, had overtones of the settlement house crisis. Possibly Mr. Burn was telling Ward to give his efforts to the loyal ones in "the shadow of the fold" and their circumscribed local church financial problems.

In 1904 Ward was transferred and became minister of the Union Avenue Methodist Church. His longest pastoral tenure was here, nearly six years. Upton Sinclair was actively writing to advance reform at the time. He knew Ward and acknowledged his good work several times in his writing.[3] Graham Taylor, Raymond Robbins, and others of good intent were also active, coming to the aid of those victimized by John J. Coughlin, popularly known as Bathhouse John, with his corrupt political practices. The destitute faces and twisted bodies and minds caused by the greed of a few was George Mead's "significant other" for the rising self of Harry Ward. Theodore Dreiser was writing his observations and experiences and producing characters that revealed his protest and rage over a society that created a Sister Carrie. James T. Farrell would be coming along.

Ideas about socialism were permeating the thinking of the larger and smaller community. Workers were organizing unions that hailed the brotherly and sisterly commonwealth—a type of government they hoped would bring them relief from long hours and low pay. Even the middle classes in the smaller textile, coal, and steel towns were sympathizing with workers' plights and job actions. The writers, poets, and intellectuals joined in criticisms of capitalism. More people voted for Henry George for president on a platform of property income tax, more read Edward Bellamy's *Looking Backward* (published in 1888) and formed "Nationalist" and "Social Science Clubs" than is mentioned in most contemporary history texts. There were Socialist congressmen, governors of states, and mayors of cities, as well as a socialistic Populist movement. The Populists were so numerous that the northeastern trust manipulators became fearful that the movement might unite the poor blacks and whites of the South and the West against the monopolies. Social Gospel ministers preached in the pulpit that one's soul was in danger of hell fire if the cruelty to the wretched continued.

These Union Avenue Church years are most important in many ways to an understanding of Ward's life, philosophy, and un-recognized contribution to the awakening of the consciences of religious adherents in America. His decision to extend this awak-ening—to make it a life goal—came just after the turn of the century, and his Chicago church experience confirmed and strengthened it. His expressed aim, however, was to eliminate the dichotomy between progress and poverty, to forward one gospel: the building of the Kingdom on earth.

What did he preach and how did he behave in his slum church sanctuary? His sermons were typed, for doubtless he had trouble reading his own tiny, difficult handwriting while at the pulpit. They were filed in labeled envelopes that listed on the front when and where he had used them. All of them, almost without exception, dealt with the burning social issues of the time. Semiliterate Polish, German, and Italian immigrants were his neighbors. In simple English he gave relevancy to topics like "Aliens and Americans," "The Unemployed," and "The Citizen and the Primary." When he talked to his congregation about cleaning up the city, a subject that brought a cruel beating by thugs to his fellow minister, Raymond Robbins, he was courting trouble. "Christianity and the Anarchist" was a sermon in which he sought to explain Emma Goldman and her colorful hobo-physician-paramour Ben Reitman, who also identified with and sought to help the lowliest on the Chicago class ladder. Ward furthermore praised Lincoln, as indicated by the February-twelfth envelope in his archives containing several sermons related to the Emancipator and to slavery. "Lincoln and the Black Man" was one. Throughout the sermon he used "Black man," not "Negro," as if he sensed the revolt to come sixty years later. One such sermon begins "The Black man is the great sufferer of history." Children's sermons were frequent. Now and then, in good Methodist tradition, he gave sermons on temperance in which he attacked the saloon as a destroyer of family income, pleaded for "local option" because liquor was a soporific for workers and should be banned from the district, and grew righteously indignant at the employing of small children in and around the bars. Sometimes he preached of his beloved out-of-doors, and sometimes he used "Song Sermons" in which his sentences were interspersed with illustrative hymns.

The Union Avenue Church also had a busy program to be carried on by the Wards. Two services were held on Sunday, as well as a children's church at two-thirty, a men's program at three-thirty, and Epworth League for young people at six-thirty, just before the evening "call to worship." During the week there were women's meetings, gymnasium programs, and a prayer meeting each Wednesday evening. These were standard activities in most evangelical churches no matter the denomination. What was far from standard was the substantive quality inserted into them by the young preacher who went outside his sanctuary for involvements that kept his messages factual and pertinent. "Sociology," he wrote, "is the antidote to sectarianism" (57).

Christian Sociology was a name often given to the churchly endeavors of which Ward was a part. Some have written that its greatest exponent was Walter Rauschenbusch, who was a dozen years Ward's senior. This writer of prayers, hymns, and prolabor sermons for the workers visited the Wards in their modest stockyards-district home in 1907 to preach and to speak at labor rallies. The two men became fast friends, with Ward and Rauschenbusch carrying on long discussions when either was at the other's home. Though these occasions were infrequent, because Rochester, New York, was far away, their meetings were not unlike the more extended dialogues of Coe and Ward later at Lonely Lake. Despite the barriers of distance, the two were friends until Rauschenbusch's death in 1918.

Ward found that he could extend his Christian Sociology by becoming involved with the famous City Club of Chicago. This organization was preceded by the Chicago Civic Federation, formed by such men as William T. Stead, a crusading British journalist who in 1894 wrote *If Christ Came to Chicago*; Albion Small, who trained for the ministry and organized the first sociology department in the United States; and the street preacher,

Graham Taylor, who later became a sociologist in the Chicago Theological Seminary. Whether or not Ward joined the Civic Federation cannot be precisely determined, but notes and brochures about the federation are in his papers. Ward knew the men and women in it. He shared the views of Albion Small on the unethical nature of private property and talked with him on occasion about Karl Marx.

Ward did become an active member of the City Club of Chicago. This organization had a broad base of interested citizens with goals of "community improvement" and the "promotion of public welfare." Well-known members were the self-labeled "curmudgeon" and probably our most enlightened secretary of the interior, Harold Ickes; Jane Addams; Charles E. Merriam, the pioneer political scientist at the University of Chicago; Mary McDowell, social worker; and George Herbert Mead, assistant professor of Philosophy at the University of Chicago. Most graduate schools in social science or philosophy today present the "symbolic interactionism" of Mead, but very few seem to know or mention his activity in social reform and the labor movement. Mead served several years as chairman of the Standing Committee on Labor Conditions of the City Club and wrote a philosophical paper defending trade unions. Ward was a member of this committee for six years (1904–1910), serving part of his tenure as chairman.[4] In this capacity he rallied the entire City Club to support the protected-machinery bill that he had been lobbying for in Springfield, the state capital. His Labor Committee gave support for aiding and educating neglected children, mentioning the Chicago newsboys who were on the streets hungry and mistreated and slept in alleys. His articles were published in the *Union Labor Advocate*, and Ward also had them appear in the *Methodist*.

Out of this interaction socialism appeared to become for many of these persons a realistic—in a time of growing realism—theory of gradual social progress. The ethics of the idea, they insisted, were identical with Christianity. These friends, colleagues, and admirers were coming to accept Jesus, as the Wards did, as a carpenter, a workman, "the son of man" as all persons could be. Their summary of capitalism was Richard Ely's "To the biggest beast the biggest bone" (277). They felt that all men should earn their bread by the sweat of their brow and those who would not work ("sweat out greediness" as a modern Chinese writer exhorts) should not eat. Harry Ward's sermons expressed these sentiments as well as the ideas John Dewey philosophically stated in defending Margaret Haley's teachers' union in Chicago. In Ward's words, "The Labor Movement was the most advanced point at which the divine energy was operating in the higher evolution of man" (64). If the church was to minister well it must identify itself closely with people who labor and produce. There was divine energy, he thought, in their labor, their reforms, and their organizations. On several occasions, his wife called him "the man with singleness of purpose."

When men or women center on a search for the grail, their family, friends, and health often suffer. Harry Ward had generally robust health as a result of his relations with nature, experiencing its drama, beauty, and invigoration. His love for rugged outdoor activities such as camping, building, canoeing, fishing, and gardening, all came to his rescue when he did overdrive himself. When his health was breaking in the energy-sapping stockyards' church, his physician warned that once every year he must have a two-months "complete vacation." Stirred by the insistence of this medical advice, he wrote a letter to the Canadian government Department of Lands, which owned a vast acreage of wilderness, giving an approximation of his needs. He wanted lakes, hills, woods, and a guide. Between one Sunday sermon and the next in the summer of 1904 he made his pioneering trip to the place called Lonely Lake, near Echo Bay, Ontario. Immediately, the Mormon mantel-words of Brigham Young, "This is the place," assumed living light for him. Mormons consider "the place," first Salt Lake and then their individual home, sacred; so Lonely Lake became a special retreat for the Wards. Because the cost was only fifty cents an acre, enough land could be purchased to prevent crowding. Since the family was the first to settle in the remote area, Ward had the idea of inviting one or two of his closest friends to purchase land nearby. And who might these be? Yes, "Uncle George" Coe and "Uncle John" Gray, as they were soon called. In 1904 it was necessary to travel a rough wagon road from the railroad to the foot of Lonely Lake to arrive at their isolated woodland home.

Figure 2.1 *From Lynd Ward's Wild Pilgrimage.*

Long before Mao Tse-tung instituted the practice that intellectuals could learn much and keep clearer heads by returning at times to labor with the providers of food, clothing, and shelter, Ward thought of his Lonely Lake experiences as a work-ethic opportunity. A course in carpentry and cabinet making at Chicago's Rush Institute in 1900 had helped prepare him. At Lonely Lake roughly half of each day, five to six hours, was devoted to manual work such as putting the roof on a comfortably large log house, installing windows and doors, and putting down hardwood floors. This was followed by building cabinets and furniture inside the house, planting a large garden, and chopping and splitting wood for a cookstove and fireplace. The second half of the day was designated for "play," which included fishing, reading, playing games, hiking, and later music with son Lynd using the accordian for song fests. Included, of course, was an abundance of good talk among the family members, including the children. The select neighbors were often part of the story telling and serious evening discussions.

John Gray was there. In later years he introduced a note of pessimism occasionally and expressed feelings of being glad to be away from "the corporation ridden, politically infested" Warren Harding world, but yet concluded how "exciting to live in this age, if not very inspiring." George Coe, whose wife had died in 1905, found his cabin in the Lonely Lake woods a rest and the discussions a refreshment. Representative of his part in the high-level deliberations was an answer to "What is religion?" Several evenings later "Uncle George" came back with "Religion is a valuation principle which operates through a whole spectrum of values. It is an ever new and vital process." John Dewey was insisting that democracy at best is a process, a way of thinking and acting. Coe suggested that religion was much the same.

This continued summer after summer for almost forty years, philosophical punctuations between efforts to find the seeds and fruit trees that would grow in the far north and learn how to care for them. When Coe came into the evening of his life he was almost totally deaf. But his use of a hearing aid meant that the discussions could continue, sometimes out in the center of the lake, away from children's romps and other digressions. One chilly afternoon, with their knitted wool caps in place, Ward had to shout, with Coe answering in the same manner. They were working on some Marxian ideas and everyone in the three cabins of the Shangri-la knew Methodist pietism was giving way to Marxist theories.

There seemed to be good humor too, enjoyed by everyone. Daisy called to Hal on one occasion to say Uncle Josh Ward from Utah was coming for a visit. Dislike for impractical visitors at the retreat was reflected in the levity of the answer: "Better tell him to learn to row a boat." Professor James C. Bonbright, a member of the Columbia University faculty and another close friend of the Wards, reported a yarn spun by a fishing party of six of them on a week's excursion to remote lakes. Dr. Gordon Ward, the older son, was a participant in the event and has written the story as follows:

Six friends, among whom were . . . Ward and son Gordon . . . paddled across Bass Lake and portaged over to Island Lake where they camped to fish for grey lake trout. One day they went over to the far side of Patten Lake to a farm for fresh vegetables, eggs, and milk. There they saw a bear skin tacked to the wall of the barn for curing.

Upon enquiry, it was learned that the father and grown son . . . had been over to Stuart Lake on a patrol and seen a yearling bear which they had shot. Since the fur was in good condition, they had skinned the carcass without bothering to skin out the feet and claws. Dad knew from experience that young bear meat is as good eating as beef. So he decided to go get some of the meat. . . . Fred Sheets Junior offered to go with him.

[When they found] the bear carcass, Dad cut off the loin steak meat and the rump roasts and round steaks from the legs and wrapped it and put it in packsacks to carry back to camp along with the four paws with their claws. . . .

On the way home to Lonely Lake the group concocted a tall tale to account for there being no feet with claws on the bear skin. They told that Dad and young Fred Sheets had gone over to Stuart Lake to catch some bass for their supper. At one point they placed the boat alongside a big pine tree trunk that had fallen over and extended out on top of the water so both could fish at the same time. Dad hooked a good sized bass that jumped several times and thrashed on the surface of the lake as he tried to land it without a net. Just then, Fred Junior heard a grunt and saw a black bear on the log just back of Dad reaching out pawing the air trying to get the fish flopping on top of the water. Fred instantly pulled his single shot 22 pistol from the holster on his belt and shot. . . . The bear toppled over into the water and enraged, clawed at the gunwale of the boat trying to get at the men. They fended off the slashing paws with their hunting knives until Fred could reload his pistol. Then, taking careful aim . . . he put a bullet in the brain and the bear collapsed. They dragged the carcass out on the shore and Dad butchered the desirable cuts for meals in camp and for the folks at home. Dad declared that Fred had saved his life by killing the bear with his pistol. (11)

Told in decorated details upon arrival home that evening with bear paws as exhibit A, the womenfolk were half convinced. Daisy thanked Fred for his marksmanship and gave him a cheek kiss. Then the truth came out. The chagrined women doused the men with buckets of water and threw pillows at them as they ducked behind trees.

Horseplay there was, woven into the fabric of pleasant and constructive activities at the rugged retreat. Ward knew how to do many things of interest to children: to find the way to the spring with its water of cool and special taste; to go on longer and longer hikes with bars of chocolate, crackers, and raisins in their pockets; to fish and untangle a line patiently; to observe woodsmen who, like the Indians, know how to carry an axe through the woods; to blaze trails to sparkling lakes; and to learn how to read for wisdom by not reading too much, hence leaving space for musing.

He had urged his "Dear Miss Kendall" in 1895 to read Robert Louis Stevenson, and in 1896 sent her books for her birthday, some humorous, some grave and for "staunch weapons in the great conflict." He always seemed to be instructing his wife, the children, later their mates, and in time, the grandchildren. Added to this was, "find time for recreation with all-round development." By 1925 he wrote "too much reading spoils thinking." By 1932 he was more convinced that when he read too much in preparation for his classes "my mind feels like a sewer."

The Lonely Lake years spanned three generations of Wards, and it is little wonder they feel the lake to be almost a sacred

Figure 2.2 *Daisy and Harry Ward with their children at the family summer place on Lonely Lake, 1908. (Ward family photo collection.)*

place. Those favored by being invited for a visit left knowing that the calloused hands of a competent carpenter, with some help from family and friends, had built the shelters, the cabinets, and the furniture. They knew that from these activities lasting impressions had formed, building themselves into their lifelong values.

Ward wrote "The Call of Lonely Lake" in 1908:

There's a call come down from the North today
With the whirr of the wild-goose wing;
It whispered softly at my desk
On the street I heard it sing.
Who calls? The cabin on the hill
Whose great logs stand with folded arms
To guard my sleep.
The wide hearth in the twilight, reaching hand
Of light and cheer across the shadows deep
The hills along the shore—those wondrous greens!
 Who laid
Them clear to far horizon, shade on shade.
Come away, come away.

Who calls? The rhythm of the dripping oar, the pull
　of straining sail.
The ease of the pack well-hung, the joy of the new made trail.
The plunge in the deep cool tide, the ring of the axe swung true
The lure of the distant lake, the glide of the lithe canoe
The calm and gentle converse of the trees,
Making plain to man the ancient mysteries—
They're all a calling. Loud they say
"Fling far the worry and the care
Come and play in the open air,
Come away, come away." (11)

At this point, Ward's personal attitudes, prejudices, and familial interactions may be understood further by a study of the letters he wrote home and Daisy's replies during Ward's long trip around the world in 1908–1909. It had become a possibility because a wealthy Methodist in Chicago wanted a secretary and companion for such a sojourn. Moreover, Ward had been ill, probably from overwork. Living among the underprivileged, jammed as they were into the inhospitable derelictions of the industrial megalopolis, he spoke of an excruciating "pain in the neck." This could have been sociosomatic. Could the trials of the streets with the crudities and cruelties and their cancerlike spread be responsible for wracking a neck? Hardly was it the locale for a contemplative man who loved fresh air and the beauties of nature. Or could it have been the confusion of three small children around, as exasperating to many meticulous philosophers as Xantippe was to the pondering Socrates? Whatever the cause, he accepted the invitation.

Daisy went to California to live with her mother and took the three children: Gordon, the oldest, aged five; Lynd, whose family baby name was Bunting, aged three; and Muriel, in her first year. Daisy received fifty dollars a month from her husband's writings; the steady inflow came from the *Epworth Herald* and the Sunday School teaching aids. On shipboard Ward wrote poetry and articles in an attempt to increase the family income.

The letters to Daisy found in the Ward papers at Union expressed sorrow in leaving her alone with three children. He missed them and he "got seasick often." That it was important to be properly dressed for dinner in First Class with his wealthy host troubled his conscience. He wore a blue shirt and was indirectly reminded of it by the social looking glass of formal Britishers who had already isolated the Americans at a special table. "I wish I had traveled second class," wrote Ward.

There were many comments on the people he saw and the wonders he visited. "The coliseum dwarfs St. Peters," he noted in Rome. The imposing stadium was symbolic to him of the dominance of the material over the spiritual in Western society. This dualistic note, still a factor in his thinking, tended to disappear as he became older. He resented the "fakes" in Jerusalem perpetrated by Jews, Muslims, and most disappointing of all, by Christians.

Probably the visit to India had the most profound effect on his feelings. India—its ancient customs, the use of cow dung, some practices unhygienic to Western eyes, the spicy food—created a culture shock as it does to most first visitors. The poverty confronted on all sides he took in a manner deeper than sympathy, approaching empathy combined with anger. He noted the tropical flowers, trees, and birds of India. He refused, however, to enter "one of the vilest temples," the Varanasi temple on the banks of the Ganges. It was filled with Mithuna art that illustrates sexual intercourse as symbols of the creative in Hindu religion (Indians, it is said, used it for sex education before books, films, and literacy). It was a bit much for a Methodist living fifty years before the denomination's youth magazine, *Motive*, attempting to change uncouth attitudes toward the subject, headlined an article, "Sex, Ain't It Fun." The "hideous idols" were viewed by Ward out of their context and probably in relation to child marriage. He condemned both. He probably accepted the missionary interpretation of child marriage. The Hindus themselves, as do other cultures and religions where arranged marriages exist, explain it as an interfamily ceremony and agreement leading to cohabitation many years later after a second nuptial ceremony.

Calcutta oppressed him most with the swarming population, beggars, mistreated widows, and ugly tenements. He referred to it as "the only place in India where I have felt anything like a missionary feeling toward the people, strange to say they have not moved me elsewhere. Unconsciously one adopts a superior attitude towards the lower classes as the missionaries do. It's the only way you can get anything done." He thought that in India one succeeded only by being patient, "but when it is said and done about equality there is a difference. You feel that you are of the dominant race, and perhaps proud of it." Although his earlier notions of Kipling and "Chinese" Gordon were still in his thought, the trip was adding much to his experiential reservoir.

Another illustration of ideas Ward was living with on this tour that would change because of his experiences in foreign lands was his conclusion that he preferred "Gothic towers to the domes of the Taj Mahal." This might sound ethnocentric to modern ears, but it underlines that new sights and sounds have to wait to be assimilated and integrated into most peoples' being before anything approximating objectivity can be accomplished. Another example was his writing to Daisy that he was shopping for a "little jewelry" for his "true heart." He had to do some negotiating, probably not realizing that "bargaining" was a respectable kind of game in the Near East and Far East alike.

Also on several occasions he rode with his host in a rickshaw pulled by another human being. Possibly this experience led to his firm resolve later to free the coolie and working class everywhere from such degradation. Sin has been defined as "holding on to outworn ideas." Ward freed himself from most such "sins" as he grew older and gained consciousness-raising experiences.

By the time Ward reached China he was making extra effort to meet as many working people as possible, although it was difficult to establish rapport through an interpreter. Even on the ocean liner enroute to China he asked to visit the workers' quarters on the ship. He referred to the Chinese in these youthful days as "John Chinamen," not to denigrate them but to try to break through culture barriers. Ward liked the Chinese people and wrote that they were "fiends for work and very honest" and would "eventually run the Orient," a prophecy that might come true. He concluded, "But the Eastern question possibly comes next to the Labor question in importance to our children and a little first hand knowledge of it will be of great value." How right he was, is, and will be.

The travelogue type of letters this serious young man wrote also tell something of his role as father and husband. Usually at the end of each letter there was a studied note or short paragraph for his wife and children. "Gordon take care of mother," he advised; "Bunting save your money"; "Muriel, read well." (She was less than two years old!) As for Daisy, and this urging came quite often, she must keep her health and vigor. From the time he departed on his trip, he almost teased her about dieting and not gaining weight. "Then she might go looking for a younger man," was his pointed humor.

Probably her becoming more plump troubled him and brought guarded suggestions about taking exercise, playing with the boys, staying outdoors as much as possible, or boasting that his own weight was only 135 pounds.

As many mates are prone to do, he often brought up matters that proved to be unwitting pressures on his busy wife. "Have you done this or that thing?" he would write and follow his checklist with the admonition "don't get tired." "Have the children been vaccinated?" "Have you finished the pennant for the cabin in Canada that would bear the name 'Ward' in the local Indian language? It would be 'Mah-gah-gua-yah.'" One letter explained that she should tell the children the Bible stories rather than send them to Sunday School, an early inkling of a growing distrust he carried for theology and the established church.

As the world tour was nearing its end Ward was wishing to hurry to Lonely Lake. Perhaps he needed time to assimilate all the experiences; also, his benefactor died suddenly in Hawaii, and Ward had to arrange to have the body sent to Chicago. "Are you going to Canada with me?" he pressed. Daisy wanted to go June 1, rather than May 15. "Very well," replied Ward, "I can't blame you if you don't want to because the bites [black flies] are not fun. Gordon and I will go."

Ward almost suggests in this collection of family papers that his love for the outdoors takes precedence over other concerns. In a March 1909 letter, he wrote that Daisy may wonder why he can't linger and reestablish his habit of reading the Sunday funny papers to the children, why he sees her and rushes away so fast to Lonely Lake. Answering his own question, he adds that he wants to see the May colors, and if she doesn't come "what can I do?"

Perhaps the camp in Canada was something of a pressure for Daisy, not only in 1909 but other years as well. She kept irregular diaries. In one of these, 1920–1922, there are amusing incidents about the automobile and other travel problems. Daisy had taken a course in auto repair in return for Ward's promise to buy a car. Seventeen-year-old Gordon acted as a mechanic and was helpful, but a great deal of the car responsibility was Daisy's. Roads were not good nor well marked; so the round trip each year could be onerous. Daisy's diaries reveal some of the pleasures and vicissitudes. On July 2, 1920, she noted after working a half day checking the car and necessities "we left the house at twelve— but stopped for lack of gas before we got out of the driveway." On March 22, 1918, she wrote:

I know as well as can be that if we go to the country now we will stay there. The older Harry grows, the more the outside work of gardening will appeal to him, the less he will want to go out evenings, to speak or to social affairs. If I only were content to live that way—I can make myself do it and make the best of it for strength always is given, but I feel under constraint all the time. I suppose it's because the garden work hurts my neck and back so, that I can't enjoy it, for I love the outdoors, the trees, birds & flowers, but I also need friends. (11.1)

On their tenth wedding anniversary, April 20, 1909, according to the frank letters found in the family archives, each wrote a letter to the other. These give considerable insight into their personalities and convictions. Ward wrote he first loved her as "a successful and influential college student," but he confessed that his love had grown deeper for the mother of their children. With admiration and respect there was also love, and then this insightful sentence, "It is hard for me to express love. More likely am I to be stunned into silence." Some would say this short apologia confirms a puritanical clergyman who may be tied into a tangle of emotional knots. Probably this reticence, this affection from a distance was a twist of Ward's English acculturation. In an early courtship letter he had explained, "The wife is the queen of the home." He continued in his letter, "We English boys are taught to respect women, to reverence them. It is not true over here. There we stand afar off and worship." Perhaps he went a little too far with his vestigial paternalism, or perhaps he was not too serious when he added this comment on divided opinion in the family, "My rule is to yield where there is no question of principle."

Daisy was a person in her own right, a personality equal to the ability and intense sincerity of her mate. She did on occasion question a principle as being so firmly right. True, after a year of study, she gave up medicine as a profession to marry Ward, although the decision made the Kansas City girl feel "weak in giving up a career." Ten years passed and she wasn't sorry she had made the decision. Instead, she gave her husband ideas for sermons, read his speeches and made comments and suggestions, and offered him advice and support. Her tenth-wedding-anniversary letter was longer than Ward's and in many ways more sagacious. She persisted in getting the family to call Lynd, now in his fifth year, by his right name rather than "Bunting" with its connotation of "baby bunting." She had her own hobbies, projects, and a small bank account. She reviewed the decade with personal summaries about the two of them. They must not try to settle things by "worry and ambitious struggles," "Name, place and money do not tempt you, and I am so thankful." "People who really know you, love and honor you for your singleness of purpose." "Your life is so clean and pure." Then in an attempt to reassure Hal in his inability to express his love for her in words, she wrote: "Our companionship is so much more precious, and perhaps because you are less demonstrative than some, when you do say what you feel, it is all the more valid." Sorry, she said, that she "gets cross" too often. The year away from one another had helped her see her faults, and she had a plan to change. The plan she won't reveal, but Ward was to see if he noticed any change. She was hurt when he wanted to take Gordon and go to Canada without her after nearly a year apart. Now on this special day she "wipes away a tear" to write that "you are going to be a dear, sweet boy, and follow the plans that seem best for us."

The social process in which Harry Ward lived in the Chicago years informs us on his central purpose as well as his most intimate judgments and behavior. His central purpose was involved with the setting and full meaning of his Social Creed of the Churches, to be discussed in the next chapter. There is a line in Daisy's letter that marks a second related issue of considerable importance. Ward shared only with her that he got little, if any, credit for initiating and writing the Creed in 1907, the first social principles for the churches ever written for any religious body in America or elsewhere. Reassurance from his wife came with this sentence: "Appreciation is sometimes delayed and is all the larger when it comes."

Notes

1. Carl Sandburg, *Selected Poems* (New York: Harcourt Brace and World, Inc., 1954), p. 29.

2. "We find that Christian Socialism is a possible thing among women," said Hester Richardson at a meeting at Smith College in 1887 to organize a nationwide "College Settlements Association." Six of the "seven sisters"—Wellesley, Smith, Bryn Mawr, Radcliffe, Vassar, and Barnard—were represented. "Man [sic] is a product of his society," they agreed; "his influence is Sociological." Some very useful women in our history responded to this sociological influence—Mary McDowell, Vida Scudder, Mrs. B. T. Washington, Alice Hamilton, M.D., and Mary White Ovington are a few.

3. See especially *The Goose Step*, 1928.

4. A year before this, 1903, he had written a prize-winning essay in a contest by the *Chicago American*, entitled "How to Make Chicago a Better City." He asked for the curbing of selfishness and the encouragement of public devotion.

3
A Magna Charta
for Church-Labor
Relations

> *The divine aspect of existence is the socially-unifying aspect of it. This point-of-view is not the view of a social gospel that accompanies an individual gospel; there is no gospel but the social.*
> —George A. Coe

A creed has dangers. Even though it makes a social movement or a faith more explicit, it also tends to posit absolutes that become oppressive. For this reason, combined with a skepticism about personal theology and mysticism, Harry Ward resisted calling his theses affixed to the ugly gates of the factories and the grand doors of the churches across America a "creed"—the Social Creed of the Churches. Some church historians have accepted this document as "the first comprehensive statement of social principles by a church body in the United States" (298). But it was more than that because of its wide impact on Catholic, Protestant, and Jewish religious bodies, on college campuses, and on social legislation up to and including the New Deal reforms.

Ward had been working to bring the church house into the middle of the road where humanity would pass through it. The side of the road seemed to serve those seeking personal escape in a seductive, oriental Garden of Eden. George H. Mead, the Chicago social philosopher, at a "Labor Night" session of the City Club of Chicago underlined Ward's approach when he pointed out that public sentiment cannot be informed without considering the common interests of all.

The two men agreed upon the following statement by Mead.

We know that our political parties [and religious bodies—EPL] really erect barriers between those whose interests are common interests. We know that classes and groups and organizations of all sorts keep people more or less apart. That makes it almost impossible to formulate that public sentiment which, if we could get rid of some of these barriers, would be sure to formulate itself and lead to just that form of government which democracy represents.

We have not had the great mass of the community represented, those that come, perhaps, under the caption of labor. We have discussed housing, but we have not had the great mass of the people who live in just those houses that ought to be pulled down. We have undertaken city planning, and that city planning has not taken into account the great extent of the city itself. It has considered only a certain part of the city. (313)

The same, Mead stated, had been true of transportation, sanitation, and health where groups in the community had not been asked to participate. Ward, as chairman of the Labor Committee of the City Club, insisted that the church must break through these barriers and its members find themselves by losing themselves in serving the people.

John Dewey speaking to his union members, the American Federation of Teachers, in 1912 struck the same note that Mead and Ward did.

We should have a body of self-respecting teachers and educators who will see to it that their ideas and their experience in educational matters shall really count in the community; and who, in order that these may count, will identify themselves with the interests of the community; who will conceive of themselves as citizens and as servants of the public, and not merely as hired employees of a certain body [viz., the ecclesiastical church—EPL] of men. It is because I hope to see the teaching body occupy that position of social leadership which it ought to occupy, and which to our shame it must be said we have not occupied in the past, that I welcome every movement of this sort. (322)

It was the way of social order and a down-to-earth salvation. The sociological thinking around Chicago supported those wishing to build a more cooperative community.

"The Church the Servant of the Community" was the first slogan of the Methodist Federation for Social Service (to be referred to as the Federation), which was founded about five months after the appearance of "The Social Ideals of the Church," the name given to the Creed Ward, with suggestions from several associates, outlined.[1] There were, of course, forerunners, somewhat like the organization and purpose of the Methodist Federation. From England came the ideas of the prolific novelist Sir Walter Besant, whose uplift ideas provided Palaces of Delight to attack the monotony of slum dwellers. Later these were called Palaces for People. Their purpose was to improve—by recreation, technical schools, art schools, and gardens—the condition of the London underprivileged. The Palaces were too much "do for" rather than "do with" to last long.

The failure of Besant's ideas in 1875 was related to the failures of the British Christian Socialists who had tried to bring the clergy together with the laboring classes. Like many of our modern liberationist theologians, these socialists laid emphasis on "brotherhood in God" as their appeal rather than dealing directly with the economics of "misery, poverty, unsanitary and dangerous habitations to which the new industrial conditions had given rise."[2] They had not informed or educated the upper classes on the plight of the poor. Their schemes were nice, but the working classes were not up to using them. What they needed was what Ward later was to insist upon in the United States, namely "the cold statistical facts about social conditions." Their efforts lacked vitality as a result of too much theorizing and too much debate with the Manchester school.

From his experiences in Britain and his life among the empirical-minded around Chicago, Ward was learning that the Christian socialism of the forerunners was not specific, it was deductive. Maurice and Kingsley were the a priori kind of reformer, using a theory from the Bible, not from the workers in their work places, situations that the savants did not know. Jacobs, in his book cited in footnote 2, states that Edward Denison, Arnold Toynbee, and Canon Samuel A. Barnett were exceptions in that their reform grew from scientific investigations. "They didn't stress man's relation to God, but man's to man." From them came the settlement-house movement and its practical service that captured the imagination of Harry Ward. Josiah Strong in this country, with his American Institute for Social Service

(1898–1916), might be mentioned, but his personal racism and his racist "manifest destiny" theory have caused most of his fellow Congregationalists to bypass him. Charles Stelzle of the Presbyterians, who initiated the Department of Church and Labor for his denomination and was a principal founder of its famous Labor Temple, should be noted. The related Federation of Churches and Christian Workers, organized in 1895 in New York City, was too localized and proselytizing. Some of these church efforts blended into the Federal Council of Churches after 1908.

As early as 1900 Ward brought representatives from his Northwestern Settlement House to sit with the Chicago Federation of Labor meetings at Hull House. The purpose was to unite in pushing legislative action on bills to reduce hazardous work and to limit child labor. He believed the churches should cooperate and do as the Settlement House people did, back labor directly. The formation of a national unity of labor and religion was in his mind several years before the first buds of a relatedness appeared. An apparent mutuality was not innate consciousness of kind as Professor Robert Handy of Union Theological Seminary has implied, but was rather a sense of the growing solidarity with the laboring people in behalf of the Kingdom of God on earth.

If doubt persists that Ward was in fact the central figure in organizing a social-service federation for the Methodists, the doubting Thomas could consult the early minutes of Federation meetings, preserved at Drew University (8). Elbert Robb Zaring, an editor of the *Western Christian Advocate* in the winter of 1906, suggested an organization patterned after the Wesleyan Methodist Union of England. Worth M. Tippy, pastor of the Epworth Memorial Church in Cleveland, Ohio, went abroad to study the English counterparts. When he returned he visited Frank M. North, secretary of the National City Evangelization Union in New York City. Tippy was informed by North that he and Ward in Chicago were considering such a plan.

It was agreed to call a meeting in Cleveland on September 13, 1907, of five persons: Zaring, Tippy, North, Ward, and Bishop Herbert Welch, president of Ohio Wesleyan University. Only three could attend; so they agreed to call together a larger body on December 3, 1907, in Washington, D.C.

Invited to this founding meeting were, among others, Governor Frank Hanley of Indiana; Professor Edward T. Divine of Columbia University; Dean George Vincent of the University of Chicago; John R. Commons, labor historian from the University of Wisconsin; Judge Ben Lindsay of Denver; I. J. Magruder, general secretary of the Federated Charities of Baltimore; John Williams, commissioner of labor, Albany, New York; George A. Coe from Northwestern University; and Mary McDowell, Chicago social worker. The five initiators were pleased to have twenty-five, out of forty-two invited, respond favorably to meet at Ebbit House in the nation's capital.

The conference was called to order in the Red Room at 10:30 A.M. by Frank North. Welch was elected chairman *pro tem*, and the group voted to invite Charles W. Fairbanks, vice-president of the United States, to visit sometime during the day. A series of introductory speeches mentioned England's work in social service, the spreading of the settlement-house movement, and the burgeoning concern of churches for social betterment. Then Ward, the youngest among the leaders, spoke, and it became clear from then on who had done homework for the occasion, who was bursting with ideas, who was, as Bishop Welch stated, "the creative mind in launching The Federation."

Students of Ward will recall an often-used phrase of his. "First you must get your facts straight," he proclaimed, as his blue eyes blinked in a rather fast, but irregular, way beneath his bushy eyebrows. This seemed to happen at moments when he was peering far off while presenting a thought. His remarks on the founding day underlined study that stressed getting and organizing the facts. Tippy, the acting secretary, wrote that the young man from Chicago "advanced a comprehensive scheme of publication for the consideration of the society," including a social handbook covering necessary social history and theory. Ward outlined a manual for organizing purposes, which suggested the formation of social training under the direction of colleges and seminaries. The church colleges, it should be noted, he believed must be included with the social-betterment upsurge and develop trained workers. (This was his general style of effective procedure most of his life. It would appear a quarter of a century later when he organized New America and firmed up the League for Peace and Democracy.) In 1907 his was the only carefully prepared plan for action.

In the afternoon Tippy spoke radically about the church being out of touch with socialism, with the poor, and with the masses of foreigners and intellectuals, but his action proposals were unrealistic or missing. He and Bishop Welch were later to criticize Ward for being too radical, even though both, Welch in particular, admired the basic efforts made by the younger leader to propose action after sufficient thinking. Following more discussion and planning it was moved by North and seconded by Magruder that the Methodist Federation for Social Service be organized. A standing vote approved the motion by unanimous decision.

Ward gave the committee report at the evening session detailing the plans for organization. A member of the body objected to using the word *Methodist* lest the federation be offensive to some in the denomination. Ward moved to retain the word. Later there were those who preferred the name "Alliance," "Guild," or "Fellowship." Ward prompted Tippy to move for the name "Federation." After debate the motion was passed, again unanimously. Certainly it is evident that it was Ward, at age thirty-four, who laid the foundation stones. At the close of the day he moved the appointment of a nominating committee to report the following morning. He was placed on the program committee that would also report the next day.

The morning session on December 4 convened at 9:45 A.M. to allow time for the committees to prepare recommendations. Welch was nominated for president; John Williams and Ward as first and second vice-presidents; Tippy as secretary-treasurer; and additional executive committee members mentioned were Magruder, North, and E. J. Helms, a Boston minister. Again it was Ward who gave the program committee report, which typified his ways of thinking and action, making it more difficult than ever not to believe that he was in most ways the father of the Federation. The impression remains, after reading the early records, that he came prepared with proposals and planks for the new church body. Here is his outline for proceeding:

A. Education: (1) Leaflets to explain the Federation, telling "What It Is," "How to Organize," how to prepare a list of speakers, how to produce pamphlets on urgent social questions, etc.
B. Organization: How to involve other groups (like trade unions) across the country, and how to involve college and seminary students.
C. Publication: (1) Of a Manual and (2) a book that would be an "Introduction to the Study of Social Questions." Its orientation must be social history and theory with its monographs written by authors who are specialists in this approach. Sociology, History, and Religion must integrate.
D. Study: Meaning the preparation of ways to start the church and related groups on the more careful study of social religion.
E. Investigation and Service: Locals in each community should study the social and racial groups around them. They should list problems and *start some work on them.* College Economics Departments and the Social Sciences in general should be called on to help investigations and services, or in other words, gather information and then act (or serve) in some important way. (8)

The entire report was accepted, after which Ward moved that a general convention of the Federation be held sometime before January 1, 1909. Before adjournment the body voted to send greetings to the Wesleyan Union for Social Service in England.[3]

The social backgrounds of people who attended this founders' meeting must be distinguished in order to understand better the statements and proposals of Ward. Few, if any, had ultimate aims in view. Professor Milton J. Huber, in his doctoral dissertation on the history of the Federation (331), states that Frank North's talk to the delegates expressed the need to bring the laborer and employer to a better understanding of one another. It could be summed up, says Huber, as "more in the spirit of Jacob Riis than Karl Marx." They were "liberals," he writes, who accepted the social order with the change of a few things. Some were conservatives, putting soul before body. Only a few were radicals. Tippy and Welch, both of whom had certain disagreements with Ward, wanted social reform with "the spiritual force of love," whereas Ward and Magruder wanted "social salvation" through social service to "transform community life," specifically to relieve the plight of the poor, the sick, and the prisoner and to eliminate poverty, disease, and crime. They dared wish to develop and make better the social institutions that they might more nearly approximate the City of God on earth.

The first somewhat clumsy statement drawn up by the founders reflects the conservatism of some: "The objects of the Federation shall be to deepen within the church the sense of social obligation and opportunity, to study social problems from the Christian point-of-view, and to promote social service in the spirit of Jesus Christ" (8). Harry Ward accepted these sentences *pro tempore* in order to proceed toward a recognition of the Federation and its goals at the twenty-fifth General Conference of the Methodist Episcopal church to be held in Baltimore in May 1908. Here a better statement appeared necessary. Ward criticized the old one as too abstract and unsatisfactory. A group of Young Turks— meaning Welch, Tippy, Magruder, and Ward—undertook to write a draft to be identified as "The Church and Social Problems," a call to action for the conference delegates. What was to become the Magna Charta for church-labor relations, the Social Creed of the Churches, was aborning.

The Federation committee sat down around a press table and began, with Ward as secretary urging that they join in stating clearly what the Methodist church stood for in our industrial society. Although he always insisted it was group work, in actuality he composed most of it earlier, writing it out on the back of Western Union telegram forms. At age seventy-five, in a letter to Professor Huber (June 9, 1943) he admitted as much. Frank North was so heavily involved with other church policy matters at the conference that he bobbed in and out taking little time to contribute. The committee members tended to lack the labor experience that Ward possessed. It is evident why Bishop Welch, who tended to differ with Ward at times, wrote, "His was the preeminently creative mind. He was the most largely responsible for framing the Social Creed." Later Welch repeated that Ward's mind was the "most fruitful in suggesting and phrasing," his was "the creative mind" (309).

North, who has been incorrectly credited with the authorship, had little to do with it.[4] Because of his contacts at the Methodist conference and at the Federal Council of Churches meeting in

Philadelphia later that year, his contribution was to pilot the statement through both bodies. Ward recognized North's help at these points, but was stunned and hurt that the author of "Where Cross the Crowded Ways of Life" never acknowledged the primary writer of the creed. When North died in 1935 neither the *Christian Century* nor the *Christian Advocate,* national church journals, mentioned him as author of the Creed. Neither did they mention Ward. What happened?

To begin with, in a letter to Daisy dated February 17, 1909, Ward referred to the *Outlook* magazine (vol. 90, Dec. 19, 1908, pp. 849–851) statement reading: "to Frank M. North, who drew and presented the resolution and to Rev. Charles Stelzle, who retains his trade union membership as a mechanic, great credit is due for initiating and guiding this momentous procedure." The writer of the statement, whoever he was, called it a charter, a bill of rights on behalf of toilers and society. Later in the spring of 1909 Ward heard that the Federal Council of Churches had adopted the document on which he had worked so thoughtfully and with diligence and for which he got so little credit. His disappointment was shared only with Daisy (11.1).

Have been amused at something more to see in church papers now other men have been reaping glory from the little labor platform that I drew up at General Conference. It was my idea to begin with, that we should have a definite platform that should mean something to labor men and I drafted it with a few minor changes from Magruder. Now at the big church Federation Council North gets great glory for preparing the Labor report and he did a fine piece of work, but he incorporates my platform with a few generalizations and the Council adopts it and the Labor men get on it, see that he means something and enthusiastically, this wipes out all the present indifferences of the Church. Hence North is a great man [illegible] but I am waiting to see whether he acknowledges my credit to anyone else. I suppose a man ought to be satisfied to do the thing and let other fellows get the credit, even though he does get the kicks. . . . Well, if I'm spared I hope to show these fellows something yet.

> With fondest love,
> *Hal*

One thing that pleased and surprised him upon his return from the round-the-world trip was that Federation President Welch had secured a member of the International Blacksmiths' Union to sit on the executive committee. Cheering, too, was the adoption by the American Federation of Labor of the second Sunday of May as Labor Sunday. The Presbyterian Department on Church and Labor also approved these Wardian ideas.

Nineteen nine was a year seeded with ideas for making the church aware of its social ecology. Ward edited a handbook for the Federation with articles by Mary McDowell, social worker; George Vincent, sociologist; and the "children's judge" of Denver, Colorado, Ben Lindsay. He arranged for the *Social Questions Bulletin* to publish what he called "the social biographies" of Arnold Toynbee, John Ruskin, Saint Francis, John Wesley, Charles Kingsley, and Guiseppe Mazzini. Other materials included were "social information" covering views on labor problems and injustices together with guidelines for a lecture series in the colleges, which he called "social evangelism." He was the first to organize college branches of the Federation at Northwestern and the University of Chicago.

Considering all of these efforts and successes, attention should be given to highlighting the words and the far-reaching influence of his "Social Ideals of the Church." Even though Ward said he did not like "social creed" any better than "social gospel," because both suggested a dualism unworthy of his pragmatic faith in one creed undivided by a personal way to be "saved" and one gospel undiluted by the search for personal immortality, the title "The Social Creed of the Churches" was adopted by the action of the Federal Council of Churches while he was out of the country.

The original Creed read as follows:

The Methodist Episcopal Church stands:

For equal rights and complete Justice for all men in all stations of life.

For the principles of conciliation and arbitration in industrial dissensions.

For the protection of the workers from dangerous machinery, occupational diseases, injuries and mortality.

For the abolition of child labor.

For such regulation of the conditions of labor for women as shall safeguard the physical and moral health of the community.

For the suppression of the "sweating system."

For the gradual and reasonable reduction of the hours of labor to the lowest practical point, with work for all; and for that degree of leisure for all which is the condition of the highest human life.

For the release from employment one day in seven.

For a living wage in every industry.

For the highest wage that each industry can afford, and for the most equitable division of the products of industry that can ultimately be devised.

For the recognition of the Golden Rule, and the mind of Christ as the supreme law of society and the sure remedy for all social life. (54)

The "mind of Christ" in the last principle was unusual for Ward and must have been added by others, just as such interpolations were added to Solomon's Old Testament love songs. Ward would more likely have used a phrase like "the teachings and actions of Jesus." *Mind*, as a special, discrete entity, means little to most social interactionists, and concepts of Christological theology that removed the Carpenter of Nazareth from history were foreign to the thinking of Harry Ward. All the other principles are workaday guides, down-to-earth in attacking the sins of greed, arrogance, and exploitation in "the living present."

Issued as Pamphlet No. 5 of Federation publications, its name became "The Church and Social Problems." Important introductory statements written in Ward's report to the general conference had disappeared. He had urged the elimination of the profit-making economic system and the recognition that the fundamental purposes of the labor movement are ethical and that workers have a right to organize.[5] Though these are implied in all eleven of his principles, they faded as the Creed took wings throughout Methodism, making it possible for the Federation to write, "It is an advanced document and as such has been received by the nation at large with marked interest and approval. Its influence has been particularly favorable with social workers and with the leaders of the labor movement." A surprising statement to be made so soon after "the Creed" was written, but it was more than confirmed by events in the years to come.

The Federal Council of Churches adopted it in December of 1908 with the floor leadership of Frank Mason North and others. Minor modifications were made, the most serious being a new name, "The Social Creed of the Churches." For the next quarter century—from four years before the Progressive movement through the early years of the New Deal—many of the Creed's principles were made the law of the land. In the interim it was adopted by major religious bodies and the Student Christian Movement (YMCA and YWCA) active in the nation's colleges and universities.

After twenty years of the Creed, Harry Ward wrote an article about it in the *Christian Century* (152). It grew, he wrote, out of the "impulses of the time": booming industrialism, a growing awareness of "how the other half lives," the "back to Jesus" movement and away from "pie in the sky," the vocal religious critics Gladden and Rauschenbusch, and finally the upthrust of the fist of labor, through its unions expressing its demands and ideals. The orthodox church had never been aware that its underlying goals were similar, if not identical, to those of the settlement movement and labor. "How could Jane Addams not be a Christian when all she gave her neighbors was her life, while declining to offer them the choice of coming to Jesus or going to hell?" queried Ward. Helpful, too, he added, was the strength of the Socialist movement and the Populist farmer movement. This was the milieu that fostered the Creed. The church must be saved by labor, and the Federation was an instrument through which Ward and like-minded people in other religious bodies would make a grand attempt.

With minor change the National Council of the Congregational church in 1910 endorsed the Creed. In 1911 the Northern Baptists, with an addition or two, and the Presbyterians, including those in Canada also joined those approving it. In 1912 Ward revised the church's "bill of rights for labor," urging people to be activists and to uphold unions that faced blacklisting and lockouts. Before closing with a plea for a gospel "working for the regeneration of communities," he added a daring new plank to his Creed that urged "democratic control of industry, both process and proceeds." He must have known that most church people would not comprehend nor grasp the impact of this addition. They would, however, be pressed to find out—to learn—and that was the educator Ward's aim.

The new crusade kept spreading to encompass the Southern Methodists, the Reformed, and the Episcopal denominations and, in 1920, the Friends (Quakers), who added the idea of limiting the return on capital. The Central Conference of American Rabbis joined in, as well as the Roman Catholics with the endorsement of Bishops Muldoon, Hayes, and Russell. Robert M. Miller in his *American Protestantism and Social Issues, 1919–1939* (299) writes that the Creed was read from the pulpits during the great steel strike of 1919 and at labor conclaves. It gave the clergy guidance on issues of vital importance to working people. More important, it was used as authority for action.

In the New Bedford, Massachusetts, textile strike of 1928, Winifred L. Chappell, Ward's loyal prolabor colleague, wrote that the pulpits in the area referred to the Methodist Social Creed and like pronouncements from the Federal Council of Churches. One minister drew headlines by proclaiming that the present economic system was "obsolete" for "it fosters greed, distrust and injustice to workers" (11).

Ward was constantly traveling, lecturing, preaching, and writing letters, pamphlets, and short books to stimulate and guide. In a kind of recognition of the quantity of his writings, especially of tracts and pamphlets, the Press Club of New York, through J. J. Wohltman, invited him into membership. Ward declined, for how could he deviate from his central purpose?

In 1916 he had pointed out that the publishers of Methodist literature and books were paying substandard wages and using nonunion labor. Though he lost in his effort for unionization at that time (the continuing endeavor will be further described in Chapter 4), the wave he created had the force to move working people and to show that the church could be on the side of organized labor; it would lead to the Federal Council of Churches being represented, with permission of its representatives to speak, at several of the national conventions of the American Federation of Labor. In fact, the wave brought a response from a faraway Australian labor paper recognizing Ward's work in making the church aware of the economic scene. All accomplished, said the paper, by "a progressive and far-seeing young clergyman" who finds himself supported by the highest authority in his church (11).

If Harry Ward got the attention of trade unionists, he captured also the college and university students in what then was called the Student Christian Movement (SCM) aligning the campus Young Men's and Young Women's Christian Associations. His Methodist Federation and other denominational bodies approximating it, with the Social Creed as the "little Red Book," swept through the campuses creating a kind of missionary zeal. YMCA crusaders like Sherwood Eddy, international leader; Kirby Page, editor of *World Tomorrow;* and J. Stitt Wilson, a friend of Ward's since his Harvard days, visited colleges to plead justice for blacks, for Colorado and Pennsylvania miners as well as those in Ohio, and for Indiana and Chicago steel workers. Norman Thomas, graduate of Princeton Theological Seminary, felt at home in the movement too, as he visited the colleges with his effervescent socialism. Auditoriums filled and even college gymnasiums resounded with the fervent oratory for reform of the stark realities of industrialism.

Many were involved in aiding this movement, but again it was Ward who proposed that students, through their SCM, their social science clubs, or social services clubs, be dedicated to a new College Evangelism, as he called it. David R. Porter and A. J. Elliot, nationally prominent "Y" men, were approached for suggestions on how best to spread this gospel. Porter responded by agreeing to send out to all the SCM locals, to concerned professors, and to YMCA board members a speech on social justice he had made at a Northfield, Massachusetts, conference. It affirmed the ideas of the Creed. The national meeting of the YMCA at Detroit, Michigan, in November 1919 responded favorably to a motion by another Mr. Big in the organization, Ben Cherrington, to adopt the Creed as guidelines.[6] The YWCA followed in most of this; in fact Grace Scribner, the first executive in the national office of the Methodist Federation, until her untimely death was half time with the Federation and half time with the YWCA national board. Offshoots of Ward's single purposefulness were many. After all, it was he who was most responsible for bringing to Union Theological Seminary a brilliant young social critic by the name of Reinhold Niebuhr, thinking that he too would pursue the grail of justice by his teaching and his dramatic ability to stir the thinking of students.

Leadership in founding the Federation, writing down the Social Creed, then seeing that its social ideals spread far and wide was a major task and contribution. Just how major was revealed in Samuel McCrea Cavert's *The American Churches in the Ecumenical Movement, 1900–1968* (270) where he wrote: "The Creed was of 'Prophetic quality'. It brought to sharp focus Christian social concern that had been developing during the two preceding decades." Though he does not seem to know of Ward's central role, mentioning him only in a footnote, he adds that the Creed became a common platform for the churches in the fields of social education and action.

When letters arrive and comments are made on how much a person has influenced lives and thinking (called consciousness-raising today), counterideas arise, especially if the issues involve entrenched power. To be sure Ward received some plaudits, but recognition also was the beginning of serious attacks upon him. As mentioned, Worth Tippy turned against Ward and announced his views at an executive meeting of the Federation on November 22, 1920. Tippy made it clear he could not follow in the direction Ward was going, which was dangerous to the Federation, to the denomination, and to society. The executive secretary, he exclaimed, seemed certain that "revolution is sure and desirable," so the executive committee should have a vocal minority to "give some restraint to HFW, who needs it" (11).

Churchmen who adopted the Creed and preached it were called by the National Civic Federation "Bolsheviks," a pejorative word in those years. This federation of business tycoons was organized for the specific purpose of opposing the growth of organized labor, social reform, and socialistic trends. The *National Civic Federation Review* was its expensive trade journal. The

Review gave warm support at election time to Warren Harding, who spoke against collective bargaining. Of course Ralph Easley, its editor, knew the central person to attack was Harry F. Ward. Forty-five years after the social rocket was propelled, both the Creed and Ward were again criticized by a group of Methodists calling themselves the Circuit Riders, who proposed adding the sentence "free enterprise gives larger opportunities for the development of personality and freedom and the Christian spirit than any collective system" (11).

As teachers and educators generally had taken up John Dewey's progressive education with slogans "learn by doing," "meaningful experience," and the "activity school," but without solid understanding of what it meant in practice, so preachers took up the Social Gospel to keep up, as Ward stated, "with publicity fashions." A flow of vapid utterances about better education eroded Dewey's true meanings. Just as Ward had warned, turning the "Social Ideals of the Churches" into a creed resulted in "words," "mere statements" to be called "the Social Gospel." Ward called these preachers "pulpit weathervanes," who hung on to personal salvation at the expense of community.

In Ward's 1928 article in the *Christian Century* (152), he stated that workers and farmers were on his mind and his intent was to bring the churches to face the life of the larger community. Individualism (a narcissism approaching that of the 1970s) was rampant, which was due, Ward suggested, to the frontier experience and to puritanism. It had made U.S. citizens the most individualistic people history has recorded. The church, with artisans and all kinds of workers as members and participants, must assert moral authority, in the face of vast injustice. It must lead the middle classes toward the sustaining community. Pulpit orators generally insisted that "the permanent in life is the mystic communication with the eternal or the esthetic satisfactions of beautiful services," while to work in the here-and-now social scene was to deal with the temporary and shallow. The Creed was the clarion call to discover one's self in the only place it can possibly be found, in interaction with "the other" and "the others," the community, in ever-widening circles of fascination, dedication, and creativity. Perhaps it is a law of history that to serve the people, to protect the sheepfold—expounded so often in religious and scientific volumes up to our own day—is the better path. Ward's Creed made an imperishable contribution to those seeking guidance for action as the Industrial Revolution swept across the continent. He had become an important figure in the attempt, through the churches, to form a countermovement of humanitarianism.

Notes

1. The name "Social Ideals of the Church," as well as its content, changed as Ward's document was adopted by various church bodies and national denominations. For awhile it became known by the Federation as "The Church and Social Problems." When the Federal Council of Churches called it "The Social Creed of the Churches" in 1908, that name tended to prevail.

2. Leo Jacobs (286) discusses these failures in detail.

3. This session over, the twenty-five members were invited by President Theodore Roosevelt and Vice-President Fairbanks to a reception in the "New West Annex" of the White House. "Teddy," it was reported, did most of the talking, saying how important their work was, "more important than a tariff high or low. The negro [sic] has need for an industrial education and the need to keep educated men in the South!" This was the first and only time the president of the United States entertained the Federation (8).

4. Charles H. Hopkins (284) seems to have accepted Tippy, who gave too much credit to North. Tippy became a conventional clergyman and an implacable opponent of Ward and his goals.

5. In passing it might be noted that some basic aims printed on the masthead of the *Social Questions Bulletin* for several decades have, in recent years, disappeared.

6. Ben Cherrington later became director of the Social Science Foundation at the University of Denver. With this sinecure for financial support he became well known, at one time holding a high office in the State Department in Washington. His associate in Denver was Elizabeth Facht, a product of the YWCA and the college movement. She was always a firm advocate of Harry Ward.

4
Whirlwinds
in Boston

We are with the Poor. They are the Church.
They teach Christianity to others.
—Gustavo Gutierrez

There is every reason to believe that Harry Ward was motivated to move his family to Boston and accept an invitation to teach at Boston University School of Theology by his longing to spread his social evangelism eastward. To remain in a pleasant, middle-class church in Oak Park, near Chicago (his post after the Union Avenue church), was alien to his purpose. To have access to the minds of larger numbers of youthful, prospective clergy in his classes led Ward to join a teaching institution. He could influence ministers and reach into the Student Christian Movement even more. In the winter of 1913 he became the Boston seminary's first professor of Social Service.

These were days of other major decisions. Although at one time he debated leaving the formal church and Methodism altogether, he stayed with both (see Appendix A). If the Social Gospel leader Washington Gladden, a Congregationalist, could wonder if God hadn't selected the Methodist Church to lead the social movement in the United States before prophet Ward had reached his peak of influence and if the towering social Christian, Walter Rauschenbusch, a Baptist, could affirm that Methodists "have not backed away from a fight with Diabolus and when they march, the ground will shake" (11), why should the youthful Ward abandon this sturdy support group?[1] In the Boston days he swept across religious skies like a meteor, leading Elias B. Sanford, honorary secretary of the Federal Council of Churches, to refer to Ward's "prophetic social leadership" (8). He had put "the Methodists at the front in facing the social problems of the

56

hour." And this was 1916, three years before he joined the faculty of Union Theological Seminary in the heart of the Great Babylon.

His experiences in Chicago had helped in forming his convictions. Living in slums, helping to organize the Packinghouse Workers' Union, and participating in their strike in 1905 led to his close identification with labor. It was in Chicago that he and his friend Raymond Robbins tried to rid the city of a corrupt mayor and, a little later, of "Bathhouse John," a councilman who tried to sell city bus lines to high-finance circles for leases of ninety-nine years.[2] These experiences, combined with the creativity of the vibrant city, were internalized in Ward, and he came to serene and solemn Boston and its School of Theology with credentials seldom mentioned in a vita. They were made up of actions and thoughts that, like white-hot sparks from his meteor, would illuminate and spark the minds of his students. "We need ministers with social concerns," Ward said in 1914, "for too many students find useful work outside the church" (55).

The labor movement and the church were his hallmarks, and in that order of priority. He always identified himself by either helping organize a union or by joining one, but in later years never any other organization. For a brief time (1919) he was a member of a Masonic Order, but his other growing involvements eliminated that too. In Chicago he helped organize the Meat Packers' Union and the Teamsters, and when he became a teacher he joined the union of John Dewey, Albert Einstein, and other notables, the American Federation of Teachers, now affiliated with the AFL-CIO.[3] Though his participation in labor disputes and strikes often led to accusations that he had joined political movements, he never did so. Neither did he join the Christian Socialists or the Communists. Beginning with his Northwestern days, he resolved to avoid political entanglements, believing they would limit and weaken his objectivity and his wish to criticize freely as a student of ethics. He felt party affiliations could tend to splinter and divide people. Both sectarian theology and sectarian politics could be invidious.

The importance to Harry Ward of the labor movement, of course, did not develop instantaneously with his experience in the settlement house and his first churches in Chicago. He had pondered over the Thames River longshoremen's strike before he was sixteen, sitting on a high stool working on his father's records of meat sales. As he thought of the difficult working conditions of these men, the first signs of identification with labor appeared. It was not, however, until he arrived in America and became a teamster and bookkeeper for his uncle at Salt Lake City that his personal experience ripened into a devoted concern. He read of Kingsley in England, of course, but in 1898 he went to hear Eugene V. Debs. "What to do about it?" he pondered. In 1905 he read *The Communist Manifesto*. He began doing something about it in his first churches. And his labor identification continued to grow.

Boston wanted this unusual minister because he had become highly regarded as a labor evangelist; he had brought the church and labor closer together. It was difficult to proceed as an agitator in the quiet suburban church of Oak Park, Illinois, so Ward had written a small book called *The Labor Movement* (64) in which he defined sin as the opposite of brotherhood. Unions were brotherhoods and sisterhoods. They were forces for good; their goal was the "full development of personality."

Ward made many speeches on these themes, stating and elucidating the need for cooperation between the church and the unions of working people. He recalled that on several occasions the Methodist Federation met at Hull House and asked a speaker from a union to give an address. In Chicago, Boston, and on his lecture tours Ward invited union leaders to share the platform with him.

In fact, the Boston University School of Theology wanted him on the faculty so much that they decreased his teaching load to half so that he could advance the work of the Federation. Bishop Francis McConnell had nominated him for the new chair at the seminary, and Professor George Coe had urged him to accept. They knew that the Federation was important to Ward as a seedbed for his social message, therefore it had to be moved eastward with him. They even furnished him a free office at the seminary. From this new base of operation with a seminary salary of $3,000 per year, a Methodist Federation recompense of $1,500 offered annually, and the skilled aid of the remarkable associate secretary, Grace Scribner (with a half-time annual salary of $1,080), Harry Ward was able and ready to present sin as "the lust for profits" and the destroyer of brotherhood.

The indefatigable energy of his Boston days, from 1913 to 1917, appear in a Federation clipping file preserved at Drew University (8). Ward called his travels "campaigns for social evangelization," and in each city he tried to give one speech in a labor hall and another in a local church. Members of the Federation at each stop had prepared for his visit. Sometimes laborers came to heckle the preacher, whom they expected to utter nonsense, but most applauded what they heard. In Seattle, Washington—the state where a physician, Hermon Titus, had at the turn of the century edited a militant, socialist paper with a large circulation, as if to prepare the soil for the seeds of the Federation—Ward persuaded ministers to endorse a strike and to establish a Federation chapter that is active today. If profiteering was the great sin, action-not-talk was the moral corrective for religious torpor. "Jesus' strength was in the action of the people in struggles on many fronts not in the church," was one of his emphatic statements.

His addresses were praised for their frankness and power. After pointing out the need for immediate collective bargaining, he proceeded to criticize the evil in wage discrimination and the immorality of child labor. Then he continued to stress the importance of the eight-hour day and the rightness of the IWW (Industrial Workers of the World) and the organized labor movement, but not in the use of sabotage. Next, he would ask why the saloon should be abolished when no place is provided in the community for men and their families to gather. Also, why abolish the pool hall (then considered by the upper classes as a den of sin just as the saloon was for his denomination) and have no community recreation for youth? Ward believed children's problems arose largely from economic deprivation, far more than from genetic qualities. Thus healthy, noncommercialized recreation was more essential to their well-being than moralistic sermons.

The *Social Service Bulletin,* started in January 1911, was to act as a clearinghouse for the various methods of protest and reform, to offer speakers and suggest topics, and to provide readily all kinds of information, progress reports on activities, and advice on social legislation for Boston and the whole country. A Layman's

Figure 4.1 *Harry F. Ward as first professor of Social Service, Boston University School of Theology, about 1913. (Ward family photo collection.)*

Missionary Movement was activated, and the Bible notwithstanding, a new wine of social religion was poured into the old flavorsome evangelistic wine skins. "Men and Religion Forward Movement" was selected as the name. In every conference (a geographical governance area) of the Methodist Episcopal church there must be an industrial evangelist whose task was to get the message to the middle and upper classes and recruit members for the Forward Movement with its objective "to live for the sake of those to come—this motivation was to be stimulated by the Church" (51).

By efforts like these Ward had founded the Federation. During the first year and a half in Boston he addressed 347 meetings, conducted 36 group conferences in 17 states, and traveled to the West Coast to large and small communities, to labor and church groups, to high schools, and to colleges, all of which led Professor Milton Huber to say that Ward's travelogue sounded like Wesley's *Journal.* Under his guidance his three staff associates also traveled, visiting mills, mines, and timber camps to advocate a shorter work day and week, a sufficient wage, and collective bargaining. These combined enterprises were called, by their initiator, social evangelism. "Faith, hope, and love, yes plus work is my creed," he wrote in 1915 (57).

Ward's indictment of "sin" and its effects reached to the wealthy (he called them "wage shavers") and his own denomination's publishing houses. The charge came that the refusal of the publishing houses to pay wages and to provide working conditions similar to those in their home cities of Cincinnati and Kansas City was causing the workmen to lose faith in the gospel. And when the church refused to give active support to the eight-hour-day campaign in these cities, some of the workers in the mines, mills, and factories also began losing confidence in the message of Jesus. The problems of the workers in the Methodist Book Concern were a challenge to Ward. He proceeded to go beyond "preaching" and put his ideals into action. Accurate information was the first priority. He was meticulous about gathering facts and requested from the Cincinnati publisher, among other information, a list of the workers and the wages paid to each. Then he made efforts to bring the two unions involved, the Printing Pressmen's No. 11 and the Press Agents'

No. 17, and the employer together. His negotiating items included (1) union conditions throughout the plant; (2) a "preferential shop" rather than a full "union shop," which meant that union members would receive preferential treatment in hiring, and if approved by the union, consideration could be given to proficiency (a member of the Methodist Church could be employed at any time); and (3) a union foreman would be the head of each department.

This first effort at collective bargaining with the publishers was only indirectly successful. The Federation leaders were divided. Welch, for instance, did not favor a closed shop; so Ward had to "educate him," or so he said. Tippy was shifting to the right and wrote to the secretary in April 1914 that labor was not to be trusted, that it should be brought under control "as we do the trusts" (11). McConnell was ready to compromise more than Ward "just for this time."[4] North advanced a "weaker alternative," so that the executive secretary had strong support from only I. J. Magruder and H. Franklin Rall in fighting the uncooperative administrators at the Methodist Book Concern in Cincinnati.

If the resistance of Cincinnati could have been overcome, a domino effect on other religious book houses might have been created. "A Survey of Salaries of Religious Publishers" initiated by the Federation had revealed that none had a union, a wage scale, or tenure (two-weeks notice for dismissal prevailed) and none had a promotion plan. Among these publishers were the Congregationalists, the Presbyterians, the Baptists, the Reformed, and the Lutherans. Their policies were justified by references to the factory girls of Lowell; "we are one big family here" under the command of "Christian Kindness." Others called it "mutuality," claiming that the underpaid assistance of wives was a "work of love" (8). A letter was sent from the Federation office to its union-leader friends in Ohio asking them to write immediately and report information about the effect of the church's pronouncements on organized labor.

Many people—for example, sociologist Emory Bogardus at the University of Southern California—wrote to Ward to compliment him on his work and the effectiveness of the *Social Service Bulletin* and to suggest that it might be well to add some employers to the board of the Federation. However, the larger number of church members resisted associations with unions. Undeterred, the Federation pressed on with Ward's plans to publicize conditions at the book houses and to involve the higher councils of the Methodist church. A year later, in 1917, the denomination's publisher faced a strike for an eight-hour day but still refused to yield, and thus added strike breaking to the list of antiunion policies.

The Federation in this same year prompted a discussion of the need for a preacher's organization vis-à-vis the church officials as employers. One issue discussed was the need for a minimum salary for ministers. "We are brothers," or so it was said, whether serving large or small, rich or poor congregations. The pay should be the same. This daring proposal must have set the minds of those unconcerned for the book workers to project their "selves" into unexplored "others" in the "sustaining community," as Mead called it. (Ward, significantly, used the salutation "Dear Brother" when addressing his union friends. Other correspondents, except a few very personal friends and students, were "Dear Rall" or "Dear Niebuhr.") Could the idea of an equal wage for preachers have been a strong stimulus to create more sympathy for workers by the men of the cloth?

The testing of ideas in the community for their relevance and effectiveness was accomplished during the Boston years. Ward had often left his sanctuary in Chicago, and in Boston he tried to reach the people by speaking and answering questions at Ford Hall forums. The hall was a stronghold of Boston liberalism at Fifteen Ashburton Place in the shadow of the State House. The forum in 1914 was attracting large numbers of workers, especially at the noon sessions running from twelve-thirty to one-fifteen. To time himself accurately for the midday sessions Ward wrote out each talk for his series. Other speakers were leaders of the city's American Federation of Labor and the Industrial Workers of the World.[5]

The titles of Ward's speeches usually revealed their substance: "Trade Unionism," "Socialism," "Syndicalism," "The Demand for Leisure," "The Demand for Income," "Violence and Its Cause," "Labor and the Law," and "Democratic Control of Industry." Usually they were printed and circulated. One of his first was entitled "The Challenge of Socialism to Christianity." It appeared in the *Ford Hall Folks* on March 22, 1914 (11), and dealt with the question "Was Jesus a social reformer?" The answer was, "No, not a conscious social reformer, but the whole outcome of Jesus' life and teaching was social reform and reconstruction." In his lectures around the country as well as at Ford Hall, Ward said that Christianity was revolutionary and not reformist. After all, he was speaking to and commanding the attention of IWW members. When asked once at a forum meeting how a person can accept a good salary and at the same time work for a new social order, he replied, "Use the money to destroy the system by which it was made." This belief was expressed more than once in his later years.

A friend of Ward's has written that Ward became Marxist after moving to the New York City area. In the light of the Ford Hall lectures and considering earlier remarks as well, it is difficult to be so definite about it. Carl Sandburg, William Z. Foster, and Eugene Debs had been early influences in Chicago. The Wards had more than casual contacts with these socialists. Before them were "Uncle John" Gray, a conservative economist who presented Marxism at Northwestern along with other major economic theories. The specificity of applying a date to mark a change in philosophy is like trying to push the creation of the earth into one week and date it. Such cannot be done. It is better to say that one of the outcomes of his life was Marxism.

More orthodox religionists who attended his lectures and talks raised questions. Bostonians asked in 1915, "Are you an infidel?" "Do you believe in the Trinity?" and "Is Christ Divine?" The answer came, "I must decline to answer any question on theology because while I teach in a theological school, I am not a professor of theology. I am not a theologian. I am in social service and that is what I answer questions about" (11).

Charles Beard has pointed out that often reform movements in U.S. history have been smothered by war. Populists, Socialists, and Progressives were pushing reforms before 1917. With America's entry into World War I impending, Ward had stated his view that "there is no room in America for the principles of militarism" (8). "War Must be Destroyed!" was the headline in the March 1917 issue of the Federation *Bulletin*, and the church must get involved in doing it. Ward's pencil wrote small script to gain speed as he prepared *Social Duties in War Time,* published by the Association Press (65). Distributed by the YMCA, YWCA, and the Federation, it revealed the moral, ethical, and social costs of war for church people and activated the peace movement of the 1920s in American colleges.

"War dissipates the social passions," he wrote—in the vein of Beard—"while social needs are increased." "The world's misery prevails as social justice is violated." "Suffering produces a callousness of compassion and a drying up of sympathies." "Labor is exploited by longer work days and weeks." "Great profits are made by speculators" (65). Religion is violated because there is no free speech, no civil liberties, hence no free religion. Beard had proclaimed truth to be the first casualty of war. For Ward the final casualty would be every human being nailed on Calvary by denial of the rights that give rise to manhood and womanhood. Another example of the reactions he drew with his zealous speeches and his critical remarks during the Boston years can be noted. He called San Francisco, while on a visit there in 1917, "the most pagan city on the continent," and the statement appeared in the press. It riled many and he was asked to prove it! Ole Hanson, the strikebreaking, chauvinist mayor of Seattle who boasted that he "saved Seattle from Bolshevism," also caught this caustic kind of criticism, and a verbal donnybrook arose. Ward was attacking complacency, and it gave himself and his friends a chance to educate by stirring debate.

As for the war, he gave support at once to those who struggled to stop it. Hundreds were jailed in federal prisons. Both the United States and the Allies, along with the Central Powers, he thought were seeking underlying economic advantages that were the basic causes of war. On his lecture tours in 1917–1918, sponsored by the YMCA in the colleges, he began to expose these economic bases. Hackles arose everywhere with unpleasant letters being exchanged among members of the national administration of the "Y" and affluent sponsors of the organization.

Although the mercury in the social thermometer rose to torrid temperatures from Ward's speeches in 1918, warm support did come in February of that year from people like Charles O. Lee of the Purdue University School of Pharmacy. "We were all deeply impresst [sic] with what Dr. Ward had to say." His subject was "Making a New World." ". . . we hear so much about our patriotic duty in war. Dr. Ward pointed out to us our greater Christian duty in peace." From the student secretary of the "Y" at the University of Colorado came these words: "May I not again express my deepest appreciation of your invaluable service rendered in Colorado. . . ." "I find no bad reactions. . . ." "I hope many states will have the privilege of your instructive and timely lectures" (11).

For the most part letters from YMCA executives, at least those in the college division, endorsed the Ward lectures. One of these was from William H. Tinker, writing in March 1918 to Dr. Robert E. Speer, one of the most important Presbyterian leaders of the day:

> His [HFW] message was most timely and intensely interesting. . . . It is safe to say that in several institutions where Mr. Ward spent some little time, no series of meetings have proved of greater value. From the national standpoint also it would be difficult to overestimate the importance of Mr. Ward's point of view. . . . suffice it to say wherever he went, with possibly one exception, both faculty and students expressed themselves as profoundly grateful, and the doors are wide open for other visits whenever he possibly could spare the time to come.

Many letters like these from administrators, faculty, and students may be found in the Ward papers at Union Theological Seminary (11).

Even though Ward was stressing the positive by looking forward to reconstruction after the maelstrom of violence, critics kept up a hot fire. The YMCA at 19 South LaSalle Street, Chicago, then one of the largest of its kind, decided to sponsor a "course of study" for university students on reconstruction after the war. Ward was to lead it, but by the end of February 1918 he was appearing on blacklists that warned administrators about him. An official, R. H. Garner of the University of Minnesota, wrote to Tinker at the LaSalle address:

I might say by the way of comment that judging from reactions we have from some of our students here, who heard Ward, that there is a decided danger of disturbing the morale of the administrative staff in the War Programme. Several of our men have spoken as if the Administration were not on the right track, that we should not be in the war, and have shown considerable sympathy with the socialistic, non-partisan league, etc., movements. Of course, this is not to be deplored, it only shows that men are thinking and that these movements have great significance. The main question is whether this proposed study of social problems and social reconstruction, etc., is going to aid or hinder our national programme? (11)

Other administrators at the University of Minnesota who had planned to sponsor the "course of studies" now decided to have them canceled. Deans consulted presidents and letters were sent to the national leaders of the YMCA, persons such as Speer and Mr. Y himself, John R. Mott.

One letter to Dr. Speer was from Arthur E. Bestor, a national leader in the adult-education movement. George Creel, the professional prowar propagandist who in 1918 directed the federal committee on public information, had Bestor at his service. Ward's work and words were so effective they seem to have disturbed some university presidents as reports were brought into their offices. The following letter from Bestor to Dr. Speer informed Speer that Dr. Ray Lyman Wilbur of Leland Stanford University had just wired Creel as follows:

Food Administration speakers here find campaign of Harry F. Ward in colleges detrimental to development of war spirit. He seems to be playing Germany's game by preaching disorganization within our democracy, talking war and plutocracy when we need solidarity. Says he is sponsored by Speer and Mott and talking Christian democracy or some such thing. Can you look him up? (11)

Ward was to be "looked up"—investigated—at the instigation of a well-known president of a large university. This was the first federal-government attempt to throttle Harry Ward; others were to follow. By the time Martin Dies appeared, then Joseph

McCarthy, Ward had gained the experience and confidence to confront opponents and make their probing more ineffective.

The Chicago course-of-study lectures were canceled even though Mrs. Harlan W. Cooley, an influential member of the Chicago Council of National Defense, had sought Creel's opinion on Ward and had received a letter dated March 15, 1918, with the sentence "He is to be trusted with the largest number of people who hear him" (11). On the very next day, however, she wrote a letter to Ward notifying him that the lecture series would not be held. Gratuitously, she offered partially to reimburse him for losses due to the cancellation. On March 27, 1918, Mrs. Cooley received another letter from Creel, completely retracting his letter of a few days earlier and withdrawing his endorsement. The letter read "He [Ward] puts continual emphasis upon the class struggle and his speeches are responsible for a great deal of bitterness" (11). "We are," Ward explained, "opposing the autocracy of Germany, but we should fear more the autocracy of money in our own country" (11).

One thing students remember about their teacher Ward was his relentlessness in tracing the source of all charges made against him. He wrote personal letters to everyone making accusations, stating exactly what he had, in fact, said and asking each person to state explicitly the source of the false information. He prided himself on gathering accurate facts and uncovering hidden motives. It was said he never used information himself that had not been checked with great care.

This petrel of increasingly serious storms flew rather well above the rough waves, but there was trouble also in the theological offices at Boston University. Ward stated it in a letter to his friend George Coe, then teaching at Yale University (6). The "money bags and reactionary preachers are after me," he wrote, "and they are wondering why Dean L. J. Birney keeps me around." What could a note from this dean to Ward in October 1915 really mean that stated he wanted to maintain Ward's association with the school because "we and the country need his message"; so he hoped to "have his services full time soon." Was this aimed at dissolving the Federation as a means of clipping the petrel's wings? Or was it the ever-recurrent attempt at the degradation of humankind by trying to divide thought from action—a "back to the carrel, monk" for reading and prayer?

The charges against the outspoken professor became more frequent. Letter files grew mostly because of his unusual Ford Hall lectures. Homer Albers, dean of the law school, asked university president L. H. Merlin if anything could be done about "Ward's peculiar doctrines." They are "hard on the name" of the university. The letter came to the professor through Dean Birney, and in his usual manner, Ward prepared a careful answer pointing out distortions and misquotations and presenting evidence for what he did say. Dean Albers replied with some pugnacity, closing his letter with the advice that Ward could have said what he did, but not let it get into print.[6]

On another occasion Dean Birney was informed by a self-styled "Christian Employer" in the Philadelphia area, W. S. Pilling, that he had heard Ward say in a New York City speech that one of Pilling's coal miners received only four dollars for two weeks' work. But information from laborers could not be trusted, Birney thought. So he wrote to Pilling. The mine operator obliged and loaned the dean a copy of his payroll so that he could check it over with his Social Service professor. Ward, in returning the payroll, found corroboration for his statement and pointed out other inconsistencies and misstatements. All the same, Dean Birney concluded that this faculty member was less critical of labor and unions and "was not quite fair to a great number of Christian employers."

In addition to these disagreements there were those over the war, as have been noted, and the circumstances that always gather to overwhelm a faculty person with charges. For example, it was reported that Professor Ward passed to the dean a note received from one of Ward's students, which stated that "a man was working at the seminary 73 hours a week for $8." Ward was said to have scribbled on the edge of the note, "is it true?" Because the hours and the pay were crucial, the question needled and embarrassed the administrator. Another instance dealt with the Social Ethics professor's responding to the flattering request to write the Federal Council of Churches' position on the War. In the same month of November 1917 when he was doing this, the dean questioned him about absence from faculty meetings.

This subtle harassment grew when Dean Birney sent Ward a telegram the next June inquiring about a newspaper charge that he was connected with Emma Goldman, the anarchist leader, and with the anticonscription movement. Birney must have known his faculty well enough to answer without bothering Ward. Instead, he used the inquiry as a threat, writing that he must know the answer at once because of "a meeting tomorrow to consider the tenure of faculty members."

The situation would have become more ominous had it not been for invitations coming from distinguished Union Theological Seminary in New York City for Ward to lecture there. Union was considering persons to teach Christian ethics and following a Columbia University policy of inviting professors who might be called to the faculty at a later date to lecture. Dean Birney as early as November 1917 seemed to have known of Union's approaches to Ward, and it was probably this that influenced President Merlin not to call Ward to task over the issue of Christian employers as he had planned, but instead to write in April 1918, "I do not want any misunderstanding or ill-feeling to cloud the pleasant relations we have had during your stay at BU" (11).

How pleasant the associations were with the dean and president could be equivocal, but during Ward's tenure at Boston new friends were found among the faculty and students, some of whom developed into cherished lifetime associates. Before arrival on the campus Ward had known of Professor Bordon P. Bowne, the head of the Philosophy Department. Like Ward he was a rose grower who enjoyed the out-of-doors, but more important, the two men tended to have similar ideologies. Bowne used the pragmatic test of life just as the younger man was learning to do. From Hermann Lotze, the German philosopher, Herbert Spencer, and others Bowne developed a system called "Personalism" that influenced Ward and affected religion and philosophy at Boston for another generation. A phrase like "the world of action is the realm of values" caught Ward's immediate attention. He was not surprised that Bowne was tried for heresy by people Bowne called "theological obscurantists." Because of Bowne's death in 1910 Ward was deprived of being his teaching colleague.

Edgar Sheffield Brightman came to Boston two years after Ward, and a lasting friendship developed. As Bowne's successor he argued that personal experience was the only way, that God was "inexhaustive creative process," the resourceful energy of life. "Life as change was an absolute" (5). The realm of possibilities that Mead and Dewey emphasized was unlimited. In later years Brightman would step forward to defend his companion Ward, to call him in 1937 "a battle-scarred veteran," and to declare that he was "proud to be enrolled in his ranks." Brightman contributed regularly to the financial support of the Methodist Federation.

An interesting exchange between these two friends in 1941 can be read in the Ward papers. It concerned a Greek scholar's view that Jesus's disciples were more influenced by their economic class than by Jesus's teachings. Ward had brought A. D. Winspear's 1940 book *The Genesis of Plato's Thought* to Brightman's attention. In commenting on it Ward had asked what influenced Plato: was it Pythagoras or the society of the time? What facts were there? Then he expressed his concern about the way in which many modern thinkers use Plato's philosophy and the consequences of it.

He agreed with the Winspear discoveries of the social genesis of Plato's ideas. "Isn't it," he asked his friend Brightman, "a deeply imbedded kind of theology that works against social change? Isn't it contrary to the Gospel?" Brightman tended to defend Plato by writing that the Greek believed in and sought social change. Moreover, "the bosses were against him. Let's don't make Plato into our enemy." This touch of humor lightened an interchange between the two in which it was evident that Ward disagreed with Plato both on epistemology and on social ideas.

A contention between minds was welcomed by Ward provided it was friendly in spirit and searching for truth. He had no patience with intellectual jousts for mere argument's sake. Sincere group searching, including those who disagreed with him and needed patience and cool repartee, was eagerly sought. Students liked him and his occasional bluntness of speech. Repeatedly throughout his life they testified to his perspicacious thinking in the midst of some seminary obfuscators and to his courage in presenting the truth as he saw it.

Many inquiring young minds at Boston were attracted to Ward's views. One was Bromley Oxnam, who later became a Methodist bishop. In the late 1930s as the congressional investigating committees sought to throttle socialism in this country, Oxnam "trimmed," by moving toward the views of Sherwood Eddy and Reinhold Niebuhr. In so doing he compromised his teacher's values. Jefferson first employed the word *trimmers* to describe those who failed in their loyalty to democratic procedure, and from Ward's point of view this is what happened. Oxnam's dealings with Ward involved hedgings, double meanings for words, and clever dodges such that his behavior, as a former student, became disappointing to Ward.

However, other Boston students did not follow Oxnam's model and the inertia of greed, competition, and ego inflation. Charles Webber, who later came to teach at Union with Arthur Swift and Ward, is an example. Brightman wrote of Webber, during the inquisition of the thirties and forties, "My enthusiasm for Webber is boundless. He is tactful and presents the social gospel the best of all the others" (5).

There were other devoted students whose personal testimony or combined student body recognitions were sent to Ward before he left for Union to take up the appointment he had accepted for the fall of 1918. One of these wrote: "Your work in Social Service has been one of the strongest drawing cards I have known to hold out to men why they should come to Boston University School of Theology." A group of them expressed doubt about Boston making a serious effort to keep their professor. "Your resignation . . . has brought real pain to the hearts of the students" (11).

> You have meant so much to our thinking on the social gospel that many of us have had an experience intellectually which is equivalent to being "born again." This coupled with your excellent Christian spirit and fearlessness for truth, makes it hard for us to understand why a school which boasts that it has kept its loyalty to these things undimmed, should be at all willing to let you go.

And still another: "We [theology students] felt that the question was not merely losing one of the finest men from our faculty, but also involved the wider question of independent thinking and uncensored presentation of truth as men saw it."[7]

Almost thirty years after he left Boston the Harry F. Ward Cooperative store was organized and named in his honor. The students added, "all the work is done by the co-op members." He left large footprints after his four years in New England.

David D. Vaughn, a friend since student days at Northwestern University and a worker in the Chicago stockyards district, became Ward's successor at Boston. Dean Birney offered a salary of $3,500 and a three-months' contract. Vaughn had asked for three years. He wrote at once to Ward asking if he should accept: "What were the disagreements you had with him?" Ward wrote back to say the main disagreement was over the war and added generously, "If he comes to believe in you he will defend you to the limit." As for the lack of tenure, Ward advised Vaughn to accept anyway. President Merlin could make it for three years, but probably would not. Come without it, for there is "great opportunity for influence and leadership" (11).

Vaughn came to Boston. He said of his friend and predecessor that he was "the greatest social teacher in the church today." "He is Bunyan's character 'great heart'" (27). Pauline Rauschenbusch, widow of Walter, had heard of Ward's harassment by the "powerful." Her husband had just passed away that year of 1919, and she wanted to place his mantle on the shoulders of a new prophet. "The attacks made you a prophet," she wrote, for,

> After Walter published *Christianity and the Social Crisis*, the president of the Board of Trade a gunpowder manufacturer millionaire tried for six years to get Walter out. When he didn't succeed he got out himself. Walter has gone on and is out of this phase of the strife and so I'm doubly glad you are still here. Ordinary preaching seems not to sink in. Do you suppose if some modern prophet would go around like the prophets of old, sandals and barefoot, dressed in skins or a cowl and cry out the injustices, they would be heard? If Walter had not had his family, he would have done just that. (11)

Certainly these comments from a family friend gave Harry Ward much pause at the end of his Boston days. Now he was about to continue his work in one of the most affluent and respected seminaries in this country.

Notes

1. Both Gladden and Rauschenbusch died in 1918.

2. Raymond Robbins later became Colonel Robbins, a more-than-casual friend of Lenin and after that an adviser to President Franklin Roosevelt on Soviet affairs.

3. As early as 1902 he spoke at an anthracite miners' strike victory celebration and was criticized for preaching politics, not salvation. After his retirement in 1943 he joined the State, County, and Municipal Employees of America.

4. In the summer of 1917 McConnell was invited to Lonely Lake "to fish," or better to talk things over. Almost always throughout his life he was a staunch defender of HFW.

5. Ford Hall Forum was begun as part of an adult-education movement at the turn of the century. Started by the inspiration of Cooper Union in New York City and aided by the benefactor Daniel Sharp Ford, its first session was held on February 23, 1908. George Coleman was its first director. For a time such a forum dealing with the stresses of industrial culture was operating in Manchester, New Hampshire.

6. It was alleged that Ward had shouted his defense of a "framed" labor leader with ". . . to hell with the law and to hell with the court." This kind of rabble-rousing speech was not characteristic of him.

7. Quotes are from Clarence T. Craig and Garfield Morgan, February 8, 1918, in Ward papers (11).

5
Family Rituals
and Loyalties

Man's hands have served greatly to break up fixed instincts.
—Geo. H. Mead

No one has a right to life who doesn't fight to make it greater. I've watched you fawning on the bishop and on every good coat that sits down on a chair.
—S. O'Casey

With streetcars and ocean liners, poverty on the East Side and affluence on Park Avenue and Riverside Drive, whites south of 110th Street and blacks to the north, New York City hardly presented itself in the nineteen twenties as the megalopolis of crawling confusion it is today. The Woolworth and Flatiron buildings were not so imposing as the World Trade towers. Big Harlem, Little Italy, and Chinatown were clearly marked and discrete social jails. The flower beds of Central Park survived vandals. All stood in contrast to the cold steel and hard glass today rowed up in walls of meaningless monotony suggesting at best a giant computer manipulating the flow of a civilization into and out of it. Over there on the Lower East Side and up in black Harlem—Henry George's dichotomy of *Poverty*—abject and fetid "dumbbell" apartments, like southern sharecropper huts stacked five or six high, stood clearly in contrast to over here on the West Side with the conspicuous consumptive *Progress* of Fifth Avenue, the Metropolitan Museum, Broadway and the theaters, and the Riverside Drive leading up to famous institutions like New York University, City College, and Columbia University. Union Theological Seminary was snugly surrounded by Progress, the very best of Morningside Heights. On the west the terraced Riverside Park; on the north, Julliard School of Music; on the east, Columbia University; and on the South, Barnard College for Women.

It was something of an accident of interaction that Harry F. Ward had arrived to teach at this posh West-side seminary, where he could maximize his singleness of purpose by clearly contrasting vast poverty with the progress of a few whom he prophesied would be held accountable for the hiatus. On his arrival in the Great Babylon his undivided purpose to criticize and replace the profit economy was uppermost in his mind. So clear was it to him that it pierced the increasing confusion of a dying orderliness. As if standing on the North Pole, all parts of his mental compass indicated one direction only—the inevitability of increasing collectivism. The need was to demonstrate the inevitable process and prevent it from becoming fascistic. It was his religious imperative to make straight the way toward a more humanistic community at home and across the continents.

* * *

However, Ward still lived with the warning that he must protect his health by regular exercise, a healthful diet, and a rhythm of work and play, of classroom and garden, of Union Seminary on Broadway and Lonely Lake in the Canadian wilderness during summer. Perhaps the tension over the nature of the agreement with Boston School of Theology exacerbated his illness. For reassurance he wrote another of his poems in the winter of 1919. Understandably he called it "Consolation":

Where there's no profit in the words of men,
Barren & bitter as a winter breeze;
I will take counsel of the silent stars,
I will hold converse with the friendly trees.

When there's no gladness in the hearts of men,
Whose ceaseless cares have banished mirth;
I hail the welcome of the joyous flowers,
I greet the laughter of the genial earth.

When there's no purpose to the paths of men
But idle trackings of their wandering wills;
I seek the solace of the abiding sea,
I claim the comfort of the unvarying hills. (11)

But a new social-medicine health program was recommended to support his search for consolation. It led to the exploration of the services of one of the truly beneficial, total-medical-care programs that spring up periodically. The Life Extension Institute was headed by Irving Fisher, an economist at Yale; it was planned and operated by prominent physicians of social vision like William H. Welch of Johns Hopkins and Haven Emerson of Columbia.[1] Ward got a thorough, though disturbing, physical examination with these words in the report on it: "Badly underweight," "faulty posture," "lack of muscular development," "albumin in urine," "enlarged tonsils," "some prostate trouble," and "headaches." Affixed to this dour report was a sentence that would seem hardly necessary for this particular patient, "You must have a proper diet and exercise." Certainly he had been dieting and exercising, but perhaps not *properly.* The physician at the institute so advised on April 4, 1919. By December the report from the institute indicated "albumin is normal"; a general improvement had taken place.

Lonely Lake for the three months of summer became indispensable for his physical survival. And for his wife and three children, it was essential. The family needed him for personality growth in its constellation, and he needed the family to involve him in health-giving activity and to prevent what he called the "dry rot of intellectualism." Gordon was now sixteen, Lynd fourteen, and Muriel twelve. Canoe trips of ten days to two weeks into the wilderness became a family pattern starting in 1923. When Dad went into the village of Echo Bay for supplies he was known to tie a fish line around his leg so that he could both fish and row simultaneously. On the long canoe trips, Lynd would take his sketch book, Gordon fished, and Dad did the cooking. This pattern changed some as the boys grew older. After all, Dad liked to fish, very much so, but he later rowed while Gordon would fish. Lynd dropped out of these pack trips after his marriage. Dad summarized his philosophy of fishing with this sentence, "Holding a line from a boat has had a long

Figure 5.1 *(Opposite page) "North of the Height of Land," near Hudson Bay, by Lynd Ward.*

association with the demijohn, but whipping a brook for a trout is a job for men—and for men who can really love the outdoors." Practically speaking, fish—especially fresh bass—was their principal meat food well into the forties at their Shangri-la.

Family rituals, such as fishing, became the colorful threads of remembrances that strengthened the texture of living and added ineffable pleasure to the senior years. Both the camp in Canada and the ten months of "winter" living in Boston and New York were underlining certain interhabituations that gave rise to distinctive selves and marked a particular family. There were many rituals to be recalled in any reminiscing session where both bitter and sweet became palatable. Here are some appearing about midway in the Ward story that may help in understanding the man's consistency and dedication.

Dad made the bread for the family, and he did so with regularity. It was real bread, too, made from whole ground flour. Just as he was proud of his carpentering skill, he was proud to create the staff of life with his hands, for they had a special meaning to him, much as George Herbert Mead traced the growth of mind to the manipulations of the thumb with the four fingers. His Chicago friend offered the insight that hands break rigidities and fixed instincts, and so make "the art of the possible," possible. Ward found a therapy and a life enhancement in the useful work of hands. "Although a thin man," writes daughter-in-law Margaret, "he had large, strong hands. I have seen his hands in many of Lynd's drawings and wood engravings." Who would know how students grasped what was so carefully pointed out to them in last week's lectures? Ward once mused. A cabin or a cabinet built and six loaves of healthful bread baked on each Saturday morning gave a sense of accomplishment and a feeling of relatedness to the workers of the world. No wonder students called it "Christian Ethics" bread. At home he sliced the bread and passed it around: the "Breaking of Bread" together.

A common ritual expected in ministers' families has been to observe "grace" before meals. Dad gave a short one much in the spirit of Rauschenbusch's prayers for working people. Once he paused to thank Mrs. Ward in a prayerful manner for her preparation of the food. At another time he sat quietly while Lynd played "Joe Hill" on his accordian. It was a labor song about hand laborers that Dad accepted as a hymn. His graces were in keeping with the simple, nutritious food.

Almost always Ward, and later Ward and the boys, washed dishes. The presence of guests seldom altered this regularity. Guests were welcomed to take a towel and help. This necessary bit of work was accompanied by a lively discussion, usually of a political nature. Sometimes the Ward rituals became a little threatening to new guests or to a prospective daughter-in-law. Reading the *Nation,* the oldest journal of opinion, as faithfully as Alice Hamilton, M.D.—toxicologist—and her sister, Edith Hamilton—Classicist—did in their home was a weekly ritual. When May McNeer, who was later to become Lynd's wife, sat down to dinner on the first evening she was filled with fears that she could not contribute to the informed discussion of social issues. Ward addressed the charming, over-awed young woman, "Do you read *The Nation?*" Under her breath, "I never heard of it, then audibly, "NO." "What do you read?" pressed the father-in-law to be. May never forgot this first encounter. "He was that way for some of us," she said. "He could scare you to death and make you feel so dumb."

Then there were certain dominant views in this family that were not rituals, but certainly, with the exception of a few possessed by Daisy, were Dad's. They were threaded into the family texture sometimes to become principles, or to be forgotten, or in some cases to be later laughed over. For one, Dad disparaged bridge with a dash of emotion: a little for diversion maybe, but very little. "The bridge parties of these fool women are second only to the bigger gambling parties of their fooler men in the business world," he snapped as his old-fashioned Methodism combined with his modern economics. "It is better," he added, "to be outdoors spending time that relieves stress and brings sleep."

Opera, as has been mentioned, verged on being an effete art form, although he reported enjoying a production at the Bolshoi. In general he agreed with Tolstoy in finding opera distasteful. Other forms of classical music and the Woody Guthrie and Peter Seeger folk songs were listened to and cherished.

Alcoholic beverages, including beer, were taboo in their earlier years, in conformity with Methodist tradition. Once after June and Buell Gallagher, who later became the president of City College, had returned from study in Europe, Ward asked them directly, "Did you drink over there?" "A little wine" was the answer, but their professor frowned. In later life he enjoyed a small glass of wine at the end of the day. He never smoked—none of the Wards did. It was contrary to good health and for Daisy, "It smelled up the house."

What about social dancing? Dad in the nineteen twenties and thirties, still being the traditional Methodist argued, "It is a waste of time and can lead to temptation." Gordon tried to follow his father's ideas and was worried that he had limited opportunities to find the proper girl. Lynd learned "on the qt" in high school and first met May NcNeer at a dance. Muriel learned in Canada, and Daisy—not worried—said, "with my encouragement."

Were they too puritanical? This, of course, would depend upon the definition. They certainly were not puritanical in their larger social contacts. If the Ward ideas were too puritanical on bridge, beer, cigarettes, and such issues, they were generous toward other races, religions, working people, and social concerns. Some, as the reader knows, considered Ward too "liberal" in his economic and religious views.

The Ward family developed what might be termed wholesome ideas about the natural processes of life. The family rituals stressed the development of each member's interests and concerns and respect for each other's efforts. All were expected to contribute to the common good. Their interest in and contact with nature, plants, animals, growth, and seasons caused them to be aware of the unity and naturalness of life. The complete dependence on Nature in the Canadian woods—to the extent, for example, that all members helped to dig pits for the outdoor toilets before the modern flush commodes were installed—was an ordinary fact of life. Baths could be taken in the lake, and if it were too cold, in zinc tubs in front of the fireplace. Such natural experiences can seldom be fathomed by those who live with the artificialities of the city. Procuring their own food with a garden, fishing, and with Ward himself baking the bread, the family clung to minor puritanical attitudes.

For instance, in the family letters at Union, Daisy wrote the children that, when she and Dad were in Shanghai a few days ago, the most exciting event seemed to be the flea that got down her neck and inside her blouse, leading the two Wards to become hilarious trying to catch the flea. In another letter Dad wrote of a trip on a Russian ship where he tried to request from the room steward a chamber pot for their cabin, but Ward knew only a few Russian words. The fellow acted as if he understood the request and led them to a kitchen pantry of pots and pulled one out with flour in it. When he was about to pour the flour into another vessel, Dad said, "No, no, leave the garzok [sic] as it is in simple devotion rather than get it mixed up with the uses we might have for it."

"Our family has been too serious at times in spite of my frivolous tendencies," Daisy wrote in 1932. The dash of John Knoxism in Dad—and it was only a dash—probably caused Daisy to continue: "Dad sometimes is so interested in getting things done right he overlooks the price either he or others must pay." The dominant and often dominating views of Dad were reasons for Daisy, at times, to explain him to the children. She did it with skill. When Gordon wrote to his mother that "I must resign myself to being your son," with all the problems of being an appendage, wise mother wrote back that she was glad for his decision because "you cannot help it." "I know what you mean, Gordon. I have been an appendage a good many years, yet I like to feel that I have an identity of my own. But it's worth a lot to have a father to be proud of." All of the family were tied into the patterns of an earnest man of single purpose, who probably had trouble saying now and then in work or play "to hell with it."

Lynd had married and found an entity of his own in the first successes he was having in his artistic pursuits. Gordon wrote to his mother in India that Lynd was critical of him and this "chaffed" him. With her consummate grace she answered, pointing up a difference in the two. She said "Lynd gets so involved in his work he seems selfish and often leaves work to be done by others which he should do. As he grows older, he will be better." Mother was right. While Gordon worried about getting a wife, she encouraged by writing she had purchased some nice linens and a jade pendant in China "For her—when she comes along and she will!"

Wherever Ward traveled he kept his children and their interests in mind. He kept Gordon, whose special interest was agriculture, informed on what he saw and heard on that subject as he did with art for Lynd. He advised "you had better not call yourself a radical Gordon; it will hurt and block you out." He advised Muriel at Swarthmore to avoid reading thirty books on Anatole France. That is "perfect rot," instead read *him* and not books about him. "Read the originals and make your own reactions, independently of others." He urged Lynd to read the book on Mohandas K. Gandhi that he was sending to him. The following sentences are characteristic. To Muriel: "Swimming, hiking and firing professors is better than grinding and sororities." (Swarthmore, a Quaker College, had long accorded to its students the right of free speech and criticism of the faculty.) And in playful humor "If you will revolutionize Swarthmore, Lynd will humanize Nicolas Miraculous [President Nicholas Murray Butler at Columbia] while Gordon reconstructs Virginia and the rest of the universe. Meantime I'll boss the triple job." Gordon won a prize in oratory in his senior year in college and gained Phi Kappa Phi membership. Ward himself, as will be recalled, was a prize orator and in earlier years proudly wore his Phi Beta Kappa key. Now he offered to pay for Gordon's fee into the honor society for agriculturists and earth scientists. Ward must have felt his sons and daughter were "measuring up" quite well and just possibly due to his didactics.

The appendage feeling of Daisy, especially after her progeny completed college, was softened by the availability of more time for her interest in problems of women, their work and their freedom. She wanted to "be herself" and not solely a wife and mother. If she differed sharply with "Dad," as she always called him in later years, instead of giving in so easily, she would "wager on the differences." The children recall an occasion when she openly resisted her husband at Lonely Lake. She disliked sitting on the front porch of the cottage with a one-to-a-dozen ratio of herself and mosquitoes because there were no screens. She requested the bug barrier. Dad was hotly resistant and argued that fresh air was fresh air only without screens. Ward, no doubt, was indoctrinated with the English idea of the necessity of fresh air and the campaign, at the beginning of the century, for the prevention and cure of consumption with open air. The men folk went off on a two-week fishing expedition. When they returned screens were neatly in place, made by the carpenter hands of Mother this time, with assistance from other women left behind. Dad nursed his anger in silence for several days.

While travelling in Asia Mrs. Ward met with women's groups and began to address them on her own. Two speeches she gave about India, while in Japan, were better than the addresses of two bishops in the week before, according to members of her audience. She spoke clearly, in a matter-of-fact way, and now was being called upon both abroad and at home. Her long and detailed diary on this trip notes again and again the scenes of suffering in China and India from famine and exploitation. The emaciated bodies and arduous puffing of the rickshaw puller were noted with the comment "Who could ever let a half-starved human pull them over the hot roadways?" One entry that undoubtedly helped her self-image was that she was more rugged than her mate on the trying travels. She confided to her diary her wish that she had contracted malaria instead of her husband.

Before leaving on the Asian trip in 1925, attention had to be given to the rite of security in case something should happen to the parents. Dad wanted Mother to go, for he relied on her more now for companionship and care. In their early fifties they still played tennis, two sets each time "to relax and have fun" even though her wrist and his bifocals were bothering. However, they must be certain that the three children would have a little security in case the travelers suffered serious injury or death. Bonds were purchased, some from "the greedy Bell Telephone Company." All of them averaged about 7 percent interest. Daisy was the adviser on this little capitalistic adventure and the one who divided the assets into three portions equally, which came to $1,823 for each person, when they returned.

The Englewood home that Jane, the cook, cared for during the world trip (receiving, in addition to her salary, half the money she made by selling fruit from the trees) was never quite what the Wards envisioned. They sought vista in nature as well as in the unfolding of history; so they looked for an expanse of water, nearby woods, and more garden space. In 1925, wanting to reduce the travel time between home and Union Theological

Seminary and feeling much more secure with President Arthur Cushman McGiffert than with the president in Boston, Ward undertook to build an attractive English cottage–type home on the Palisades above the Hudson River with the vista, the woods in which to walk and picnic, and the space for a large rose garden. For over forty years, 1116 Arcadian Way became the home for the family.

The more secure feeling with President McGiffert was due partly to the fact that the Union president was something of a pragmatic philosopher and an independent thinker himself, who had been reprimanded by the Presbyterian denomination for suggesting that Jesus might have made a mistake or two and that the Last Supper might not have occurred. Despite such heresy Union Seminary was one of the three in America noted at that time for their quality of faculty and their rigorous scholarship. Ward was aware of this and of the seminary's bountiful endowment replenished and protected by the wealthy men who were on the board of trustees. Noting these factors, Ward felt he and his spouse could design and build with confidence the cottage house of their dreams.

New rituals and patterns of family interaction began to add to the old ones, transforming the Palisades cottage into a home. First there was Ward's extensive rose garden. Rose culture was a very special hobby, which doubtless was a vestige of his English background. This can hardly be appreciated until travels in England reveal that almost every household has a rose garden. But he cultivated roses of rarer varieties like "Helen Traubel," "Eclipse," "Dr. Debot," "Mirandy," and "Crimson Glory," bringing them in from nurseries far and near. The New Jersey Cooperative Extension Service in Agriculture tested his soil not only for the best for roses but also for advice on feeding his pin oak tree to bring out coloration. A folder in his file was labeled "Gardening." In it were *New York Times* clippings and others from the *Home Garden Front* and the *Journal of Economic Entomology* on the control of crabgrass, on spraying, problems with iris growing, and a letter from his agriculturist son, Gordon, on the use of fertilizers. In a neat 3-by-5 card file in Ward's handwriting were separate entries for nearly every plant he grew, giving instructions for watering, fertilizing, and cropping—some blos-

Figure 5.2 *Harry and Daisy Ward in Harry's rose garden, Palisades, New Jersey, 1935. (Ward family photo collection.)*

soms and pods may be picked, others must be clipped. Written instructions for the care of house and garden were left each May for those who rented the Palisades home in the summer.

After a decade of living at Arcadian Way the house had become an unpretentious home in a neighborhood of more affluent households, comfortable to the degree of inviting informality and relaxation. Those favored old hats and coats hung in the hallway with raincoats and sturdy walking sticks nearby. Throw rugs were in place on unpolished floors. Ashes from the fireplace, a favorite gathering spot of the family, often sifted to outside the screen. The brassy was missing. So was other show-off bric-a-brac from places the family had traveled. The couch was used, as were the lounge chairs. They looked that way, and over the back of the couch was a heavy wool coverlet for use during a nap for these early risers. The kitchen was small for this family, whose food was as simple and adequate as the rest of the home. No big dinners were served, but instead guests gathered in the dinette, enjoyed rich conversation over homemade bread ("holy bread," as Daisy called it, "because it was made by a preacher") and a delicious vegetable soup. Newspapers, journals, and books were everywhere, for they all read widely. Mrs. Ward was warmly attentive to guests. Ward—without meaning to—tended to create a little unease because of his knowledge of facts, his insight, and his ability clearly to cut through nonsense and uncover the essential. With a bit of trepidation students sought him in his relaxed moments to try their intellectual interpretations of the meanings of current affairs against his analysis and prophecy. This was an oft-repeated happening in a home that was as functional as one's favorite forty-year-old Harris tweed jacket.

Before leaving the descriptions of the family rituals that help in understanding Harry F. Ward, the one on "family communism" must not be overlooked. Ward gave it this title in the days of the Great Depression when a "hard rain" fell. In 1932 Lynd and May were in economic difficulties. Ward faced up to economic problems with his family not in a new way, but in an informed one that anthropologists describe as always used when a culture group is threatened. When the steppes of old Russia were struck by drouth, the Cossacks traditionally pooled the horses and divided the mares' milk equally. The principle was a universal one, applied consistently in wars, famines, and other human tragedies down to the present day. The plan outlined for meeting the Ward family financial needs was to place father's good salary into a common fund for family members to draw on as need demanded. "Family limitations," said the man who always voted for Life, "mustn't be settled on the basis of money."

Notes

1. The institute was located at 25 West 45th Street, New York City. Emerson was the physician who stood almost alone among leading colleagues to defend Prohibition, not on moral grounds but on the basis of careful, extensive laboratory studies he made at Columbia to show the pathologic reaction to the drug, alcohol.

6
Building the American Civil Liberties Union

Political without economic democracy is unworkable wholly.
—Harold Laski

Speak the truth and base men will avoid you.
—William Blake

Some historians have felt that the founding fathers of this nation were not thoroughly consistent in their democratic philosophy. Most of the forefathers defended democracy in religion, government, education—even the family. However, with a few notable exceptions, such as Thomas Paine, Benjamin Franklin, or John Taylor of Caroline County, Virginia, the democratizing of the institution of economics was largely neglected. One need not read economic histories of the United States to note that the economic processes have become dominant in American society, giving rise to a status-seeking individualism and a devotion to seeking unearned profit that have left our country less than an economic democracy and with a system that has often violated our political democracy.

Ward noted this movement of our history. He gave energy and time to help others to see the dangers ahead as corporate juggernauts seemed to monopolize the roadways of life with the throttle of the economy (the GNP)[1] nearing the floor for rapid growth. Traffic lights for economics were too often declared by legislative halls to be illegal. However, there have been attempts to defend Jefferson's warning, "without vision the people perish," by insisting upon the right to free speech, free press, free assembly no matter what might be its effect on economic gain. One of the most effective of these countermovements was the American Civil Liberties Union (the ACLU), whose stated purpose was to defend the Bill of Rights. The first chairman of its national board of directors was Harry Ward (1920–1940).

Passage of the Conscription and Espionage acts of 1917 and the attempts to ban the Industrial Workers of the World (IWW), to arrest and imprison conscientious objectors, and to eliminate socialist literature and activities were some of the reasons for the formation of the American Civil Liberties Bureau, the forerunner of the ACLU. Antilabor activities included establishing the open shop, harassing through the Palmer Raids, convicting Eugene V. Debs in the courts, expelling Socialists from the New York legislature, and deporting and imprisoning Communists. The bureau had been harassed at one time and raided on another by Mitchell Palmer's men from the Justice Department. The ACLU was formed by an amalgamation with the Liberty Defense Union, the American Union Against Militarism, the Workers' Defense League, and others. A conference was called for October 18, 1919, by Elizabeth Gurley Flynn, the labor leader from the Workers' Defense League. The goal was to unite money and strength against moves to repress American workers. The minutes of the conference on October 23, 1919, read, "We are not associated because of any bonds of common belief other than the defense and protection of unpopular minorities" (11).

Ward served on the committee to establish goals and priorities and the recommendations clearly reflect his views and procedures. The aim was to be a champion of freedom of expression in which *labor must be included.* This was one of Ward's first opportunities to make his imprint, the inclusion of labor. The organization was to be national in scope and to contain various interest groups. Three specific categories of labor-oriented people must be represented: (1) those directly engaged in the labor struggle, (2) those involved in writing and speaking on the labor problem, and (3) those liberals who favored the freedom of expression. In the first category on the national executive council, from 1920 to 1940, were people such as A. J. Muste, William Z. Foster, and Rose Schneiderman. In the second were Felix Frankfurter, Father John A. Ryan, Elizabeth G. Flynn, and Ward; and in the third category were such progressives as Harold J. Laski of England, who was teaching at Harvard in the thirties, James Weldon Johnson, and Senator Robert M. LaFollette.

This reorganizing was hardly settled when the national committee of the ACLU invited Ward to be chairman of the board of the new organization that he had helped to create and to define its responsibilities. It was to be named the American Civil Liberties Union. Jeannette Rankin, a pacifist, represented the liberals as vice-chairman, and Duncan McDonald, the other vice-chairman, represented labor.[2] Fifteen years later Ward used this same strategy of broad representation to launch his third successful major effort, the League Against War and Fascism (the first being the Federation and the Social Creed of the Churches and the second the ACLU).

Ward's contribution to the ACLU was possible because major cases of violation of civil rights in the United States were brought before the board, giving him the opportunity to leave his mark on the debates and decisions. He never missed the Monday weekly meetings except when ill or away from New York City, and he wrote careful reports on the infractions of liberties discussed. Because many members of the board attended irregularly, a great responsibility was left on the chairman's shoulders.[3]

Labor problems were many. There were attempts to suppress the IWW in southern California. There was direct legislation to throttle labor and its unions. The Lusk Committee of New York was threatening unions whose members might be socialist or communist. Teachers in classrooms were being warned their jobs could be in jeopardy if they so much as mentioned the new proletarian government in the USSR. The laws that produced these cases were under various Criminal Anarchy or Sedition statutes that existed in one form or another in thirty-nine states. They grew out of laws opposing Socialists, Communists, immigrants, and conscientious objectors of World War I. However, according to Ward, "These have been used entirely in industrial disputes and always against those who are trying to improve the conditions of labor" (327).

Ward had many other opportunities to participate directly in advancing the cause of labor and economic democracy by reaching a wide audience in speaking at many public meetings and to church groups. For example, he went to Pittsburgh in March 1920 to address several meetings of the Committee for Organizing Strikes. The ACLU gave him money for this trip from the Garland Fund. He addressed steelworkers committees on the issues of free speech in their campaign.

In 1930 there was an attempt by the Veterans of Foreign Wars to hold a counterdemonstration to threaten those celebrating Labor Day. "While we recognize that no working class organization has an exclusive right to the use of this public property [Union Square, New York City] nevertheless custom establishes a strong precedent," Ward wrote (1). The ACLU appealed to Mayor Jimmy Walker, and Ward explained the left parties and the unions should not be molested in their desire to protest unemployment.

In most cases the freedom of speech and labor issues appeared inseparably interrelated. Henry Ford's agents, for example, were physically abusing workers because they wanted freedom to organize, while at the same time Ford was claiming the freedom to express himself by circulating antiunion literature on factory bulletin boards. The "liberals" on the board who defended free speech without regard for critical interrelated issues voted for Ford's right to free expression; Ward, and a minority, voted against and proposed a substitute statement reading in part:

> . . . that the restriction imposed upon the right of the employer to express himself to his employees concerning unions is occasioned and limited by his restrictions of the right of the workers to organize. . . . Restrictions on the employer will cease as soon as restrictions on workers cease. When the employer grants freedom and democratic procedure, *then* his right of expression may be approved. (1)

The National Labor Relations Board soon after ruled in favor of the Ward view and called upon Ford to cease and desist.

As Ward's chairmanship progressed it was clear that he was more concerned with basic issues like the Ford case than the civil-rights cases, which were legion, but of less fundamental importance for economic democracy. He defended, nonetheless, every variety of encroachment on liberty. There was the espousement of Emma Goldman's right to speak freely on anarchism. Although Ward in general opposed her philosophy, he wrote, "We can afford to endure a good many Emma Goldmans rather than imperil that right" (1). There was also the ACLU petition to the attorney general of the United States to free political prisoners who had resisted World War I. The organization provided

Figure 6.1 *From Lynd Ward's* Wild Pilgrimage.

legal advisers to assist Clarence Darrow in the famous Scopes trial. It gave money and aid to save the lives of Sacco and Vanzetti and the nine Scottsboro Blacks who were to die for the alleged rape of one white girl. It publicized acts of police commissioner Grover Whalen as "Whalen Espionage" because he used police to spy and report on New York City teachers' remarks in their classrooms in an attempt to uncover pacifists, pro-Russian or prosocialist advocates, or even members of the ACLU. The defense of the men of the Bonus March who went into the battlefields near the White House was still another active concern for Ward's board.

There were cases in which freedom of press and right to read were involved. The Post Office Department was opening letters and mail of citizens to seek out revolutionary or communistic literature and identify subversives. There was the attempt to ban a widely used textbook, *Modern History*, written in 1923 by Columbia University historians Carlton Joseph Huntley Hayes and Parker Thomas Moon. The ACLU board protested vigorously, and the chairman wrote in part:

> In the first place, it is absurd to throw that book out after it has been used seven years. If they have any reason to throw it out now, it is a confession of delinquency on the part of the superintendents. There is no question about Professor Hayes standing as a competent, fair-minded historian, and he ranks with the leading historians in the country.
> The complaint that the book confuses democracy, nationalism, capitalism and religion is ridiculous. If we were to have no criticism of any of these, then we had better shut up the schools and have no history. (1)

In some respects protection of religious freedom was almost as difficult as upholding laws to control cartels or to regulate international banking. The ACLU had tried for years to protect the freedom of religion and gave, for example, wholehearted support to the Jehovah's Witnesses in their struggle to live their religion. Ward, an ordained Methodist clergyman, had no reservations about finding a person to help test the legality of widespread Bible reading imposed upon children in the public schools. "The ACLU," he wrote, "offers its services free of charge to any Catholic, Jewish, or agnostic family" interested in testing the constitutionality of such behavior (11).

In reading the minutes of the ACLU the conflict between the reformist liberals and the progressive social-change groups becomes more and more evident. The first may be represented by Norman Thomas, J. H. Holmes, and Roger Baldwin. The progressive wing, in contrast, was led by Corliss Lamont and Elizabeth Flynn. The conflict seemed to grow out of a difference in perception of the basic issue. Freedom of speech for those who dwelled on predominately noneconomic issues was different from freedom of speech for those who worked with labor and minority groups, unemployed persons, and political associates concerned with economic issues. The latter needed equal rights to speak, to picket, and to *organize*. They deserved the more careful protection.

It might be interesting here to note the actual political complexion of the board. For example, in 1931 eight were members of the Socialist party of Norman Thomas, seven were Republicans, six were Democrats, four were Farmer-Labor, and one, Elizabeth Flynn, was a Communist. Four were either not members of a party, or they preferred anonymity. When asked to state their vote in the election that year the tally showed eleven Socialist votes, nine Farmer-Labor, six Democrat, two Republican, one Communist (again Flynn), and one Single Taxer.[4]

To state Dr. Ward's position fairly one must make clear that he was concerned always with minority rights, but he insisted all civil rights for these groups must be defended, not just freedom of speech. He protested the segregation of the American Indian and the black Gold Star mothers when they were taken by the federal government to visit their sons' graves in Flanders Fields and thereby anticipated the revolutions of rising expectations in the sixties and seventies. He fought injunctions, yellow-dog contracts, industrial spying, use of the third degree in jails and prisons, and lynching. A case in which emotions ran high, marking the division in the board, was the report that Communists attempted "to break up" a meeting addressed by a paid professional anti-Soviet by the name of Viktor Chernov. Earl Browder, then the national leader of the Communist party, explained that the liberals were permitting Naziism by not resisting vigorously.

He argued that Chernov could speak freely, but if Communists protested it was interpreted as "breaking up" and therefore contrary to the ideals of the ACLU. Browder felt Communists and others should raise "angry protests" and participate in "demonstrations of disapproval." The "liberals" on the board resented the idea of the Communist leader and would not accept the view that the USSR would play a major role in overthrowing the Nazi dictatorship. Baldwin warned Browder that such demonstrations should cease for "if you wish to hold present middle class support, better reconsider."

Ward continued his defense of minority rights in the late thirties by initiating through the ACLU board an effort to defeat the proposals of the Fish Committee to outlaw the Communist movement in the United States. Files of the organization in Princeton Library reveal that its chairman wrote:

> The proposals to outlaw the Communist movement on the grounds of its political principles, not because of any acts charged against it, strike squarely at freedom of speech, press and assemblage. The inevitable result of these recommendations, if adopted would be to drive the Communist movement into an underground of conspiracy. It would produce results far worse in disorder and violence than the policy of letting the movement advocate its principles freely without restraint.
>
> The proposals are absurd on their face. The immigration and deportation laws concerning communists are already too comprehensive. The committee's "investigations" show no conditions in this country which justify strengthening the already too stringent laws against free speech enacted during and since the war. Only fear to face the economic conditions which produce Communist protest could possibly prompt such a sweeping and hysterical program of repression. (1)

The ACLU backed away from this declaration and in 1940 disavowed the man who wrote it.

The reformist-radical conflict took a great deal of tact and time on Ward's part. He felt the "liberals" were unsteady, chameleonic, and required an inordinate amount of "research," or they required hours of patience when they quibbled over word meanings or when at times they formed a block of stubborn opposition. The nub of the conflict between the factions was made explicit by him: "Our traditional doctrine of civil liberty grew up with laissez-faire economy. With the coming of planned, cooperative living it must be rewritten in terms of social controls necessary for the fullest freedom of development for all. Meantime civil liberties must be defended not as personal rights but as the indispensable instrument of social change" (1). It was frustrating and tiring for a man of action like Ward and others of his views, but together they made the ACLU effective for many years until the Red Scare stormed the board meetings.

A definitive history of the ACLU has not been written. Extant writings have been cold war marred and have overemphasized the role of Roger Baldwin, leaving the impression that he was the central figure in the American Civil Liberties Union.[5] Most letters and documents written for the organization were signed "Roger Baldwin, Director." One writer concluded that "the ACLU *is* Baldwin," and still another wrote that "Baldwin was the moving spirit behind the ACLU." He played an undeniably strong role, but Ward's contribution has not been fully presented.

Peggy Lamson, in her *Roger Baldwin* (291), presents an interesting portrait of Baldwin. She found him concerned, dedicated, but at times somewhat too breezy and temporizing. He could never understand people who found the labor movement to be a philosophy of life and a fundamental way to a better day. (While speaking prolabor he made uninformed remarks that Jews, for example, were not prolabor in the nineteen twenties!) Two clashing motivations dominated Baldwin's personality: a desire to hobnob with the rich and wellborn on one hand and a passionate desire to eliminate poverty and injustice on the other. He seemed never to reconcile the two. In his later years he summarized his life and activities, "I took the Christian underdog doctrine for the ACLU." Lamson summarized him as "a contrary fellow with a simple purpose."

Ward was in contrast a contemplative man with a single purpose. He was prolabor and molded the structure of the ACLU in that direction. That Baldwin and he would clash was almost inevitable. It surfaced several times before the ugly final separation in 1940; for instance, in 1926, when Baldwin was preparing for an extended trip to Europe, he spoke of "the stalwarts" who made it easy for him to go. The organization was "in good hands," he wrote, with John Haynes Holmes as vice-chairman and Norman Thomas influential on the executive board. Actually neither man was reliable about attending meetings, but that aside, Director Baldwin made no comment about Chairman Ward. Similarly Donald Johnson in his book *The Challenge to American Freedoms: World War I and the Rise of the ACLU* (287), written for the Mississippi Valley Historical Association in 1963, makes no mention of Ward's leadership and contributions. The chairman's devoted and fundamental work has tended to be painted over by uncritical praise of the debonair Baldwin. The rift between them grew as the ACLU moved into its second decade.

Off on the horizon a storm cloud was moving toward the Civil Libertarians. The "great scare" that President Truman predicted would be required to turn the people into haters of an ally in World War II was on its way. The actual political complexion of the executive board was quite balanced, as noted previously, as the tornado approached.

However, criticisms had been coming from many sources. Most were pointed at Ward. As early as 1921 twelve questions came from Huntington, Indiana, from an ACLU member, the Reverend Frank Day, Methodist. "Do you mean to say that the capitalistic system cannot insure justice and human rights?" "What do you mean when you say the Roman Church sought to translate into human life the vision of a povertyless [sic] world and had almost achieved that end in the middle ages; or as you say they lived under the shadow of that spiritual unity?" To which Ward replied tersely and briefly, stating an answer would require too much time and "If I had time, I should not feel inclined to do it—can't see answer would be of any possible use" (11). He usually dealt with what appeared to be arrogant stupidity in this way.

Calvin Coolidge attacked Ward by misquoting him in *The Delineator* (1921). The future president wrote that Ward said, "I am a member of the ACLU and our aim is to get a fair trial for all our people who are arrested in their efforts to bring about a new order." Mrs. William Brown Maloney, editor, was sent Ward's reply. "I did not make this statement, which is a misrepresentation of the nature and purpose of the American Civil Liberties Union as repeatedly expressed in its printed matter"

(1). Coolidge apparently quoted one of Ward's books out of context, suggesting that it argued the need to use force and violence in change. Ward was about to send a copy of his answer to President McGiffert of Union, when he received a phone call from his supportive superior that included the advice not to trouble to send it, for the misstatements from the White House had already been noticed. This kind of reassurance from an administrator foiled the rapiers of critics.

The superpatriots also began to attack through the Better America Federation. Its newsletter in 1922 carried this item: "The ACLU was founded and is headed by Roger Baldwin, who served a year in jail for dodging the draft, and the chairman of its press bureau is none other than Reverend professor Harry Ward, the ultra socialist propagandist who filled Methodist publications with economic and political poison until he was deposed" (1).

The charged words of advocating "force and violence" were repeatedly hurled at those suspected of being Communists. In 1923 a J. H. Hansen on the prairies of Nebraska kept alive what the *New York Call* dubbed the stupidities of Coolidge, by writing that H. F. Ward urged the West Virginia miners to use guns. Characteristically Ward replied that he had never advocated violence "in personal, international or industrial relations" and asked Hansen to send him the names and the dates of the newspapers where he found this material. No reply. Ward could not have avoided noting the darkening sky with the promise of the storms of Martin Dies and, later still, of Joseph McCarthy.

More organization was his answer to threats. He called in June 1931 a "Conference for Joint Action" to find the issues on which all participants, twenty-six organizations, could agree and work. Included among others were the American Jewish Congress, the American League to Abolish Capital Punishment, the Cooperative League of America, the Fellowship of Reconciliation (a peace organization), the National Association for the Advancement of Colored People, the Consumers' League, the Amalgamated Clothing Workers, the Federal Council of Churches, the National Education Association, the Urban League, and his own Methodist Federation for Social Service.

At the first meeting Ward gave the keynote speech. The body then selected a general committee, with Ward as chairman, to arrange for (1) better research and fact finding, (2) more expert consultants, (3) prevention of the waste of overlap in printing and mailing, (4) wholesale purchasing, and (5) joint lobbying. The stated purpose of this social combine was "to promote better cooperation among agencies in the field of social action." Its name was to be The Joint Conference for the Defense of Civil Liberties. This larger group plan never matured, but it is indicative of Ward's insistence on organization that would give power to more people and revealed his basic anxiety about the erosion of civil liberties in the country.

In 1940, however, after twenty years dedication and service in the American Civil Liberties Union temple where a "walking, not talking" religion was advocated and practiced, Ward was moved to resign. By refusing to bow to the current dogma of pillorying people not bathed in the grace of patriotism, he must resign on principle. Communists were being called economic witches, murderous hobgoblins, and rapists of body and mind and were considered subversive demons that lived on the red blood of the body politic, the body "free enterprise." He no more believed such things about the socialistic minded or the Socialists than he believed atrocity stories about the labor movement. The patriotic protectors of the libertarian laissez nous faire creed in government, in church, and in the organization he had done so much to advance became intent on checking his effectiveness. When liberals closed in, and he saw that he could no longer "worship" by defending the rights of all, he resigned.

Three books have appeared in recent years that have helped to keep the record straight on what happened in the ACLU leadership at the end of the thirties. Peggy Lamson's *Roger Baldwin* (291) has been quoted. Lucille B. Milner, whom Baldwin called a "field director," had the advantage of knowing Ward well from the regular Monday meetings.[6] She presented him as a man of few words, a fearless fighter for freedom. He stood out in her memory among all the others because of her profound admiration for his leadership, marked by great energy and insight, and his influence, "so necessary" to the work. She wrote of him as follows:

> Our first chairman, was Harry F. Ward, Professor of Christian
> Ethics at Union Theological Seminary, who had spent more than
> twenty years in religious activities, as teacher and preacher. He
> was a thin, wiry little man with a sensitive face and thoughtful
> eyes, set deep under bushy eyebrows, they seemed to be searching
> unceasingly for the many problems that beset us. He was a man
> of few words, but I had the feeling Dr. Ward would be in the
> vanguard of fighters for freedom until they put him in his grave.
> "You and I will die standing up for the civil liberties fight,"
> Roger once laughingly said to me. I was certain that if we did,
> we would be standing with Dr. Ward at our side. (301)

In his *The Trial of Elizabeth Gurley Flynn* (290), Corliss Lamont, the Columbia University philosopher, offered in 1968 the verbatim record of the Flynn trial. The volume was dedicated to Harry F. Ward because Lamont knew that Ward drove himself to exhaustion and illness in trying to prevent the ACLU from splitting. In 1976, the Bicentennial year of our nation's founding, the ACLU voted to rescind its charges and reverse its decision against Elizabeth Flynn. Ten years after his death, thirty-six years after the incident, Ward was vindicated.

Reading the Baldwin papers at Princeton and the Ward papers at Union Theological Seminary supports the views of the three books and throws more light on Ward's detractors. From this study he emerges as the one of insight and courage. The writers Sydney Hook, Eugene Lyons, and Benjamin Stolberg were presenting the idea that the Soviet Union and Nazi Germany were fundamentally the same types of government. The polarity of the two systems escaped them. A left socialist system on one hand and on the other a largely capitalist order of fascism were treated as the same kind of dictatorship, to be equally condemned. A number of ACLU board members saw that this cloudy thinking could wreck their unity and serve only reactionaries; so they requested their chairman to join in writing and signing a letter to criticize the view. Hook, who had begun as early as 1934 to attack Ward in what Lamont called "the most extreme and bitter terms," took up the cudgel in October 1939 by answering the ACLU board in a speech at a large meeting in New York City. Hook then wrote to Baldwin that Ward had "besmirched by the foulest means" those who criticized "Russian terrorism" and that he lacked "emotional balance and a judicious mind" (1). Lamont was certain that Hook's remarks "verged slander" (290).

Hysteria prompted by these writers and the fears aroused by the Dies Committee caused former friends, says Milner, "to hatch a plot to force Harry Ward out of the ACLU because of his beliefs" (301). Norman Thomas had come to Ward in 1919 and urged him to be chairman of the ACLU because of his close contact with labor. But now, in 1939 in his Socialist paper the *Call*, Thomas was one of the first to cry "resign" because Ward was to him irresponsible in not criticizing the Soviet Union in the same way he did the Nazis. Baldwin was asked about the spreading of poisonous rumors among board members. Five weeks after the Hook and Thomas blasts, he assured Ward's friends that no acrimony prevailed. Moves to force out Ward were "quite without foundation," he wrote, and all such talk must not be released to the newspapers. Both Norman Thomas, who led the attack in executive-board sessions, and Roger Baldwin knew this assurance of normalcy was not true.

The principal actors contrasted, one with the other. Ideologically, Ward and Thomas did not get along well. Students reported that Ward stated in class that Thomas was driven more by a desire to destroy communism than to attack the profit system. Thomas did speak for a *partly* socialist society where only four or five basic needs, like energy and transportation, would be provided by government. Ward, on the other hand, felt this middle way, the mixed public and private sector idea, could not work because of the ever-present corrupting influence of private gain.

In some respects Baldwin and Ward had similarities. Both enjoyed canoeing, fishing, and gardening, activities they both said Thomas would not like. They agreed Norman shunned "roughing it." He was more sedate and proper, an intellectual who married into wealth. His children attended fashionable schools and no more enjoyed mingling with workers and slum dwellers than did their father and mother. John Haynes Holmes came closer to being Thomas's counterpart, except even more formal, almost pontifical with his pressed suit, white shirt, gold-chained watch, black bow tie, and pince-nez. These were the three principals who carried on at times what came close to being hypocritical machinations against Ward. Letters reveal consciences that must have caused pain, because in correspondence each tried to rationalize away, in later years, a culpability for the behavior.

Morris Ernst, an FBI lawyer on the ACLU board who boasted of being J. Edgar Hoover's personal attorney and a treasured friend, supported Thomas in board meetings that led to the purge. They seemed the least contrite afterwards. For the ninetieth-birthday celebration of Ward, Thomas, for example, wrote a sentence stating that differences existed, but he wished to acknowledge the "friendship and instruction" that had existed between himself and Ward (11). Baldwin, during an interview with me in 1973 (13), kept repeating phrases like "no doubt a man of principle, a man of great probity and high personal conduct." "One of the boys who tried to put a red cap on the Cross." A revealing remark he made at the time was less a judgment of Ward than of himself: "He never knew who his God was."[7] Baldwin was saying that his former friend, with whom he exchanged flower bulbs and occasionally roughed it in the woods, couldn't choose between Jesus and Marx. This statement, coming from one who had difficulty finding a unifying loyalty in his own life, is not surprising. A follower and friend of Emma Goldman, Baldwin was tinged by her philosophical anarchism leaving him to believe in freedom with no text, context, and at times no sense of responsibility.

As for Holmes, his conscience seemed to intrude even more. On December 4, 1939, he wrote that he wanted no purges of his associates. One month later on January 2, 1940, he made his most serious charges against Ward. He "couldn't hold things together," even though Holmes could not say that Ward was a Communist "in either the party or the doctrinaire sense of the word." The ACLU chairman could not manage those who were Communists; he could not "instill good manners." Then Holmes added that Ward was "shrewd, calculating, able and brave, a scholar of high academic rank" (1). This double talk was damning with faint praise. It grew more disturbing when it questioned

Ward's usefulness to Christianity, "which he is supposed to expound and represent in Union Theological Seminary." Twenty-three years later Holmes wrote that he would be glad to be a sponsor for the ninetieth-birthday celebration, but he admonished Mrs. Ruth France, a solid friend of the Wards and organizer of the celebration, for mentioning "a break" between him and Ward. "I mourn when I see somebody dropping out of my life because we have had some disagreement or dispute which is taken for granted as an occasion of separation."[8] With some conscience cresting, Holmes still blamed "his friend" Harry Ward for the whole disreputable mess.

Quietly guiding the controversial policies of the American Civil Liberties Union for twenty years was the second of the three major contributions that Ward made in his active lifetime. Several highpoints of historical importance need emphasis. "Divide and rule" is a pervasive policy in efforts to destroy democratic procedures. Was this method of dividing the leadership successful in changing the whole course of the ACLU? Martin Dies, congressman from Texas and the chairman of the House Un-American Activities Committee (HUAC), wrote to Professor Lamont on July 20, 1955, and admitted that Morris Ernst and Arthur G. Hayes, ACLU lawyers, did call upon him and that he advised them as liberals to join the conservatives in exposing Communists. In fact he urged that liberals take the initiative in the exposé. The liberals did, with some private investigation done by Joseph B. Matthews, the well-paid investigator for the HUAC.[9] Dies proclaimed that the ACLU was not protecting Communists and would not be investigated by his congressional committee. The ACLU lawyers, by yielding to Dies, permitted the departure of Flynn and Ward as the price to be paid by an organization set up to defend the rights of citizenship in the United States. ACLU would not be posted in the newspapers of the land as a red-front organization.

The intrigue with Dies split the ACLU. More than that, for the first time in U.S. history it pointed out which citizens or organizations could enjoy "certain inalienable rights." Nazis, pornographers, advocates of child abuse, and racists could have certain rights the politically recognized Communist party members could not. This conclusion was the basic reason why Ward felt he must resign, and he made it clear in his letter of resignation. He wanted no "doctrinal tests" for citizenship. There must be no "test of consistency in defense of civil liberties," no creating of an "orthodoxy of belief." He alone, no other board member, walked out of the ACLU boardroom forever. His social religion made him firmly confident that rights are inalienable.

In these years, too, he became "Doctor Ward," an honor bestowed upon him by a progressive-minded university president, Glen Frank, through the official action of one of America's outstanding liberal institutions, the University of Wisconsin. His honorary Doctor of Law degree in 1931 was awarded because of his significant public services where as "chairman of the ACLU you have valiantly defended those basic rights of free speech, free press and free association without which neither scientific advance nor social progress is possible." Earlier that same year Ward visited Madison to help William Gorham Rice, noted law professor and civil libertarian, activate the Wisconsin Civil Liberties Union. The Reverend George "Shorty" Collins, the YMCA director on the campus, was the first president, with Rice as chairman of the board.

Later in the thirties Ward suggested that the recently founded New School for Social Research, an institution established to help employ scholars who had escaped the tyranny of Hitler, should introduce a course to train those who "go into social action." In the same vein he gave his support to "Reconciliation Trips" run by Clarence V. Howell, a fellow Methodist and former student, who led carefully planned visits to the slums of the Bowery and to the minority sections of New York City, like Harlem, Little Italy, and Chinatown. Howell kept his groups, mainly composed of graduate students, together on the subways and in the crowded streets by blowing a small Swedish post horn. Mrs. Howell's and his simple living (he charged hardly enough to buy their food) and complete dedication to bringing thirty to sixty people at a time to see, feel, smell, and hear how the poor and the racially and nationally exploited lived and worked, many claimed was the most important "course" they took while on Morningside Heights. This social-action teacher, known and trusted by so many in Black Harlem and the Lower East Side, has had little recognition. Ward would announce

Howell's tours each week in his classes and urge the students to go and "feel into the situation," as the University of Michigan social philosopher Charles Cooley expressed the experience.

Ward's crowning achievement of the twenty years was the solid groundwork he built for the American Civil Liberties Union. With consummate skill he took charge of the grievance procedure that was the central function of the union. As Lucille Milner's important book adds, "We were not committed to any program or to any cause, but we soon found ourselves forced by circumstances on the side of labor. Labor denounced the war as capitalistic, and capital arrested, imprisoned and mobbed labor on patriotic grounds" (301).

As his family correspondence indicates, Ward was shaken by the lack of recognition of his efforts. He reacted in two ways. "Tell Daisy" was the abiding one since the Social Creed injustice, and the second was to have a psychosomatic setback that involved both his overworked body and his bruised self-image. Just after his resignation, his physician urged a complete rest in Mexico. Muriel, to protect her father's health, did not write to him about the ACLU board's final expulsion of Elizabeth Flynn and the board "trial" at which Holmes, the new chairman, broke a four-to-four tie to support the expulsion. Ward wrote to his daughter asking her to formulate a true version of why he resigned for the news media. The "purgers" had, according to the board secretary, Lucille Milner, tried to change and rewrite the minutes over her protest. They also attempted to release as little as possible to the press. Muriel, with the help of her brother Lynd, followed the request of her father. Their announcement to the press prompted a letter from Baldwin saying he was sorry the two had to do this. It was an "unhappy task which we could have spared you."

Many of Ward's friends came to his defense. One was Franz Boas, who, besides being the author of groundbreaking books in anthropology, was a teacher who respected the minds of women and encouraged his students Ruth Underhill, Gene Weltfish, Ruth Benedict, and Margaret Mead. He signed a protest against the treatment of Ward, as did Robert Lynd, one of the *Middletown* sociologists, and I. F. Stone, the watchdog journalist who sniffed out media distortions and printed the other side of the news. Carey McWilliams, who later became the editor of the *Nation*, was another. And there were lawyers, too, who thought the ACLU machinations were illegal. Counted among these were the Darrow-like A. J. Isserman, Osmond Fraenkel, and Russell Chase, a founder and president of the National Lawyers' Guild.[10]

Members of the board and of the national committee of the ACLU signed a statement at the time of Ward's resignation. Some of the better-known signatories were Corliss Lamont, Quincy Howe, Walter Frank, Nathan Greene, Carl Carmer, Elmer Rice, and, hypocritical though it may seem, John Haynes Holmes. The statement read, in part, that they:

> Desire to express to you their profound appreciation of the devoted services which you have so signally rendered to the cause of civil liberty through the Union. In the history of organizations devoted to the public welfare, it has been a rare service marked by painstaking attention to the Union's role and activities, by unqualified fairness in dealing with the many controversies which have risen and by unflagging energy in the promotion of the cause which we all serve.
>
> We trust that in retiring from the chairmanship of the Union after these twenty years, you will feel, despite recent unhappy divisions among us, a sense of accomplishment both in what the Union has done under your leadership and in what we have stood for in American life. (1)

Milner, present through all of Ward's tenure with the ACLU, wrote that the chairman's treatment was a turning point in the American liberal movement. "A superb job he did; not the least being to keep things stabilized between two Socialisms." "He had," she continued, "great tact and could be firm, even stern, but always fair. A practical idealist, he was spokesman for neither side. He helped us free ourselves of erroneous beliefs and old myths. I learned high standards of courage and fair play" (301).

While in Mexico Ward wrote to Muriel, house-sitting on the Palisades, to send a manuscript chapter for what would be a part of his last book. "You will find it back of my chair in the study, underneath the shelf below the books, in the center pile." The tired scholar then turned to his everlasting love of flowers and added, "when your snow is gone you will see some snowdrops and soon there will be days warm enough for Johnny to trim the hedge." Then would come June and Lonely Lake where he always renewed body and mind. The double cross of rejection and disappointment he bore in his last year with the ACLU would be eased by his knowledge of how history moves. The experience would strengthen him for further leadership in the morality of social action. He was only sixty-seven.

Notes

1. Gross National Product.

2. McDonald was leader of the United Mine Workers in Chicago and head of the Illinois Labor Council.

3. Barton Bean (327), p. 143, said "it was a working board" and "Board members still pay much more attention to minor details than is customary."

4. Bean's thesis (327), p. 165, states "the number of clergymen who served on the National Committee is striking, even more is the bishops. This undoubtedly reflects not only the desire for 'good' names but the strength of 'socialized Christianity,' and the influence of Harry Ward, outstanding exponent of social gospel at Union Theological Seminary." His many tours throughout the country, both as Chairman of the Board of the ACLU and on behalf of other causes, notably the League Against War and Fascism, strengthened his acquaintance and influence in this regard.

5. Bean (327), p. 50, wrote in a footnote: "Most biographical treatments of Baldwin tend to be uncritically laudatory, e.g. Jensen, *World Tomorrow*. Dwight McDonald, *The Defense of Everybody* has the most research and is unfriendly in tone. For example, 'Baldwin . . . is an unsure philosopher, too much attracted by power.' " Bean is not sure he agrees with this. He feels Joseph Freeman, *An American Testament*, is the best "point of view of a pitying communist."

Bean interviewed twenty persons for this thesis: among them Baldwin (at length), J. H. Holmes, Scott Nearing, Norman Thomas, Alan Reitman, Morris Ernst. He especially thanks Arthur Garfield Hayes. He did not interview Ward or Lucille Milner (see footnote 6 this chapter).

6. Lucille Bernheimer Milner was a founder of the ACLU and the wife of a successful New York City real estate broker. After her devotion as executive secretary for twenty-five years she wrote *The Education of an American Liberal* (301), which revealed more exactly what transpired

in the inner circles of the ACLU in the first twenty years. The *New York Herald Tribune* carried a review of the book in the July 11, 1954 issue. It in part read that the author "participated in key cases which made civil rights history during the administrations of Wilson, Harding, Coolidge, FDR and Truman." The *New Yorker* of August 28, 1954, called it one of the few of that kind that was inspirational. Her obituary in the *New York Times* (Aug. 18, 1975) stated her one book to be a significant "history of liberal America after World War I."

7. There is considerable evidence in the records that many people confided in Ward even though he was reserved in personality. One confidant was liberal activist Marguerite Tucker, whose letter tells us even more about the unsteady pattern of Baldwin's life than Lamson has revealed. Tucker describes his changes of wives and the stark tragedy of his two adopted sons. She wrote Dr. Ward on March 10, 1940 as follows: "You must know the very important place I had in Roger's life—formerly. Although I was hidden away, it was none too easy a position, and I blame no one but myself. But I do feel that had Roger followed the inclination of his heart rather than his head, matters might have turned out differently. But perhaps this is only my conceit." The purpose of the letter was to say that Ward's leaving the ACLU was "painful to her" and that she regretted the break between two fine friends and workers. Ward was ill and away for rest and recuperation. Muriel, who was helping him with his mail, wrote in the corner of the letter "I did not acknowledge this for she probably expected you alone to see it."

8. However Holmes continued insisting that Ward did not resign from his ACLU post, but was *asked* to resign. As late as Dec. 15, 1966, *Time* magazine stated that Ward was "thrown out." Lynd Ward corrected this and wrote that his father resigned over the principles of civil liberties and the rights of Communists.

9. When I first knew Matthews, he was something of a roué and sensational radical, a bright young man who had taught Bible courses in a southern "hard-shelled Baptist" seminary. He was promptly dismissed from his institution in 1925 for bringing a black woman to a dance. In time he came to New York City to become an executive of the Fellowship of Reconciliation, a peace organization. From here he went on to advocate atheism, free love, anarchism, and, as the occasion warranted, left socialism.

In the early 1940s J.B., as he was known to his friends, made a Damascus-like flip-flop from brazen leftist to aggressive rightist and was quickly picked up as chief investigator for the Dies Committee. When I visited him in the House Office Building he pointed to a bullet-shaped scar on one of his windows. "The Communists are out to get me," he said, "and there is the proof." He broke with his old friends, calling many to appear before the congressional committee so that he might accuse them. Thus he ruined reputations and lives. A paranoid cynicism could characterize his outlook the rest of his days.

10. Baldwin about this time had been working to expel Chase from the Cleveland ACLU for defending the rights of the Communist party. Chase wrote to Ward about it on Dec. 31, 1941.

7
The Internationalist Experience

The young father and clergyman, Harry Ward, had his first international experience (except for his emigration from England) on his journey in 1908–1909 as a travel aide to a wealthy senior Methodist Chicagoan. Although this was an absorbing educational journey around the world, some of Ward's reactions were not so profound as those he expressed on his next trip in 1924–1925. "Dear Heart," as he addressed Daisy in letters, was with him on the second trip. Therefore, Ward had a travel aide and a wife-companion rolled into one. The Chinese Committee on Foreign Lectures invited him to lecture in their universities on ethical aspects of industrialism. He was the third Westerner chosen to speak, Bertrand Russell and John Dewey having preceded him. However, university student committees heard of the success of his lectures, and they insisted on a lecture visit also.

Since the couple traveled with a purpose in mind, they could discuss their experiences thoroughly, a maturing process used about the same time by the Beards and the Webbs. The Wards wanted particularly to learn what the average persons of the country were feeling, thinking, and doing. Avid reading of the English newspapers in the country they visited was not sufficient. They avoided the overstuffed furniture and excess food in western-type hotels and stayed in missionary compounds, homes of friends (usually former students), pensions, and hostels. They supplemented this, wherever they could, by searching for workers' organization leaders and by long walks in the lowly areas where the great majority of Asians lived.

* * *

In his first judgments about India in 1909, Ward held that the country was not yet ready for autonomy. An essay he wrote entitled "The Unrest in India" sounded in a few places like some of the biases in Katherine Mayo's *Mother India*. But when her unfair book appeared in 1928 to strengthen Britian's imperialism and give it a cast of righteousness, the Wards' world insights had increased such that they were horrified by the gross propaganda in the book.

Three years after Mayo's ethnocentrism appeared in print, the Wards were expressing sympathy and understanding toward the poverty and degradation of the Indian people. Both of them became strong defenders of Mohandas K. Gandhi, the Mahatma, and of "his light that will never be put out." These feelings were published in the *Christian Century* of June 4, 1925, in an article that Ward wrote with his wife's help, entitled "Gandhi and the Future of India." Before making the trip in 1924, Ward tried to keep alert to the little whirlwinds of dust and leaves in Asia that portended a storm. This he had done by careful reading and by correspondence with his former students, Indian and Chinese, who provided him with essential, firsthand information.

One of these was S. P. Arya in Madras, who was asked in 1922 about the Hunter Report and the accuracy of the testimony given at the inquiry about the Amritsar Massacre.[1] "The noncooperation movement also greatly interests me," Ward wrote, "I shall be glad to get your opinion as to these happenings" (11). In like manner he got reports from friends in China with the National Christian Council and the YMCA. Both organizations were sympathetic with the reform movements in Asia, opposed the practice of extraterritoriality for Westerners, and upheld leaders like Gandhi and Sun Yat-sen.

Daisy, in particular, was enthusiastic over the philosophy of Gandhi. In 1924 she was praising him in letters written to her children from Bombay; and well she might since she had to keep an appointment with Gandhi for both of them. Ward was seriously debilitated by malaria, leaving his wife to discuss her own interest in spinning and weaving with the Mahatma. He was spinning when she arrived. A few days later Gandhi himself came to the hospital to see Ward. Two weeks after this he proposed to call again on the fever-stricken American. Three more weeks passed before the nonviolent militant chose to leave an important meeting in order to keep an appointment one sultry afternoon at four-thirty with the Wards. This was a more-extended visit where issues of top importance were discussed and the like-mindedness created a rapport among the three. Should Gandhi accept the pressure to become a Christian as many missionaries suggested? The Wards did not feel at all that way and told Gandhi as much. He was pleased, for this was an indication that his guests had a more profound understanding of his unity goal for India. It meant, too, that correspondence would further develop between the American and his East Indian friend. Some of their letters are preserved in the Ward papers.

Remembrance of the two Wards by those who knew them confirms the impression that it was Daisy who was more captured by some of the Gandhian mysticism. Her husband was sympathetic, but stressed the historical and political significance of the whole swaraj (freedom) movement.[2] He, for example, wrote an article for the *Nation*, which appeared at the end of April 1925, stating pro-Gandhian sympathies and predicting that it would be impossible for England to continue to dominate India. An article published in the *Christian Century* two months later reflected Daisy's sentiments with more allusions to "soul force," selflessness, and pacifism. The following is an example of their joint writing in which the emphasis of each seems to appear:

> This attitude of complete self-surrender [Gandhi] is hard to be understood by intellectuals, whose knowledge leads them into pride. It is our weakness that while we may tolerate mistakes in a leader, we can seldom abide the acknowledgement of them. We are little able to understand and suffer such loss of faith, but with the common people it is different. When Gandhi acknowledged that he had been mistaken both as to the capacity of India

for non-violence and as to the length of time in which Swaraj could be gained by his program, when he turned his program over to others who were apparently getting results, it was additional proof to common people of his humility of soul and complete disinterestedness. . . . So it may be said that while Gandhi has diminished in political leadership he has increased not only in moral but also in spiritual authority. The common people do not follow him merely because of his political program. They give him reverence and almost worship him because of his saintly character. . . . When this little wisp of a man who looks like a holy one of ancient times, and speaks in Oxford English, gives battle to one of the greatest empires of history, with no weapons but those of the inner life, it is once again spirit and brute force in conflict. It is the great drama of soul against external things personalized once more. (117)

"Culture has inertia" say the sociologists. The two Wards had cultural backgrounds that helped them avoid mental inertia and understand, in part at least, the adoration of an ascetic, saintlike Gandhi. Though such adoration easily becomes personality worship, a corrosive cult for democratic behavior in a nation, there must be a time to recognize heroism and the leader inspired to deny self for the greater good. Ward's boyhood tendency toward hero worship may have appeared in his first reactions to Mahatma Gandhi's dedicated life.

Ward did not know at the time of Subhas Chandra Bose, who a few years later would be organizing both inside and outside of India to drive the oppressors out by force. Bose might have appealed more to Ward, since he was a hero and a more militant one. There are those who have argued that India would be more "free" today had there not been the sapping of militancy by Gandhi's arousing of a nonviolent, satyagraha, or "truth-force," kind of escapism. Whatever the answer, the Wards end their eulogistic writing with an optimism that saw spinning and hand weaving becoming so widely adopted the work could, by its economic impact, cut India off from the West. Then the writers added: "This would otherwise cut us off from the spiritualizing influences that India can throw into the world's life. Gandhi's friends elsewhere should remind him that he belongs to the world and not alone to India." (116)

So as the Gandhian mystique possessed his wife more, Ward was soon to be making speeches to students in both China and Japan that troubled the governments of those countries enough to stimulate the calling out of their secret-service agents. There was talk of having this lecturer expelled from India, just as in 1957 India asked that Arthur Schlesinger, Jr., be called home for indiscretions in lectures. The reasons for the threats were polar, however, for Ward spoke of the need for a new social order, whereas Schlesinger thought too many professors in the subcontinent were communists and bluntly said so.

Daisy spoke on the status of women in America and other countries while her husband gave lectures explaining the Marxian economic system of the Soviet Union. He wanted to demonstrate that a system of production for use works effectively to supply the goods and services people need without exploiting workers for profits. In the city of Madras both Dr. and Mrs. Ward spoke against the "Blavatsky frauds" and other prestidigitators they seemed to encounter everywhere in that superstitious country. They wanted to get away from "that crowd of blacklegs."[3] These activities and reactions were expressed in letters to Gordon, Muriel, and Lynd.

While Ward emphasized that Gandhi belonged to the world, he also was among those who urged Gandhi not to visit the United States. There were too many curiosity seekers and cynics who could never understand, only ridicule, advised the Wards. Five years later Roger Baldwin, an agnostic and yet a warm defender of Gandhi, was still advising him not to come as "Dr. Ward, my close associate has already told you." An issue of the *New Yorker* at that time carried a vivid cartoon on its front page showing the ninety-pound, nearly toothless ascetic, his legs folded as he sat in the Buddha style on a grass mat. Nothing was on his emaciated-looking body except a *dhoti* (loin cloth). Nearby were his only possessions, an inexpensive pocket watch and his handwoven shawl. The Mahatma, the great soul, held up a striped four-in-hand tie with a card dangling from it that read "Merry Christmas to Gandhi, from America." That cartoon capsulated the attitudes of many Americans toward him and affirmed the soundness of the advice given by the Wards.

Like the drama *Rain* that the Wards attended in Madras, which stirred deep emotions and caused Daisy to write home "I am reminded of it often," India's monsoons and the Mahatma lingered in their minds, too. Gandhi asked in later letters to Ward about the Chinese social scene, how the people felt about India, would "non-violent coercion" work in China?

*   *   *

A perceptibly different China existed in 1925 than the one visited by John Dewey in 1920 and certainly by Ward in 1909. Dewey left China in 1921, the same year that the Communist party was formed. Revolutionary activity had not boiled, as it would have three years later at the time Ward's lectures began. In a report called "Bolshevism in China," Dewey claimed no Bolshevism was present and "there was no leverage in the country to bring about a social revolution." There existed, outside of a few large cities, no discontented proletariat, no significant labor movement, and what did exist was only a little bread-and-butterism. As some have written about India today, Dewey felt the peasants of China were inert, not subject to rioting even when starving from famines. He closed his report with this note of pessimism: "Many hope that a political revolution is coming to throw out the present class of officials and to get a new start. There may be an upheaval of this sort which those who don't like it will call Bolshevist. But I am afraid it won't come very soon, and when it does come it will be confined to doing over again the things that were pretended to be done in 1911" (11).

The Wards had undoubtedly read John Dewey's articles on China in the *New Republic* and *Asia* magazines in the 1920–1925 years and noted his views. They also were friends of the leading authority on Mongolia, Professor Owen Lattimore, and his wife, Eleanor, a student of Chinese culture. They corresponded with each other, especially Daisy and Mrs. Lattimore, and the scholars guided the Wards into a more hopeful understanding of the awakening of China.[4] Ward wrote to his family after a few days in China:

As before, China gets me more than the rest of it [Asia]. Why?
The landscape is colorless after India, the folks not so charming,
as Japan, but it is the sense of what is in the background.
Something inscrutable. Yes. Something that you feel will keep
on challenging you and may perhaps not yield to your inquiry.
The sense of reserve power, as I said before. Yes, they were here
before us Western upstarts and may be here after. They are stayers,
these Chinese. Well I'll tell you more about them later on when
I see whether a longer acquaintance changes my impression of
something deeper elsewhere. (11)

In contrast to Dewey, Ward could write from his knowledge
of history and social forces. Dewey's pessimism, it would appear,
prevented him from seeing that which was beyond a short term
pragmatic reformism. Ward, on the other hand, was able to
predict almost a quarter of a century before 1949 the change
that China's self-reliance could bring—the emergence of a country
that could shelter one-fourth of the world's population.

Ward had arrived in 1925 to find students were being shot
down in Shanghai and Canton for protesting the violence used
to repress them. The unequal treaties forced on China by European
nations, all the ugly conditions to which people had to submit,
were reasons for the famous "May 30th" protests. Even though
the Wards were sympathetic to the students and critical of "the
imperial minded, arrogant foreigners," they were advised not to
speak at Boone University, Wuchang, "lest hotheads caused
trouble."

The empathy of the Wards with the Chinese people made
them especially sensitive to the expressions and causes of anti-
West feelings. They heard phrases from Western businessmen
like "damn dirty chinks." They noted that the Chinese language
was not deemed important enough to be learned; it was not
even taught in the mission schools. As the blacks in America,
so the Chinese in the larger cities of their own country were
segregated and were not permitted in certain parks and recreation
areas. Ward wondered about the commodious compound of the
Methodist Mission in Peking with its more than comfortable
houses, schools, and spacious grounds. Was this acquired "by
the cleverness of a missionary negotiating for a good slice of the

Boxer indemnity finances?" Christianity in China, he seemed convinced, had been propagated by the gun. There is no logic in the church holding to these gains, he commented to Bishop Frederick B. Fisher, influential Methodist in India.

Ward made an effort to break out of protected social circles like the missionary centers. Daisy wrote home to report that "Dad" spent more time with the non-Christian groups; and then Ward wrote, April 24, 1925, that he believed he had succeeded in breaking out of Western circles and hence had gotten nearer the Chinese people. His sociological techniques learned in the Chicago days allowed him always to put himself better into the role of "the other," thereby constantly widening his ability to empathize and grasp understandings that others failed to get.

Daisy included comments on Chinese women in her letters to her family. She noted their mistreatment and their inability to get an education; religion opposed it (11.1). If an educated woman married a less well-educated man, he would beat her for being "uppity" and immodest. She noted, too, that the student "mob action" over the country had "little power of organized self-direction." But they will learn, she added, from "Western athletics" and military training. Finally, she wrote that Ward wanted to join the protest marches, but "he knew a white skin would enflame." Wearing a long coat, dark glasses, and a sun hat might do, he said, but "unfortunately the Lord or someone else gave me a beak that will never pass as Chinese."

As Ward studied the social situation in China he formed interesting hypotheses. One was the thought that the country could not so well use Lenin's stress on the dictatorship of the proletariat. He observed that millions of rural peasants were starving or very close to it, there were hordes of city dwellers in abject poverty, and nowhere were there sufficient numbers of industrial workers to spearhead a proletarian movement. Mao was anticipated too in Ward's reading of movements in the China upsurge, which suggested that a rural base composed of soldiers and farmer-peasants was a wise process to develop and an important factor in the revolution against Chiang Kai-shek. This was a commonsense view of a situation where more than 80 percent of the people were rural. Sun Yat-sen's party seemed in 1925 to be right in its effort to bind the students and the rural peasants together. Ward's idea commanded a ready, enthusiastic response, as he gave support to a combination of intellectuals with peasants and farmers. It became known as "the Renaissance group," to be distinguished from the general Renaissance that started a dozen years earlier.

Economic theory and the economic system received almost all of the attention in his numerous lectures, so much so he was criticized by some church colleagues for not preaching salvation as offered by Christ. When the Renaissance group was convinced he was not disseminating Christian propaganda, they heard, read, and discussed his lectures as widely as those of John Dewey. Two Chinese papers were printing all of his lectures. They dealt largely with the immoral nature of a profit-making economy, and hence they so tightly integrated practical science and workaday religion they could not be separated.

One series of lectures given in Shanghai, for example, dealt with "The Ethics of Property." The first discussed "The Rights of Property" and distinguished the dangers of private property versus the necessity of social property to maintain the common good. The second lecture explored "Property and Personality" and argued in part that if a city provides a good library then an individual doesn't need so large a personal one. Or if a city library provides expensive reference books, then the college nearby saves by spending less on duplication. Continuing this line of reasoning, the construction of more city gardens would make personal ones less necessary; an art museum for all would replace private, less-accessible collections. Private ownership is too expensive and largely unnecessary. Most important is that personality develops better because these cultural, humanizing things are available to all. The third lecture of the series, entitled "The Future of Private Property," pointed out its inevitable decline and demise. Its growth has exposed the seeds of its own destruction. More socialism must be expected to control and eventually displace the giantism of private property. The moral imperative he urged the Chinese students to ponder was how to build a better social order and how to work carefully and unitedly to achieve it. "I came," writes Ward to his friend Coe, "at the right time. The Renaissance group can be influenced and that is why I came."

Many American students in the mid-twenties supported Dr. Sun and his large student following. Leaders of the Student Christian Movement in the United States, so deeply impressed by the Social Creed, were ready to support Ward and others of his thinking. David R. Porter, a national SCM leader, wrote to inform Ward that telegrams had gone to 256 colleges and universities, followed by a detailed letter urging Americans to write notes to Washington and to Christians in China asking that military action not be used against the emerging nation.

Student uprisings seemed to follow Ward visits to Chinese universities, and, as some thought, he was now contributing to the alertness of the students' minds as it appears he had done in India and at home. Chiang Kai-shek's police harassed his meetings, so that often he was forced to travel by night and to give his lectures in some private place. He went so far as to advise an economic boycott of foreign powers' products, just as Gandhi was doing. Thus Ward's lectures seemed to have played a small part in the vast Chinese Revolution. Certainly they created more response than those of Russell or Dewey.

No sooner had the Wards arrived home than they became involved in forming the American Committee for Justice to China (later known as the China Aid Council). Ward was chosen to be the national chairman of the new organization, surrounded by prominent humanitarians as officers and sponsors. Since the days of the Open Door policy the United States had appeared to be both friend and defender of China. It was a fertile field for missionaries in the early years of the century, when numbers of college students heard the rallying call "the world for Christ in our generation." Christian schools of all denominations were started, the YMCAs and YWCAs appeared in larger cities, and more colleges were established with the aid of Boxer indemnity funds. Ward, with his visions of a more-just world, was aware of this development from the mid-twenties to the end of his life. What was transpiring in China was to him of growing importance.

The program of the American Committee for Justice to China in 1925 indicated his concern. It included advocacy of (1) tariff autonomy for China; (2) the abolishment of extraterritoriality for Westerners; (3) the return of special concessions, leases, and

settlements forced upon a prostrate people; (4) the withdrawal
of foreign troops; (5) the canceling of all unequal treaties; and
(6) aid to Chinese freedom fighters. The sixty-one members of
the U.S. national committee included Jane Addams, Alice Stone
Blackwell, Zona Gale, Vida Scudder, James Weldon Johnson,
Lewis Gannett, Oswald Garrison Villard, and Kansas editor
William Allen White. They joined to protest the shooting of
students by British police in Shanghai on May 30, 1925. One
hundred were killed and many more wounded. Ward and journalist Paul Blanchard set out on lecture tours in the late months
of 1925 to raise funds for China aid, resulting in $1,000 being
sent in the first year of the American committee.

A year later the committee sent letters to Secretary of State
Frank Kellogg, insisting that he stop U.S. gunboats from patroling
and firing upon villages along the Yangtze River. Why cannot
America be more sympathetic, the committee asked, toward the
efforts of China to throw off its oppressors? Pressing for both
education about China and actions for her aid, the organization
protested an American loan offered by the banking house of
Lamont to the Japanese to build a railroad across Manchuria, an
area taken from China by force. Thoughtful Americans resorted
to the traditional friendship argument by writing that financing
still another exploiter of China would destroy friendly feelings.

As always, most of Ward's organizational thrusts for justice
stirred acrimonious counterattacks. The *National Republic*'s editor
accused the committee of obtaining money from "the communist
controlled Garland Fund," the purpose of which, according to
this status quo journal, was to aid strikers in the United States
and "to Sovietize" in China. Even though the Garland Fund
had contributed $1,000 for aid in 1925, Ward pointed out that
the 1927 gift came from the YMCA and YWCA students of
America.

An article for the *Christian Century* (September 1, 1927) in
which Ward criticized the prevailing attitudes of the governments
of England and the United States toward China, summarized
the central issues. He wrote:

If such a discussion is to get anywhere [joint China aid by
America and England], certain prejudicial presuppositions must

be eliminated at the start, even from the subconsciousness. One is the idea of the sanctity of the British empire, the other idea of the moral infallibility of the United States. Those whose thinking is tainted by these ideas are bound to fail of accord, if they do not end in misunderstanding and irritation. No real analysis, no honest judgment, is possible if one feels that failure to go along with its program is *lese majeste*, while the other reciprocates that such an attitude is evidence of moral inferiority. Both attitudes spring from the same source—the sense of a mission—in one case to govern, in the other to convert the world—always, as our international neighbors observe, with some advantage of profit, power or prestige to ourselves.

The only permanent basis for united action between governments or missionaries is the abandonment of the idea of making something out of China whether it be profits or converts, and the seeking of China's good on the same level as our own. Altruism is not mutualism. The mere doing of good is not sufficient. It is touched with the two-fold taint of superiority and of the profit motive in its most subtle form. Hence the affinity between the political views of many missionaries and those of trading interests. (147)

Up to the last days of his ninety-three years Ward's empathy for the poor and oppressed of Asia continued. He would never, for example, ride in a rickshaw pulled by a human being. His central worry was, however, that the financial empires of the West would, as he explained, make China and the colonial world more dehumanized in order to fill the voracious mouths of conglomerates. For the masters of the world as much as those of any one nation are (as quoted from Adam Smith at the beginning of this chapter) combined against the poor to prevent them from combining to raise wages. To press upon congressmen to stop sending war planes flown by American pilots to support the corrupt government of Chiang Kai-shek was another goal for Ward and thirty other leaders. They called upon the people of the United States to uphold the plan. Withdraw gunboats and marines and cease arms shipments used by the generalissimo to implement his dictatorship, was another broadcast appeal. George S. Counts, Roger Baldwin, Granville Hicks, and Theodore Dreiser were others who agreed with Ward as they noted that the

Nanking government used ten million dollars sent to buy wheat and cotton to replenish munition supplies.

While in China Ward had been consulted by Chinese friends on whether or not Sun Yat-sen should have a Christian burial service. The answer is not known for certain. The record reads that Dr. Sun had a state funeral by order of a war lord with whom he had been collaborating. A great honor came to Ward at age eighty-three when Chou En-lai cabled an invitation on November 2, 1956, for Ward to attend the ninetieth-birthday anniversary celebration of Dr. Sun. If their American friend could not come, he was to participate with a message for the occasion. Two days later Ward ended his return cable with words that many of his students felt could apply to their now white-haired professor, as well as to Sun Yat-sen: "his life challenged all peoples to seek continuously to develop the democratic way of life." Visitors to the Ward home near the end of his days noticed on a nearby table a copy of the periodical *China Reconstructs*.

*   *   *

Moving on to Japan, Dr. Ward again attracted large student audiences in that country, and the government became wary of him. His first lecture was on "The Future of the Intelligentsia" with the implication that it had little future if it tried to exist in libraries and ivied walls. His friends warned that "his message was seen as dangerous by the Japanese government." The fact that he wore his American suit was almost as threatening as his lecture, according to Japanese formality that expected him to wear a cutaway coat and striped trousers. "Did he have such a suit?" brought a straightforward "No." His Japanese friends found one for him, so that he didn't disgrace his hosts at the second lecture. Daisy wrote (Feb. 15, 1925) to her three children that "sometimes someone besides mother has to take Dad in hand. He submits quite gracefully [to this formality of dress] though he grumbles a bit in my ear" (11.1).

When word got around that the visiting professor was well informed on the Soviet Union, he received an invitation from Japan's State Department for a luncheon discussion with its entire staff. The government was considering seriously a trade treaty with the Soviets. Then the same department sponsored, a few days later, a public lecture by Ward. The Tokyo streetcars displayed an advertisement of it. The Yokohama Chamber of Commerce selected this guest of their Christian Council to give a public lecture in that city. As impressive as this visit was, it was something of an anticlimax to the friends he made and the impressions he left in China and India.

*   *   *

Through these travels to Europe and Asia between 1909 and 1925 the mind of Harry Ward was assimilating his many intensive cultural experiences, pondering them and turning them into hypotheses that related to a world of special meaning—community: the community from which arises some "selfs" that can quickly "play the role of the other" in the search to understand. Ward had left behind now the loaded word and the bit of slang that, though unwittingly used in his youth, could perpetuate misunderstanding and discord. What appeared now was a man who, like Thomas Paine, rose above nationalism with its blinding ethnocentricism to think and talk more of "world citizenship" and "fellowship" the way in which his Professor Royce at Harvard talked of "the blessed community." Such a community wherever even partially achieved would be internalized by social interaction to a "self" that could play roles with so many more of the Children of Man.

One friend asked him in 1921 about his idea of internationalism. Even before his second year in the Orient he could write: "Your suggestion about some kind of international citizenship that would still leave one's heart where it belongs, in the land of one's forbears, is very interesting and pertinent. Ultimately, of course, we shall have to break up entirely this arbitrary and artificial nationalism that is now encumbering the earth and obstructing our fellowship."[5] Forty years later, after more travels, more writings of books and articles, his goal of world unity became more realistic and more compelling. By then he had written most about the Soviet Union, where he had lived and done hand labor. Next in number came fourteen articles on China, four on India, one comparing Gandhi and Lenin, and two on Japan. With this background of internationalization, thought, and action, he wrote a statement in 1962 of less than a thousand words for a conference of the World Fellowship of Faiths. It bore the title "What Destiny— If Man Destroys Himself?"

Opening words expressed his appreciation for being invited to address the conference. The eighty-nine-year-old speaker could recall times when people on "subversive lists" were not invited, and he recalled the first subversive list he ever saw, sent around after World War I. "The first name on the list was Jane Addams who used to call me her preacher in Chicago, and the last name of the list was Harry F. Ward." Then he went directly to his famous question, What needs to be done? and asked, Why assume man has a destiny if he continues scientific designs that will destroy him? "Unless we can get rid of nuclear weapons and get complete disarmament with the different measures that are necessary to see that it is achieved and carried out," there is no destiny. His following sentences were pertinent and prophetic:

> That is why we are getting something like a formation of a world mind today. Not simply between different faiths or between different faiths and no faith. Along with all the other factors that go to make for the first time in history, the operation really of forming a world mind. This is the chief force, a force of compulsion that is in the background. . . . I don't know how any nation or group of nations can consider itself civilized when it has leaders who can talk about overkill as if human beings are a group of hogs being driven to a slaughterhouse.

The inveterate optimism of the man brought him to state "we are beginning to form a world mind" even though he shouted it in a wilderness. Hence, he continued, a judgment day is upon us:

> And it involves a day of judgment for all religions because if they have not the moral strength to make man the creator overcome man the destroyer, there is no future. Not only is it the day of judgment for all religions but it is the day of judgment also for anti-religion on the same grounds and with the same result. So this is where we really come together. This is where anti-religion meets the same test as religion.

This then is our task. Let us get to it and never stop until we win. (257)

Notes

1. The Hunter Committee was appointed by the British Raj to investigate the Amritsar Massacre of 1919, in which a crowd was fired on by English soldiers killing "several hundred" (English view), "over 1200" (Indian view). The five English members of the Committee outvoted the three Indian members to adopt a report that exonerated Brig. Gen. Reginald Dyer of any atrocity.

2. Mary Beard, collaborationist historian with her husband Charles, was the more pacifistic of the two. She was among a number of leading women from the Greeks to the present who believed that some day "women would revolt against organized killing of their sons." (Interview, June 6, 1938.)

3. An artificial hand, claimed to be that of Madame Blavatsky, a Russian mystic, rested alone on a table. When asked questions about a person's future it would tap once for "yes" and twice for "no."

4. Owen and Eleanor Lattimore wrote extensively on their observations in Mongolia and China and were victims of the red-baiting of the McCarthy period. An interesting anecdote is related in a letter from Eleanor to Daisy in the Ward papers. "He [Owen] is now with a camel caravan for four months. . . . He is thought to be an Englishman because he wears a monocle. The image of him carrying a dozen spare eye glasses into the least known portions of the earth is sending all his friends into convulsions, including his wife. We are asking his book to be entitled 'Mongolia Through a Monocle.' . . . He is a radical and I like that." (11.1)

5. Ward to G. A. Johnston Ross, Feb. 1, 1921 (11).

8

Soviet Communism:
A New Civilization?

*The organization of slick success in our age is only
equalled by the organization of political acquiescence.
Between them we shall live in a new form of society.*
—**William James**

The Russian Revolution marked the end of the autocracy of
Czars and the domineering state church, both of which dictated
to the masses. In modern history, at least, it was the first collapse of a profit-making economic system. It struck the rest of
the world with a blow like David's pebble hitting Goliath.
However, the Goliath system was not beheaded, but has lived
on. If Ward tried to maintain an equilibrium composed of
thoughtfulness and adjustment to the ineluctable changes of
history and the inevitability of movements toward collectivism,
corporate or democratic, he incited the established order even
though he tried to be objective and present the new order in
the Soviet Union as accurately as he could. In the Boston years
he confronted the rhetorical question in the title of this chapter.
It was the same question used in the first edition of Sidney and
Beatrice Webb's two-volume study of the Soviet Union published
in 1935. Ward thought the answer was Yes, as did the Webbs
in the third edition of their work published in 1937.

The scene could be traced back to as early as 1914 when the
Methodist Sunday School Journal carried a weekly discussion written
by Ward under the heading "The Social Interpretation of the
Lesson." In 1916 a series entitled "The Bible in Social Living"
began for the fourth-year senior high course in an interdenominational graded lesson. These two were Ward's opportunities
for relating religion to current affairs. The college students were
awakened to social evangelism with his *Christianizing Community
Life* through the Federation. These writings carried criticisms of

134

the United States for invading the new socialist state in 1918 at Archangel and stated the aim of the Bolsheviks was to create a state composed entirely of producers and controlled by producers.

Some early critics, irritated over Ward's identification with labor, were angry when they read that "Beginnings of a new order are upon us . . . here and there parts of it may be seen breaking through the shell of the old, which has long been nourishing the embryo." It was a new religious ideal, he stated, expressed by "from each according to ability, to each according to need" (77). Even though the respected preacher Washington Gladden praised the efforts of the Bolsheviks in a *Survey* article (July 13, 1918), William Allen White wrote that if you drive a docile cow into a corner with a whip she will in time turn and hook her oppressor, and others like Hearst wrote similar sentiments, Ward lost his weekly preparation of graded Sunday School lessons and his manuals. Bishop Francis McConnell hinted that his friend was being punished partly because he was exposing the unfair labor policies of the religious book publishers. Bishop McConnell added, "Ward is admired both in and out of his denomination and both Congregationalists and Methodists will oppose this repression of a trusted teacher, writer of widely read books and recently appointed to Union Seminary." Others, such as friend Graham Taylor, wrote that he may have overstated his views, but that did not justify the treatment given him (83).

The *Social Service Bulletin* (January-February 1919) was entitled "The Russian Question." With his usual clarity and brevity Ward explained new terms that few Americans had heard before, such as Soviet, Bolshevik, Menshevik, and Gosplan. He followed the neat lesson plans for Sunday Schools and church-related colleges that he and Walter Rauschenbusch began publishing in small-book form years earlier. Vignettes of the Soviets' leaders, with succinct statements of their policy and program, comprised the first step. Moving on, he encouraged an analysis of words like *violence, terror,* and *atheism.* He reminded readers that in all revolutions extremists have maltreated enemies. The American Revolution was no exception. People were tarred and feathered, driven to bleak Acadia, and deprived of employment. Those who contrived to undermine the new government in the USSR and to restore private enterprise were executed. Considering all this, it was not equivalent, Ward wrote, to the mass killings of the disarmed and innocent in major wars or the perpetual slow killings of the people of a nation by exploitation and induced famine in British India. As for atheism, the government had to uphold the principle of separation of church and state. No longer could a mad monk named Rasputin turn government into a mockery. John Haynes Holmes, Unitarian minister of the Community Church of New York City, who would later challenge some of Ward's ideas, wrote some lines of verse after a visit to the Soviet Union in 1931, which Ward could have endorsed:

When God was lord, and Tsar was king,
    This wall entombed the world,
And from the ramparts of its pride
    The shafts of fury hurled.

When God was king, and Tsar was lord,
    These towers eclipsed the sky—
These golden crosses dar'd the stars
    Their splendor to defy.

When God was God, and Tzar was Tzar,
    And God and Tzar were one,
Here in this templed citadel,
    The doom of man was done.

Now Tzars are dead, and God denied
    And lo, this mound of stone
A barricade of Liberty
    For humble men and lone!

Oh Thou, whose spirit moves the deep,
    And tells the toll of days,
Thou askest not for name or sign,
    Thou seekest not for praise.

Unrecognized, unseen, unknown,
    Thou waitest patient still,
Content if men unwittingly
    Contrive to do thy will.[1]

Though positive in approach to the study of "the great experiment," as William Randolph Hearst called it first in these early years, the *Social Service Bulletin* was reserved about an endorsement of the Soviet system. Still, Ward's essay created a far-reaching shock wave. The majority of the Federation board defended him, but Worth Tippy grew more sharp in opposition. There were more recriminations, with the most serious being Ward's dismissal from "the teaching force of the church."

Friends George Coe, Graham Taylor, and Bishop Francis McConnell urged him to write a supplementary article that would explain some of his statements. He complied by denouncing war atrocities in general, including "Bolshevik atrocities" that were more due to "irresponsibles than to the government." Aspects of the revolution, he wrote (*The Advocate*, Mar. 13; Apr. 3, 1919), were contrary to Christian conscience. If these aspects were terrorizing, he condemned them. But he refused to change his conviction that the fundamental principles were right and to be welcomed, the most fundamental being the abolition of, to him, the egregious sin of private profit.

At this stage in his life the Christian Ethics professor wrote that he did "not condone religious repression," which was not surprising, but he added "nor the dictatorship of the proletariat," which may be.

> I am against the theory and practice of dictatorship by the proletariat not only because I believe it is unethical, but also because I believe it to be unscientific. You cannot carry out the change to economic democracy that way, for the simple reason that you cannot control economic production efficiently in the transitional stage by means of one class alone. You have to have the co-operation of everybody that knows how to manage industry if you are going to democratize it. (80)

This subtly stated 1919 position did not spare him from emotional critics who continued to assert that he was a pawn of Moscow.

In those days Ward was critical of "crass materialism," "fatalism," and "mechanistic science" in Marx and wrote about it in *The New Social Order* (73) as well as in *The Labor Movement* (64). The insights into Marxism of his senior years were to be expressed in his last book, "Jesus and Marx" (261). In the meantime, the influence of Gandhi, which strongly affected Mrs. Ward and considerably impressed Ward, probably colored their reactions to these particular Marxian concepts. The Soviets seemed at that time, in Ward's thinking, too dogmatic and possessed by what the Wards called an "economic theology" that was not unlike predestinationism. The cases reflecting a lack of civil liberties, which after careful checking Ward found to be partly true and not fabrications by the enemies of the new state, also brought criticism from him. The Soviets' apparent use of force at some points to build their system was not wise, Ward argued, for it contained the seeds of its own destruction. Lynd portrayed this view of his father in *Wild Pilgrimage*, one of his novels in wood engravings. In imagination, the labor hero looks at the face of the capitalist he has just beheaded. As he holds the head up by the hair, he discovers the face is his own! Robert Moats Miller, who has written harshly of Ward, admits that in the 1920s Ward tried to present a balanced view and to avert the rising irrational hysteria against socialism. Instead of emotional reactions, Ward encouraged people to apply a scientific and pragmatic philosophy toward understanding the USSR. He treaded softly in his criticisms of the Soviets, according to Lynd and May Ward. He considered red baiters to be intellectually and morally dishonest cowards. Fears of becoming identified with professional red baiters and their shadow-box controllers influenced his writings a great deal.

With these reservations, and fortified with what he accepted as scientific investigation, Ward made his decision to defend a nation that for the first time in history was establishing a socialist economy. It was a new event, he wrote, here to teach and change human life forever after. It was paper no longer. If it were suppressed, like Joe Hill, it would not die.

It was wrong to ignore labor, working people and the Soviets. The Paris Peace Conference tried to do so, but it failed to halt militarism and war because "those who fought the war are not in on its settlement." These ideas were shocking in the Coolidge years. The *Atlantic* and even the social-minded *Survey* joined the Sunday School editors in refusing to publish many of Ward's essays on the new Russia. They were admittedly well written, but much too controversial.

Still nothing would deter him from his religious commitment to the ideals of a better nation because it had freed itself of profiteers, the aristocracy, the corrupt church, and their control over the Russian masses. He would say to his students that the Soviets made puzzling turns at times in their policies, but if they did not revert to profit making they were to be trusted against all the judgments made by those who lived in national economies dominated by profit motives.

He was more positive about this as early as 1924 when he wrote his book *The Profit Motive* (107) for the League for Industrial Democracy (which John Dewey had helped to found). This paragraph is representative:

> Release from inhibitions and repressions of dogma comes not in agnosticism but thru scientific faith that is grounded in reason and developed in experiment that proves itself in the laboratory of its works. This is the condition of creative activity and the essence of it in this matter of profit motivation is the belief that it is better to fail trying to live intelligently and in fellowship as developing human beings than to stagnate comfortably in the muck or to rend each other over the booty of the earth like a pack of hungry wolves.

Hence, his constant interest was in the decisions and the moves made by Russia. He decided to study the country and its people in considerable depth.

With the aid of Anna Louise Strong, an American newspaper woman who was trying to get accurate reports to the West, and former students like Julius Hecker, who lived in Moscow at that time and served as a translator, Ward in the early thirties met and talked with Soviet workers at oil refineries, harvester plants, and communes. He and Daisy had planned to eat, sleep, work, and live with the newly freed men and women, which had prompted two of his American students to give him a well-equipped tool kit upon his departure. King Gordon and James Dombrowski knew Ward planned to do carpentering on the Lenin Commune and felt this was an appropriate gift. He chopped wood for a guide and worked in one of the shops, but his frail health limited his drive to learn-by-work in the Gandhian tradition.

In Moscow the Wards lived in the simple apartment of Anna Louise Strong. Only twelve years after the Revolution, Moscow and Leningrad seemed like vast construction sites. Brick piles, chuckholed streets, whitewash splatter, and construction frames seemed everywhere. The rickety buses rattled over the rubble in the streets. Ward insisted on being accurate, his wife wrote, and "fortunately knows how to find out things, where to look. He knows some Russian, so we get along" (11.1). The obsessive drive to learn all he could overcame his earlier expressed distaste for opera. He went to one of the longest and heaviest of all, *Boris Godunov,* and according to Daisy sat through all of it until after 11 P.M. Doubtless he noted the simply dressed audience of workers and an orchestra dressed not in black-tie evening clothes but in blue shirts with sleeves rolled above the elbows.

Soviet travels took the Wards to Sochi with its warm sulphur baths and to Baku, Rostov, Tiflis, and Odessa. At each place Ward made in-depth studies by long interviews that stretched into a seven-day week. Daisy's letters mention the cold rooms and the discomforts they confronted to press their research and be able "to make the new Russia known." There was a lack of hot water, wrote Daisy. The trouble is "we like capitalists' comfort if not their economics" (11.1).

After many hours of orderly research interspersed with talks with Soviet professors, the intelligentsia, and labor, Ward began to summarize his impressions of this society. Communism, he ventured to say, was a new form of religion, which he contrasted with "the mechanistic individualism" of capitalism. Each system conditioned those under its influence, but he went on to ask, how profoundly and permanently? He was questioning, summarizing, and seeking at the nadir of the Great Depression when many thoughtful people were certain of the collapse of the old social order.

Ward concluded during his Soviet studies that capitalism had reached the end of its development. His face must have contained a blush as history's pages flipped through the forties and fifties with the old order still holding on. Almost always he interpreted the subtle twists and turns of ongoing current events with a perspicacity that fascinated his students. In fact it was one of his greatest abilities and contributions. He warned of the rise of corporate capitalism—for example, Nazism—and he considered such developments would be the terrorist death struggles of a dying order. He predicted the Soviet state would suffer repeated attacks of every variety because of the drastic changes its revolution would usher in. Early musings about the long-range meaning of Soviet Russia took an almost teleological form in his rhetorical question: "Did the providential guidance of history produce a state that brought down the mighty and raised those without the ranks or rights on the border between East and West so it could have double impact?" At the very least, Ward's visits and lectures in China helped him sense the awakening of that crowded country.

From the publication of his book, *In Place of Profit* (176), he remained a constant observer and defender of the Soviet Union. Though his mind was never tethered by a dogmatic absolute, as his accusers kept insisting, he remained a friend of the Soviets and on basic issues defended them. Some called him "the people's scholar." Others like Sidney and Beatrice Webb expressed indebtedness to *In Place of Profit* for materials they used in their monumental two-volume study of Soviet communism. Premier Joseph Stalin in 1947 wrote to Ward for suggestions on ways war-torn Europe could collectively be restored by the Allies. This request came from a leader who refused to meet six prominent clergy from the United States, members of the 1931 Sherwood Eddy party. The phone call by the premier's secretary to the student courier of the tourist group was blunt. "Comrade Stalin has no time for a group of American priests." Sixteen years later he was seeking suggestions from a seminary professor in the United States!

After World War II the campaign by certain powerful corporations, working with a responsive media, had Americans generally convinced that socialism in any form was an anathema. The working people's socialism of Eugene Debs was labeled "communism." Many notable scholars and writers who were Socialists or who advocated the theory were branded as dangerous to our "free society." It was no longer to be discussed fairly, both sides presented, in education or in politics. This produced an atmosphere in which an objective study of socialist societies was almost impossible. Serious attempts to preserve democratic principles should have dictated at least a modicum of circumspection. But the repeated tactics of Dies, McCarran, McCarthy, and others aggravated economic, governmental, and even personal fears in order to establish, as Thomas Jefferson called it, a "tyranny over the mind of man."

This remained the social setting for Ward's leadership, presenting constant threats to the effectiveness of his words and deeds from 1919, when his Methodist Federation *Bulletin* carried the carefully written explanation of the new system in Russia, right down to his last days nearly fifty years afterward. "Drop the hydrogen bomb now," shouted congressmen in 1947, "before they get too strong." Others pleased the military-industrial complex, about whose power Eisenhower warned, by advocating containment—the complete surrounding of the Soviets by heavily armed bases placed in neighboring countries. The overblown fears increased as each bill to expand the armed forces was passed. But why, asked Ward, was the hate so deep and pervasive? He answered his own question, making seven points. First, this Soviet socialist system was hated because it worked and was successful in spite of the horrible costs endured in stopping Hitler, whose one intent was to destroy it forever. Second, it was a system that threatened the continued existence of colonial exploitation, ever appearing under new guises. Third, "social democrats" hated it because they failed to achieve what the Soviet Union did. Fourth, pacifists and liberals were not prepared for the necessary harshness that goes with upsetting an old order.[2] Fifth, the capitalist system revealed a growing insecurity— a crumbling marked by increasing unemployment, inflation, collapsing money, recessions, and the need to subsidize mismanaged industries. Sixth, anti-Soviet phobia was good for business, making for puffed-up military contracts so that if the USSR reacted to this gross buildup by strengthening its defenses, the action brought out more scares and hates in the United States. Seventh, containment was wanted by both Wall Street and the military.

By this time this outspoken analyst could get almost none of his other side of the story printed. Ward was instead labeled a "commie," a "pinko," and ostracized because he defended all efforts by human beings toward building a cooperative commonwealth, imperfect though he saw the outcome would be. At age eighty Ward was asked by Anna Louise Strong to write a letter to Premier Georgi Malenkov requesting that she not be expelled from the USSR, probably because of her new interest, China. Ward complied, saying she had always been a defender of the right of the Soviets to exist. Was the independence of Ward's mind, reflected in this protest, a factor perhaps to explain why he never was honored by the Soviet Union as was the black scholar W. E. Burkhardt DuBois, singer Paul Robeson, and painter Rockwell Kent? Or could it have been because for him there was no dichotomy in religion and social morality? Religion *was* social morality, one God inside one gospel in the ongoing social process. "The synthesis between these two essentials, religion and morality, is ethical religion," he wrote (211). It was a position unacceptable to most of his seminary colleagues and perhaps equally so to the men of the Kremlin, who understandably rejected the word *religion* suggesting as it did the dualistic immoralities of a once-powerful mad monk. Whatever it was, in 1960, at age eighty-seven, Ward received a letter from Lydia Kislova, representing the Council of the Union of Soviet Societies for Friendship and Cultural Relations with Foreign Countries. She said that her nation knew of his work for peace and cultural cooperation. But perhaps because he was not a member of the Communist party, he was never awarded special recognition by the Soviets.

What did Ward do about those in his own country who were party members? What was his position on many people who were charged with being dupes and agents of the USSR? The party had a right to exist and to campaign at elections, because the principle involved was grounded on a foundation laid by those who established our own democratic government. Jefferson stated it clearly in the Declaration of Independence, a document of momentous significance throughout the world. This declaration has been used by the women's rights movement since the days of Mary Wollstonecraft, by the blacks' search for rights since the days of Frederick Douglass through those of the Panthers, by the appeals for justice in labor's struggles, and by being written into the constitutions of many nations such as France, India, and Vietnam. Ward relied on the declaration and spent his life defending the Bill of Rights as applying to all people including the Communist party:

> I have never yet seen any evidence that the Party does advocate the destruction of democratic government. In the Civil Liberties Union I have seen many disastrous results of putting into legislation general language about advocating the overthrow of government by force and violence. Time after time, such language has been distorted by interpretation in the Courts to penalize legitimate political and labor activity. Consequently I have come to believe more strongly than ever in the Jeffersonian principle of forbidding and stopping only overt acts.
>
> It follows, therefore, that I regard any attempt to penalize or outlaw any political party as fatal to democracy itself. (11)

This statement was part of his case against the Smith Act of 1940, which sought to outlaw any political party that seemed to "advocate force and violence." It was in a letter he wrote to a Methodist minister in New York City who asked why he opposed the legislation. He capsulated his answer against the measure, later to be used to imprison twelve Communist party leaders, with these words to Professor S. G. Brinkley at Emory University: "The case of the issue is in my judgment, that democracy cannot outlaw a political party for any other reason than overt acts without thereby destroying itself" (11). Vetoes by the president of the United States and a minority decision by two justices on the Supreme Court could not halt what Carey McWilliams, editor of the *Nation*, called "the great witch hunt" (294). Justice Hugo L. Black, as McWilliams reminded, noted the manipulation of public opinion for undemocratic behavior and in his dissent wrote: "Public opinion being what it now is, few will protest the convictions of these Communist petitioners. There is hope, however, that in calmer times, when present pressures, passions and fears subside, this or some later court will restore the First Amendment liberties to the high preferred place where they belong in a free society" (294).

Efforts increased to bar the Communist party from entering elections, and the small man who wrestled with big problems went to work. Ward organized a committee composed of nine prominent people: E. A. Ross, professor at the University of Wisconsin; Theodore Dreiser, novelist; Franz Boas, Columbia University anthropologist; Rockwell Kent, painter; Tom Mooney, labor leader; Owen Knox of the National Federation for Constitutional Liberties; Paul Robeson, artist and actor; Francis F. Kane, liberal Philadelphia lawyer; and Dashiell Hammett, novelist. Arguments against repression, probably written by Ward, were incorporated into a petition to Congress and the president of the United States and signed "We Who Are Not Communists." It stated, in part, that the party had been "undergoing the franchise system for twenty years; it upholds democratic procedure and expels those who advocate or practice terrorism, sabotage, espionage, force and violence; and to bar any party in a democracy is unconstitutional." Others contacted by Ward who were sympathetic but did not sign the petition for several differing reasons were Corliss Lamont, Columbia University philosopher; W. A. Oldfather, archeologist; and Mary W. Wolley, president of Mount Holyoke. Individual Communists, some of whom were Ward's friends, he tried to save from economic and social persecution. Simon W. Gerson was considered a capable administrator when he was appointed by Manhattan Borough President Stanley Issacs to be his assistant. A wrathful protest was stirred, and this time Reinhold Niebuhr, representing the Fellowship of Socialist Christians, along with William Spofford of the Church League for Industrial Democracy (Episcopal) and Ward for the Methodist Federation signed a statement upholding Issacs. In like manner, Ward as a member of the Non-Partisan Citizens Committee supported Benjamin J. Davis, a Communist national leader, to hold the seat he was elected to in 1943 and 1945 on the New York City Council.

William Z. Foster was one of the most famous of the American labor leaders of the party. Ward seemed to have respected his utter devotion to his ideals. A few days after Foster's death in 1961, Ward—then eighty-eight years old—wrote this tribute:

> I count it a privilege to have had three personal contacts with William Z. Foster. The first was in the early days of the American Civil Liberties Union. Most of its cases then were concerned with the rights of labor. As an outstanding labor leader Foster served

for a time on the National Board, making a valuable contribution. I observed closely his attitudes and with entire approval.

Several years later, when he started to organize in Pittsburgh, he asked me if I could find some preachers who would speak up for the needs and rights of labor. I found just one in a prominent church. Not long afterward he found it necessary to move to a church in another state.

Many years afterward, a national radio program concerning conditions in the Soviet Union was being arranged. Clare Booth Luce and [William Henry] Chamberlain were chosen to take the negative. Foster was asked to take the positive side and to bring a companion. He asked if I would come as a non-Communist and I accepted. In the preliminary discussion of procedure a proposal was made by the managers, after an aside talk with one of the negative participants, which seriously limited Foster's rights, and would have placed him at a great disadvantage. It was plainly the duty of the non-Communist to start the move to prevent this skullduggery from going through. The quiet, self-possessed, objective way in which Foster handled himself in this situation made a deep and abiding impression on me.

Distinguished as a labor leader and a Marxian social scientist, Foster was also remarkable as a person. It was the person who made the leader in his chosen fields, it was the nature of the causes he chose to support which matured the person. (11)

In these years when "pressures, passions and fears," as Justice Black called them, were high, a workman who lived in the slums then located in the Lower East Side of New York came across the city and took the Hudson River Ferry to Ward's home for help. The shabbily dressed man's wife had died and no clergy would help him because he was a Communist. "Could you give her a little burial service?" he asked, cap in hand. Only a few attended the service, where Marx and Jesus were compatible. The unsentimental Ward closed his eyes, and a tear slipped down his face as they sang "Joe Hill" and "Lead Kindly Light." The first hymn praised organization and unity, the second promised more loving and peaceful times. Together, Ward commented, they became the prayer for the funeral.

Roger Baldwin by 1952 had joined the chorus using the word *communist* freely in referring to those assumed to be friends.

Like Ward, he was asked to write a passage to read at the funeral of his former friend and Communist leader, Robert Minor. He did answer the request, but compared with Ward's reply it was niggardly. He wrote that the request by telegram arrived too late for a message. Baldwin expressed sorrow at the "passing of a close friend with whom I explored many ideas" on canoe trips and elsewhere, but also that "he took up defense of one State and a dictatorship at that." He closed with a sentence typical of one whose conscience is bothering: "I write this not for publication, but just as my tribute" (1).

F. Ernest Johnson, professor of Religious Education at Teachers College, Columbia, broke off friendship with Ward over the efforts to outlaw the party. "Can't you see the 'facts' of the American Communist Party?" he started off almost condescendingly. "To justify Soviet policy in the light of European history is one thing; to justify an American political party for orienting itself completely to the policy of a foreign state while claiming to be in the American democratic tradition is another. It is beyond comprehension." A terse reply from Ward stated:

> It is also beyond me to understand how anyone engaged in education could possibly think that defending the right of any political party to submit its policies and acts to the franchise of the American people, is in any sense justifying any of those policies or acts. My interest in this matter, however, goes further. The real question is whether democracy can protect itself by destroying itself. (11)

The raging fire of charges continued faster than one man could reply. As early as March 1, 1928, Ward had written on the margin of his *Christian Century* that a U.S. correspondent of a leading British newspaper told Ward's relatives in England that he was "the most hated man in the U.S." Interestingly, this was the journal issue that contained his article, "Why I Have Found Life Worth Living." Reading this, one can understand why the attacks did not stop him.

Crises in the late thirties brought a painful disaffection by Reinhold Niebuhr, from whom Ward had expected much. The abrasiveness of Herman Reissig, one of Niebuhr's devoted students and a stellar alumnus of Union Seminary, especially hurt Ward. A self-proclaimed religious Marxist at that time, Reissig was active with the North American Committee to Aid Spanish Democracy, whose purpose was to help Spain resist the invading fascist forces of Hitler and Mussolini. Ward had advised Reissig not to support the election of a Communist as secretary of the committee because Dr. Edward Barsky, "as good a communist as he was a surgeon," was the chief medical adviser. In other words, one of Ward's principles was to build a broad, united front, and to have two members from a minority political party would destroy a broad-based participation.

By 1940 Reissig had become anticommunist and anti-Soviet. In a review of Ward's new book *Democracy and Social Change* (201) in the *Christian Century* (Jan. 1, 1941), this former student wrote of his old professor "He has not been and is not a religious philosopher," and Reissig advised readers to look elsewhere for the message of religion to social philosophies.

While Baldwin and Reissig were criticizing Ward, others also fell victim to their behavior. For example, when Helen Keller resigned as chairperson of the American Rescue Ship Mission, a project of the Spanish Aid Committee, the two men reported her defection had occurred because the committee was communistic and "dishonestly administered." Keller heard of their statement and explained that her resignation was due to over-involvement in other activities. She wrote, "I am indignant that such unauthorized use should be made of my name." Both men tried to mollify the extraordinary woman, but Baldwin—who had just made it impossible for Ward to continue as chairman of the ACLU—took the responsibility to answer. He wrote Keller on August 1, 1941, stating that the phrase she found objectionable was "not official correspondence," but only a personal letter. Baldwin assured her he had not quoted her, only drawn conclusions (1).

The distortions of the meaning of words became a plague in the cold-war years, and people who were Ward's former friends must bear some responsibility for the misrepresentations. Baldwin, who once talked rose cultivation with Ward only to become later on of his "friendly enemies," wrote to William F. Cochran "confidentially" on August 27, 1940, that he distrusted the leadership of the renowned anthropologist, Franz Boas, who was then chairman of the National Emergency Conference for Democratic Rights. The reason was that "the Communist Party influence is strong" in the Boas group. When confronted with his insinuations Baldwin answered "I don't say that to detract from it, but just to characterize it."

To persuade people to sign petitions or to write letters to congressmen defending the right of the Communist party to appear on the ballot was one of the most precarious efforts undertaken by Ward and his friends. It was damaging to persons to have their name appear in the press on such a petition. Although a basic test of one's confidence in democracy, only a few lions stood firmly to defend that confidence.

If Ward knew the reasons why some religious leaders did not sign and evaded what he considered to be a moral as well as political issue, he showed understanding. Edgar M. Wahlberg of Grace Methodist Church, Denver, Colorado, confided in 1941 that he was already under harassment from the FBI and a local business tycoon or two for his social criticism and could not sign for the rights of Communists. His former teacher agreed with his decision. Always, Stephen Fritchman and certain other Unitarians would sign and get others to do so. But that was not sufficient to make much impression on those who believed in the "Red Menace."

Through his Presbyterian friend Richard Morford, Ward's petitions were circulated to that denomination and the Congregationalists. Loyal friend and former student Charles Webber distributed them in some of the trade unions. William Spofford, executive secretary of the Episcopal Church League for Industrial Democracy, tried to "get as many as he could" but added "our gang is running to cover."

Compared with other occupations, the Christian and Jewish clergy did as well on this issue as the labor unions and certain university clientele. These efforts were derided by all the media. The *New York Daily News* labeled Ward the "Red Dean" and the "chief architect of the Red drive in U.S. religion." All the leading papers carried stories from the Un-American Activities investigations in Washington where certain witnesses made unfounded charges, which were translated into sensational headlines.

One of these witnesses was Louis Budenz, who testified that he "knew from talking with him" that Harry Ward belonged to the Communist party. *Time* magazine in its Feb. 5, 1940, issue offered an unflattering picture of the seminary professor with his eyes half closed, subcaptioned "gaunt, sharp-faced, reddish haired H.W." He was sixty-seven now, his hair, in fact, snowy white.

Had his exfriends or the newspaper reporters really been looking for the truth they could have discovered that Ward had not "put the Soviet Union on the Throne of God." In his *Which Way Religion?* (167) critics could have read on p. 201, "At this point the religion of Jesus is not only opposite to the religion of Communism, but also to that of any state which seeks the welfare of mankind by the exercise of power." Then he makes a second telling argument to explain his differences with Russian views. "The religion of Communism is also opposite to that of Jesus at the point of man's relation to the cosmos. Communism denies any cosmic help to man and regards any trust in it as a superstitious faith."

The Gandhian influence emerged again with both Wards believing firmly that violence by any society would be self-destructive. Ward saw down the years the time when to loose the violence of nuclear bombs would turn the earth into an inferno. Everyone, communists included, would have to think on these things.

In summary two points must be stated. First, Ward repeatedly denied that he ever joined any political party and issued numerous notarized affadavits to that effect. For this position he had a pragmatic reason, as expressed by one of his former students from India, Professor S. P. Arya, who wrote from Madras in 1920: "Like yourself, I have never been able to tie up with a political party. One loses something in practical effectiveness by such aloofness, but on the other hand, is able to deliver an independent message and to have freedom of judgment" (11). In 1952, Ward again stated his position: "I am not and never have been a member of any political party. I took that position on principle in the beginning of my career in order that I might have complete freedom of moral judgment concerning all of them" (11). Some followers of this view have used it to avoid commitment and weaken organizational strength. Ward used it to gather the facts, analyze them to form reasonable generalizations, and then, most importantly, act on the findings. On the "American Forum of the Air" he repeated that he belonged to no party, but that he gathered the facts that led him to conclude that the Communist party had a sound right to exist and to field candidates.[3] Assailants made every effort to silence the man, and the most successful method was expressed at a meeting of the Federal Trade Commission in 1936 when a spokesman for utility interests snapped, "I would not try logical reasons, but I would try to pin the Bolshevik idea on my opponent." Secondly, Ward perceived order in the universe, and took a longer historical view, he thought, than the communists.

Notes

1. This poem, entitled "Christmas Carol," was a Christmas greeting sent to me in 1931 by John Haynes Holmes.

2. This is enlarged upon in Chapter 10. The pathological feelings toward the USSR by the United States puzzled Jawaharlal Nehru, first prime minister of free India. Before a group of Fulbright professors in 1955 in New Delhi he asked us about it. "We are next door to the Soviets," he remarked, "but do not suffer from mental disease because of it. You are thousands of miles away and yet you are inordinately afraid."

3. *The Radio Forum File* of "The American Forum of the Air," vol. 8, no. 19 (May 12, 1946) reveals the topic of the forum that day to be "Are Communism and Democracy Mutually Antagonistic?" Clare Booth Luce, William Z. Foster, Ward, and William Henry Chamberlin, a correspondent for the *Christian Science Monitor*, participated. See also the *Churchman*, June 1, 1946. It is reported that Clare B. Luce chattered and laughed derisively during Ward's summary, so that people on her side of the topic criticized her interruptions, laughs, and manners. Through it all, it is recorded that Professor Ward was patient; a few called him "a radio Christian martyr." The debate seemed to have aroused wide press and magazine discussion. Ward was "brutally attacked" and received scurrilous mail because he held that communism could be democratic.

9
Revolutionary
Trends in Religion:
The Federation

Beaten paths are for beaten people.
—William O. Douglas

If a creed were written to guide religiously oriented action through an era of industrial complexities, and if the guidelines contained no theology or mysticisms, only straightforward statements concerning one's dealings with one's fellow human beings, such a creed would need an organization to carry out its objectives. This became the *raison d'être* for the Methodist Federation for Social Action (MFSA), originally the Methodist Federation for Social Service.

The specific goal was to generate action against the politics of a profit-motivated society or to challenge individualistic plutocracy. Such action, in Ward's view, was not Radical Religion, but was more nearly religious radicalism and perhaps religious ethics for modern times. The leaders of the organization reasoned that Methodists and Christians generally needed access to the most reliable facts available about any current problem of social importance in order to put the puzzling jigsaw of events into a meaningful pattern. Then, using both facts and interpretations of facts, the Federation would help organize reasoned paths of action to solve the problems and to act morally. These were the foundation stones of the Federation.

The strict adherence to this way of operating probably explains the effectiveness of the program and the long life of the Methodist Federation for Social Action. Other organizations that Ward helped to found were dissolved at his suggestion when they no longer seemed viable. This was the fate of the League Against War and Fascism, of New America, and of the Religious Freedom Committee. To act—to act intelligently for human good—was a cardinal principle of Ward's religion.[1]

As the Federation conscientiously, almost reverently, built its program using the democratic process of noting, interpreting, and acting upon public affairs, it could also provide a kind of launching pad for dealing with unexpected issues of momentous concern. It could circulate information quickly, start action, get ad hoc groups functioning on problems of human rights. This procedure in some respects resembled the Committees of Correspondence of the American Revolution and in other ways the coalitions and labor councils of the present day.

The outreach of the Creed with its social-evangelism message to churches, colleges, and universities was like a call from the prophet Amos, "Let justice roll down from the mountains." In effect, it replaced the Manifest Destiny cry, "the world for Christ in our generation," which had nurtured the student missionary movement of earlier years. That phrase had been initiated by persons like John R. Mott while attending a revivalist-type conference in 1912 at the fashionable resort at Lake Mohonk, New York. A doctoral dissertation about the Federation has been written by Professor Milton John Huber, Jr. (331), but this chapter can list only a few of the activities that are especially illustrative of Ward's interests and procedures.

The concern to generate action against a profit-motivated society can be illustrated by the efforts of the Federation to sponsor a conference in 1922 on "Christianity and the Economic Order"— a topic rarely discussed in a church and almost taboo. Although some historians have called the post–World War I period the "period of normalcy," almost the opposite could be true. Abnormalcy would be a more descriptive word since it was a time when any reformistic bent would be overwhelmed by the pendulum swing toward the Big Business drive for laissez nous faire. To compensate for necessary wartime restrictions, the business interests were demanding freedom and a full pound of flesh. The conference confronted directly the abnormalcy of "what is good for business is good for the nation." It was convened at a mecca of Methodism—Evanston, Illinois—and was called the "Evanston Program." Bishop Francis J. McConnell presided at the high-point conference, as he called it. Again the organization man was Ward. His closest friends participated. John H. Gray, whom Ward credited for many of his economic insights, spoke on "The Economic Order"; William P. Hapgood, an American Robert Owen who organized his Columbia Conserve Company on nonprofit principles, spoke on "The Profit Motive"; Richard T. Ely, the University of Wisconsin economist, talked on "Property"; and H. Franklin Rall, a professor of religion, addressed himself to a typical Ward question, "What Are We Going to Do About It?" McConnell's handwritten report of the conference as well as Ward's marginal notes may be seen in the Federation papers at Drew University (8).

Another conference of this nature in 1926 defended the rights of workers to organize, to bargain with employers, and to speak freely in opposition to war. In reporting the conferences the *Bulletin* named some opponents, noting especially the National Chamber of Commerce and the National Association of Manufacturers. Members of these organizations promoted the open shop, blacklists, labor spying, and detective agencies; labeled the Federationists foreigners, Hunkies, and Bolsheviks; and accused some workers of spreading Sovietism in the United States.

The Federation focused on war as an inevitable product of the immoralities of the profit-motivated economic system. Ward's friend Coe supported the Federation and heartily endorsed the attack on the war system. Coe was also leading a nationwide campaign to strike militarism out of education and the Reserve Officers Training Corps (ROTC) out of the universities. The two friends wrote a report for the Federation and introduced it at the General Conference of the Methodists in 1924, stating that Christians could not support war. The report was finally adopted in a weakened version; the conference refused to reject war as a method of settling disputes.

Pressure was kept on the church publishing houses by the Federation to pay their workers adequate wages and permit unionization. A pertinent questionnaire went out to them asking about wages paid, overtime pay, dismissal, sickness pay, vacations, and pensions. Concern for these same basic issues involved the MFSA in the textile strike of 1925–1926 in Passaic, New Jersey, a strike as bitter as the steel strike of 1919.

To implement the goal of reaching as many people as possible who would be most oppressed by the profiteers, Ward, through the Federation, continued the encouragement of street preaching he had learned from Graham Taylor. He prepared a list of ten he had learned from Graham Taylor. He prepared a list of ten books for preachers who might want to use this method. Unemployment and war both seemed to result from the economic system, and Ward dealt with that subject in a series in the Federation *Bulletin.* This was followed by another series advocating the need for social and economic planning and the necessity of the church to deal with this concept.

He was continuing his civil-liberties efforts through the Federation and encouraged an exposé of the bigotry and fraudulent Americanism of the Ku Klux Klan. This was an extraordinary effort. Only older readers can appreciate the dreadfulness of the lynchings, other Klan activities, and the courage required to resist them.[2]

On the world situation the Federation warned of dollar diplomacy in Latin America and Asia. The *Bulletin* printed Ward's articles written from India, China, and Japan in which he explained the harshness of gunboat diplomacy and defended free speech, peace, and the justice of eliminating extraterritoriality agreements. These were explained more fully in Chapter 7. His articles also appeared in the *Nation,* one of his favorite journals of opinion; the *Christian Century; Zion's Herald;* and the *New Republic.* He kept urging the church to arouse itself and confront these policies in Asia. One of his rhetorical questions was, "Do the leaders of religion understand the relation of foreign investments to a big navy program, of the enormous increase of unearned income and unsocial property to the rise of militarism and the suppression of free speech among friendly and freedom-loving people?" (136) During the trying years of "normalcy," speaking for the poor created a kind of isolation of the social self. In response, the Federation developed another vital function—to give emotional and spiritual support to its members who often faced ostracism. According to Professor Huber, the historian of the Federation, the organization engaged actively in this second purpose to protect the mental health of its members.

A weekly publication to members started in 1919, called *Information Service,* was imitated by other denominations and the Federal Council of Churches. At first composed of neatly mimeographed sheets filled with summaries of important articles from journals of opinion, it became during the halcyon years a

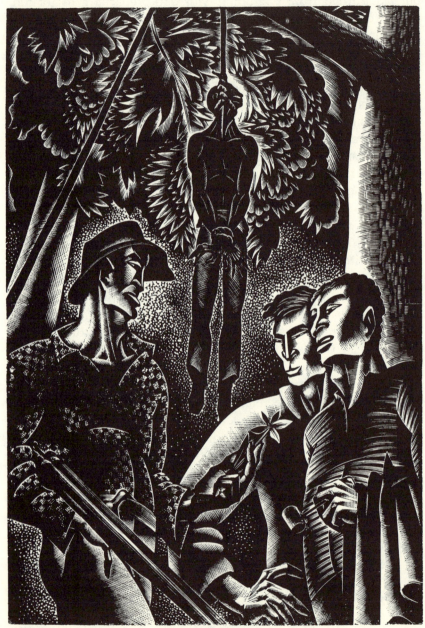

Figure 9.1 *From Lynd Ward's* Wild Pilgrimage.

publication upgraded in format and appeared more like those counterparts mailed by affluent denominations.

For a number of years small sheets called *Vital Question Leaflets* were published by the Federation to be used for community study sessions. It was a good idea, especially for city people who could carry a leaflet easily on a bus or subway. They were 3½ by 6½ inches and appeared just before *Reader's Digest* (1922), which achieved success and wealth with its functional format. The subjects of the leaflets and the adult-education method had the unmistakable stamp of Ward, for example: (1) The Open Shop, Harry Ward; (2) Disarmament, Mary Jenness; (3) Have You Free Speech? Roger Baldwin; (4) Cooperative Homes, Agnes Warbasse; (5) Public Ownership, Harry Laidler; and (6) The Nature of the Acquisitive Society, Harry Ward.[3]

At the turn of the decade, 1930, Ward wrote two books that supplemented and nurtured the work of the Federation. The first, *Our Economic Morality* (1929) (156), he came to regard as his most significant writing. Many of his former students have agreed and noted, even before the Great Depression struck, that Ward focused on the dangers of the unearned increment with the inequalities created by it. The book questioned "the myths" of *individualism* as in any fashion being able to form a constructive social force; of *laissez faire* as being proper because it balanced social and selfish interests and allowed them to serve each other; and of *competition* as salutary because it created abundance and made inequality and poverty unnoticeable.

Soon after, he wrote a sequel, or companion, volume to *Our Economic Morality*, which he called *Which Way Religion?* (1931) (167). It raised a basic question, Will religion guide the economic order or will the economic order vitiate religion? Ward stated his ideas in a straightforward, clear fashion using simple words so that the average person could understand them. These two books "full of flashes of insight," as Huber asserted, were the trumpets in an orchestration for one of Ward's greatest decades, 1930–1940.

The books and the *Bulletin* were the groundwork for a series of meetings organized by the Federation—"Call to Action" conferences. The first one was held in Chicago in April 1932. Something had to be done! Something more than reading and discussing! These gatherings would have to be different, conferences that would bring forward "the revolutionary tradition of Christianity" that would lead to an incisive criticism of capitalism.

One of the outcomes of those conferences was the "Crisis Leaflets," which followed patterns of the American revolutionary tradition. It was hoped they would appeal to the masses and would be displayed as free materials on the literature tables in church vestibules, with the usual booklets on tithing, charity, and ways to personal salvation. These "Crisis" broadsides were also to be mailed to church members, who would be stirred by their provocative sentences such as "violence from below in the social classes is a reaction to violence from above." These were to be discussed in church groups.

The turn in the emphasis of the course, from critical concerns of the profit system to an involvement for radical change in the economic structure, was brought on by the increasing human suffering in the depression. Many observers felt revolutionary change was at hand; a few were like Sinclair Lewis and Ward, who sensed the danger of an American Hitler. This change in concerns caused Ward to decide to use his second sabbatical in 1931 to visit the Soviet Union again to study carefully the first nonacquisitive economic order as a new social experience. On his return he felt he could say through the Federation and the organizations associated with it, "You see it can be done." "The USSR," he wrote in his *In Place of Profit* (176), "was continuing to exist without a profit motive."

In keeping with the new concerns Ward suggested to the executive board of the Federation in 1934 the change of the organization's name to the Methodist Federation For Social Action. The original term "social service" had been borrowed from the Webbs and other Fabians in England and denoted for them social action leading toward basic change. However, in the United States the period of "normalcy" had made the term mean little more than, as a wit in the thirties stated, "putting an uplift bra on old lady charity." The Federation, however, in the more-radical decline of the thirties boldly proclaimed that it rejected the method of struggle for profit and sought to replace it with a socialist order that would avoid depressions, sharp class distinctions, and war. Rejection of the old system was on the masthead of the *Bulletin* and remained there nearly forty years. It has been removed only recently.

The merger between the Ward and George Albert Coe social-action organizations in the early thirties may have played some part in the name change. Coe was guiding the Christian Social Action Movement centered in Evanston, Illinois. He assessed the American scene to find capitalism floundering, just as Ward had, and both men were certain of the need to work in larger groups. The Social Action Movement resembled the Methodist Federation and so no serious problems arose in considering the merger. Also Coe was seventy-two years old and was not able to give the energy such a cause deserved and demanded. Furthermore, his associates in his interdenominational organization were chiefly Methodists; so Ward suggested that the two men correspond about forming united action.

Several letters were exchanged, and then George Coe drafted a four-page single-spaced typewritten position paper dated October 14, 1934, and sent it to Ward (11). Coe suggested the merged organization should combine social progressives who were ready "to go to the limit" and get into action far beyond what would be understood in the churches at that time as "the firing line." The purpose would be to get a firm grip on the social and economic problems and increase the number who would be willing to go on this perilous undertaking.

The paper continued with four urgent issues that needed analysis and study. *Fascism* required more study so that it was not merely a congealer of emotion. What were the roots and underground sustenance and how far had it grown in America? *Violence* was a subject for more study and search for meaning. Social change often meant violence, and since persons were the object of supreme value, should not good and bad methods of social change be determined in spiritual terms, namely, what happens to people, not what happens to material mechanisms, tools, or weapons?

Coe boldly wrote that "our *social goal* is a classless society." He stated that "a more Christian economic order" was a "careless use of terms," and he suggested that an economic order was either Christian or not, and not more or less. A classless society

would demand that economic conditions that accompany such
a society would have to be declared. If "we are not sure," the
first imperative task would be to make a study of those conditions
and then follow with beyond-the-firing-line action.

A church was a place of *worship*, and Coe felt that concept
would have to be reconsidered. He wrote, "After about twenty-
five years study of worship, in general, and the consciousness
of God in American Christianity (both Protestant and Catholic),
I am of the opinion the present practice of worship almost
invariably strengthens the economic *status quo* and hinders the
kind of reconstruction to which we are already in our two
organizations committed. . . . Do we really know what worship
is or might be as an economic experience?" Almost all church
people at that time would have been at a loss to know what
these friends were talking about, just as those driven by private-
enterprise economics would have been confounded.

Then Coe dared to suggest that the writings and speeches of
reactionary preachers, bishops, editors, and secretaries should be
"devastatingly" analyzed and denounced with "infinite good
nature," but with determination. That would bring dissension,
but he asked, "Why in the world should the church be kept
from dissension at the cost of its spiritual power and significance?"

The long paper commented on the need to eliminate the
military in education (specifically ROTC) and the need to expose
the younger generation to unvarnished facts and encourage them
to do their own thinking about them. Government should be
placed in a more-religious context. "We should raise 'Ned' with
some police departments" and their fascistic tactics used during
strikes. The fascist nature of some Supreme Court decisions
needed to be attacked, also.

The final point was that class conflict existed in capitalism
and that clergy and church people could not stand above the
clash. No one could remain neutral except infants, and the
immediate problem was to ally themselves with "discontented
workers."

The hearty agreement of Ward brought a reply at once with
his revisions and additions and informed Coe these goals would
appear immediately in the *Bulletin* in an abbreviated form, and
later issues would carry detailed statements. "Meanwhile I hope

you get the Chicago fellows to approve of this. . . . The wider denominational plan which I broached to you had better not be discussed at present, I think. It was a joy and a great help to have a chance to talk things over with you" (6). Ward always had a ready organizational goal, in this case "the wider denominational plan." No doubt Coe's vigorous and bold idea that the organization become active and radical would preclude an extensive interdenominational approach, at least not until there was experience with a smaller constituency.

Winifred Chappell, the executive secretary, responded to Coe on the same day that Ward did and thanked "Professor Coe" for his check of fifty dollars as a gift to the Federation. "That was a corking criticism," she added, "that you made of the joint program and I think HFW has done a good job with all the documents he had before him—as you both always do" (6).

The *Social Question Bulletin*, after the merger, grew into a paper of twelve to fourteen pages by the mid-forties with notable contributors, among them Carey McWilliams, Franz Boas, and the humanitarian engineer-professor at Columbia University, Walter Rautenstrauch. There were articles on Rochdale cooperatives, a book-review section, and a column called "Behind the Headlines," which was Ward's column for the rest of his life.

In each issue Ward analyzed an important political-economic event and discussed the moral imperative involved. Biblical allusions were used to aid church people in grasping the ethical meanings, but he never argued *ad Biblicum*, using the Bible as authority. Rather he cited it as the experience of the Judeo-Christian past from which ethical import could be gleaned. According to Ward, Jesus united this past into a set of ethical guidelines that would not tolerate the barbarities and antilife actions of groups such as Nazis, Fascists, and Ku Klux Klan. Questions were raised in the *Bulletin* inquiring "How can a large segment of the Catholic Church support Generalissimo Franco in Spain? Isn't the Church both Catholic and Protestant more friendly to private enterprise than it is to socialism?"

The Methodist Federation for Social Action was one of the first organizations to reveal the unspeakable treatment meted to Communists, Jews, and liberals in Germany. It was the only church group affiliated with the League Against War and Fascism, later to be one of Ward's most extensive efforts. New America, an action group to revive the revolutionary tradition of Jefferson and his contemporaries and make detailed plans for a new socioeconomic order for the United States, was germinated in the Federation. In the bleak and fumbling years of the Great Depression this plan was tried, as I shall discuss in Chapter 10.

In *Action Letters* of the *Bulletin* the Federation called upon citizens to stop the lynching of blacks. It supported as well the Committee to End Discrimination in Chicago Medical Institutions. Little wonder, therefore, that Mary McLeod Bethune, the famous black woman educator and college president, and G. A. Barrett, president of George Washington Carver College, gave support to this seminal group.[4]

Much credit, of course, for the achievements of the Federation must go to associates of Ward. There were three highly capable women who as associate secretaries and coeditors of the *Bulletin* and the other publications made an inestimable contribution. Grace Scribner began in 1913, Winifred Chappell in 1922, and Helen S. Murray in 1937.

Grace Scribner was killed instantly in 1922 by a careless driver in New York City. Ward was contacted on the telephone by a news reporter, who shouted, "We want some information about Grace Scribner. We understand she was your secretary." "No," said Ward firmly, "she was the Associate Secretary of the Methodist Federation for Social Service" (11).

An essay Ward wrote has not received the same wide attention as the one that Editor William Allen White wrote for his daughter Mary upon her tragic death. Both men were deeply moved by the effect of the tragedies on the personal and community lives of us all. Ward felt that the character of our society and social organization stood "revealed." The carelessness of the driver and the unrestrained rush for pleasure and power seemed valued more than the dedicated, sacrificial life of a woman. He asked, "Does it mean modern society is on its way to destroy itself by means of the machinery that is its distinction and its boast? . . . Or shall we bestir ourselves in time to use them for the fashioning and sustenance of the beloved community?" Lamenting on the untimeliness of the sudden ending of Grace Scribner's brief life, Ward described "Into this career had gone something of the vital forces of our times and place; the urge for education and the response to it that grew out of our pioneer energy and resources; the organized religious impulse that is not ignorantly dissipated; the genuine intellectual culture that has flourished even out of our materialistic soil." This life, he reminded, had been fashioned into "an instrument of priceless value to the social order" (307).

Scribner was followed by Winifred Chappell. Ward, because of increasing professional responsibilities, leaned heavily on Chappell. She had to put in long hours to see that printings, mailings, and other plans were duly processed. Two years before his death he received a letter from Winifred's brother, Harry W. Chappell, who commented on her loyalty and devotion to the service of others and to the goals of the Federation. Credit should go to Ward, he added, as the person who helped her "find meaningful activity for her life. She had no more welcome companionship through her years" (328).

Helen Murray, Charles Webber, Jack McMichael, Lee Ball, and Mae Ball gave to the Federation unstintingly of time, energy, and selflessness. Bishop McConnell must be recognized, also. Both he and Ward would put their personal money into the Federation bank account in order to pay the assistants at union levels. Professor Huber, who wrote on the Federation, observed, "Ward carried the message and McConnell with his prestige and episcopal office cleared the way of opposition that was sure would be heard" (331). McConnell considered Ward a prophet with whom he had a cooperative alliance; the more priestly person defended the outspoken prophet through many years of more or less caustic criticism vented upon them.[5]

Bishop Herbert Welch, a founder and one who wrote on several occasions that Ward was the instigator of the Federation and the phrase maker for the Creed, had some reservations about the program and direction as it developed in the thirties and forties. When Welch was 100 years old, he wrote in his brief autobiography, *As I Recall My Past Century* (309), that the original method of the Federation was educational and the spirit was "ironic rather than controversial." He continued, "When I questioned McConnell on some of Ward's procedures he replied, 'the Methodist Church ought to be able to afford one Harry Ward.'" Welch rejoined with some trepidation, "the trouble is of producing many little Harry Wards without the strong vital qualities that brought Harry to a place of power and service."

That the church should move between opposites was the Welch position. It should not take sides, but should initiate action and act as mediator. The Federation, he felt, had turned from being educational to being a propagandist and controversial agency in politics and economics. At conferences, he claimed it pushed for "one-sided and poorly considered resolutions, not representative of the majority views, and saw some officials of the Federation showing contempt and bitterness toward those who differed with them and claiming the Federation to be 'the conscience of the church.' I decided to drop out and severed my connection" (309).

A note of pathos enters when two principal founders of the Federation part company in trying times. For whatever reasons, Bishop Welch defected. Ward did not ignore him as he did Worth Tippy and in later years Bishop Bromley Oxnam. Was it because Ward welcomed informed and mutual questing with those who disagreed with him, as with his neighbor Parlin and his friend Bonbright, both apologists for capitalism, or with his students— those who relished deliberation but rejected calculation? With calculators he was easy to anger and acerbic in criticism. He could not tolerate name calling, acts of guilefulness, and intellectual dishonesty. Those who manifested such traits during a question period, for instance, found him almost merciless in his rejoinders. At times he verged on losing his patience as he tore into their arguments with his quick mind and ready knowledge. Welch was a leader who had spoken the truth as he saw it. Ward respected him and his honesty in stating that it was Ward who had written the Creed and who had been prime mover for the Federation. On approaching ninety years of age, in 1962, Ward wrote his old friend Welch a card of congratulation for attaining his one-hundredth birthday.

As the Federation grew in social impact over the years, it was effective in arousing the social conscience in and out of religious circles, and of course the more effective it became the more the official church abandoned it. The General Conference of the Methodist Church vacillated from time to time about the Federation much as Cotton Mather did on witchcraft in his day. Proclaimed witches must be eradicated, said the churchmen around

Mather, and even though the medico-clergyman had doubts, the tragic cleansing of the community went on.

In the so-called normal days of 1924, the general conference began its exorcism by eliminating strong statements in the Social Creed. It continued to seek to capture the Federation by creating an official organization under the direct control of the conference. A few years later the Federation was declared to be an "unofficial" Methodist body and the *Bulletin* name appeared with "unofficial" printed in parentheses under it. Unable to drive out the demons, the Federation by 1950 had become so controversial that the church asked it to leave the Methodist headquarters at 150 Fifth Avenue. By 1952 it was ordered to drop Methodist from its name.

Not solely the church but government agencies, too, attacked the Federation. The operations of Attorney General A. Mitchell Palmer had their effects in 1919, but the organization survived and gained support until it was denounced by the Dies Committee in the late thirties. The first heavy blasts at the Federation came in 1935 from the newspapers of William Randolph Hearst. "Methodist Reds" who attacked profit making were the victims. The Federation was to Hearst "The Marxist Federation for Social Strife." The masses, he argued, must not acquire more money or property, because it would wreck home life and destroy the value of private property. Hearst pleaded for a return to personal religion and rallied two Chicago Methodist bankers to help him to arrange for the general conference to throw the "Reds" out. Senator James Eastland from Mississippi labeled the Federation for Social Action as a bunch of reds because they stood for racial integration.

Church and state also stood together, with few exceptions, over the position Ward took on the Hitler-Stalin Pact of 1939. It has never been easy for riders on the streamlined train of history to hang on when it takes a sharp curve at full speed ahead. The Federation and its leader had pointed out that no capitalist aid was offered in 1937 to democratic Spain to ward off the air raids of Hitler and Mussolini. Right or wrong, the majority of the Federation's executive board believed that no capitalist country would help effectively in deterring Hitler from destroying the USSR. Ward voted with the majority and asked for sounder understanding of the Russian dilemma.

Before Hitler turned his panzer divisions full force on the Soviets World War II was a continuation of World War I, Ward argued. It was concerned chiefly with trade and market advantages. As will be recalled, he took a pacifist position in the earlier war, and he maintained that economic position into World War II, until Hitler marched eastward. He perceived that the Soviets were certain that Hitler would in time attack them in full force and that they would stand alone just as Spain had against a mighty military panoply. The defensive step was to make a pact with the devil, to slow Hitler's plans, thus giving the Soviet Union time to mount stronger defenses and to evacuate citizens from its major cities. At this point Ward surprisingly was willing to forego strong pacifist principles to halt the mad man of Europe. Moreover, as he saw it, the first socialist state in the world was threatened with obliteration. Therefore, he refused to be critical of the pact, rejected his peace stance, and accepted the fact that the USSR had no wiser alternative. Even people who disagreed with him thought he took a stand that was unpopular and personally courageous.

The full wrath of the establishment then fell on the little organization with a membership of less than a thousand. One might assume it had enormous power and numbers judging by the blows that were dealt from many sources. In a memorandum in his "MFSA" folder, Ward concluded that the onslaught did serious damage to the organization, weakened the membership, and intimidated its religious leaders.[6]

Many personal friends and acquaintances seemed covertly to agree with Ward. George Coe, however, could be expected to speak out to defend his friend. Later he wrote in the *Christian Advocate* (Nov. 8, 1951) that the Federation had followed "the radicalism of Jesus more consistently than any other church body." When the name changed from "Social Service" to "Social Action," he commented, it meant not to feed the hungry but to abolish poverty.

But the Federation and its executive board were not entirely alone on the Hitler-Stalin decision. Dr. Henry Sigerist, a noted historian of medicine at the Johns Hopkins University and later at Yale, probably knew Ward only by name, but he publicly advocated full support of the socialist state. Top priority for the physician was to stop the warfare started by the fascist dictatorships of Hitler, Hirohito, and Il Duce. "I hate war too much to be a pacifist," said Sigerist. Rockwell Kent, writer and world-recognized painter, and Paul Robeson, the singer and actor, took similar positions.

As the years have passed and perspective has been gained on the era, many who were figuratively tarred and feathered as Communists or called fellow travelers have been acknowledged to have had a legitimate American point of view. The Owen Lattimores, for instance, were personal friends and defenders of the Wards. When Lattimore, the best-informed scholar of that day on Central Asia, was invited in 1967 to read a paper at the annual convention of the American Historical Association, the packed banquet hall of the New York Hilton gave him a long, standing ovation. Only ten years before he was virtually read out of many universities because of his friendly views toward the Soviet Union. Speaking of the nineteen fifties the Reverend Stephen Fritchman, a nationally known Unitarian minister, reported that Ward's letters of greetings to dinners and rallies devoted to human rights were welcomed with bursts of applause. More scholarly attitudes were beginning to replace the scare-creating name calling.

Huber comments that the unofficial status thrust upon the Federation as a reprimand by the Methodist Church was actually helpful. It made possible more candidness and greater freedom from the strings of the ecclesiastics. It became, Huber concluded, the most influential radical group in Protestantism. This judgment was based in part on a survey questionnaire he had circulated. "Which denomination do you consider has been most influential in promoting the social gospel?" he asked on plain stationery, explaining that he would appreciate the reply for his Doctor of Philosophy dissertation. The questionnaire was sent to interdenominational social-action committee leaders. Sixty-five percent of the respondents named the Methodists. The other 35 percent gave varied responses. Some respondents singled out Ward and McConnell, the leaders of the Federation, as having "enormous potency." And this response came in spite of the attacks from much of the media and the economic powers.

Huber summarized the influence the organization had during the years Ward was executive secretary and listed some of the important contributions it made. These points stressed the following:

- Considerable influence on many prominent leaders of the Protestant church.
- Important effects on conferences of individual church denominations and on their national assemblies, publications, organizational methods, and techniques. Even phraseology was "copied" from the MFSA.
- Arousal of opponents who attacked it, and learned thereby. Others were sufficiently concerned to read the pamphlets and discover the cause of the heated controversy.
- Several seminaries did not escape involvements. Garrett, Drew, and Union are specifically mentioned by Huber, but Yale (Jerome Davis), Chicago (Arthur Holt), and the Pacific School of Religion could be included.
- The Deaconess movement.
- The church curricula—Sunday School, adult Bible classes, youth organizations.
- The *Bulletin* was used by: (1) Jewish, Catholic, and civil rights groups and the liberal and radical press; (2) some religious associations in Europe after translation; (3) non-church-oriented persons; (4) the labor movement for the facts on the eight-hour day, the "living wage," collective bargaining, and other efforts; (5) students and research persons in labor unions for information on industrial controversies and for industrial and labor management courses; (6) mediators and arbitrators involved in settling labor disputes; and (7) the *Christian Century*, for example, as an excellent resource for factual materials on strikes and other labor issues. (331)

Huber complimented the literary qualities of Ward's essays. He mentioned those written from China, India, and Japan and called them classic in style, saying that they had power and point for readers.

The revolutionary tradition of Christianity Ward sensed was advancing. If continued, he wrote, it might well be the kind of religion that could survive the economic democratization of the present order. The old narcissistic religion would not endure. The new wine of a more-just community could be poured into the old wineskins of the Judeo-Christian tradition—not an act approved by Scripture, but one that sounded right this time, for it could be the preservation as Ward wished of a religious heritage in which concern for others was the goal. In the American political tradition he found, as traced in the next chapter, an old wineskin. It was, for him, a quid pro quo in the ongoing struggle for the rights of all people.

Notes

1. Ward would not permit his name to be used on a letterhead or in a list of sponsors down the side of stationery unless he could interact in a useful way with persons who were dealing with the problem.

2. Dr. Arthur Swift, also of Union Seminary and a stalwart supporter of Ward, was an effective voice against the Klan and its bigotry. Bishop McConnell declared that Ward, Swift, and Charles Webber (assistant director of field work under Swift and later executive director of the Federation) "raise disturbing questions ahead of time, they have been the most successful force in Protestantism."

3. Mary Jenness wrote several books and study guides on social problems for church young people's groups. Agnes Warbasse was a founder of the Rochdale cooperative movement in the United States and wrote books, including guides to start cooperatives. Her physician husband, James P. Warbasse, was the first president of the Cooperative League of the United States. Harry Laidler was active in the Socialist party and the League for Industrial Democracy and wrote on the history of socialism in the United States.

4. A recent critic at Union Seminary raised questions about Ward's views and efforts for blacks. In his Boston days he reminded the executive board of the Federation that there must be more contact with "our colored brethren and students." In 1943 he wrote, recalling the World War I period, "Then the black man put on uniforms and went overseas again in a white man's war to save democracy. He came home not to sit in the same seat, nor live on the same street, nor vote, nor sit on a jury." Ward concluded, "So from the black people with bright words on their lips and deep silence over their hearts, carefree in life

and careless of death, we have learned that none of us is free until all of us are free" (11). He noted, too, that black nurses were not used on the basis of their ability and training and never permitted to work with hospitalized white troops.

The Federation entered into an active defense of W.E.B. DuBois when he some years later was brought into the courts on false charges of being a "foreign agent" as a director of a Peace Information Center (see Chapter 13).

5. Considering how much time, energy, and effort McConnell gave to Ward and the Federation, one has to puzzle over the fact that Ward is mentioned only once in McConnell's autobiography and then only in connection with an anecdote. Because of Ward's role in nonestablishment organizations, perhaps it was still too dangerous in the nineteen sixties to mention any association with him. Or perhaps McConnell felt history was proceeding in a different direction, and the prophetic tradition had also shifted its course from the Ward path.

6. Other social-action groups within other denominations were also under heavy restraint. As Donald Meyer states (298), the Congregational Council for Social Action suffered as did the Federal Council of Churches itself. J. Howard Pew, a Presbyterian and an oil czar, helped finance the charges against these bodies and gave financial support to the formation of the National Council of Churches, which called for personal salvation.

10
The American Revolutionary Tradition: New America

*It is clear once again that a Socialist Opposition
in this country [United Kingdom] comes into office
with very half-baked plans.*
—Richard Crossman, M.P.
Diaries, January 3, 1965

Revolutions of oppressed classes, as the reader knows, have occurred in the past, are now taking place, and will continue to happen in the foreseeable future. They are as useful to social growth as the sloughing of casings by certain crustaceans. This truism applies to the "land of the free and the home of the brave" no matter how vehemently it is denied by those who fear change or who write history as antiquarianism. Harry Ward was as familiar with the revolutionary traditions in France, Russia, and China and those of smaller countries as he was with the American tradition of bold assertion of inalienable rights for all humanity. He taught his current-events courses at Union Seminary using what Charles Beard called the "vista" of history in contrast to the "views" as expressed by scholars cramped, even blinded, by a chronological historiography with its sterile discreteness, and he felt that history was essential to orderly living much as a rearview mirror is for safe automobile driving. The historical view could minimize or avoid the great and small crashes on the roadways of life.

The study of the history and progress of revolutions led Ward to sense a revolutionary situation as imminent in the Great Depression decade. He and some friends decided it was so possible that something should be done about it. The moral compunction to act was almost a habit with him. The plan for action in this case was in addition to those made by three other organizations Ward was leading or advising at the same time. There was agreement that no one could predict the exact year or even decade in which a transfer of power in a social order might happen, but Ward insisted on thinking and planning before giving way to random efforts that might lead to chaos, civil war, or a fascist-patterned dictatorship.

The economic system was indeed on the skids. The stock market had crashed; industrial production was lagging; long bread lines in cities, buried food products and animals in rural areas were endemic. "The Last Days of the First Republic" was the characterization make by Selden Rodman, editor of *Common Sense*. George Soule, the well-known economist of the day, titled his 1934 book *The Coming American Revolution*. There was a prevailing mood of restlessness, irritation, and groping for something better—a need for drastic change was in the air. Ward believed that this crisis with "half-baked plans" could give rise either to the man on horseback or a muddle-through policy. His hope was to use the ground swell for the organization of a better expression of democracy.

As could be expected, every imaginable kind of explanation and panacea for the pervasive stagnancy appeared. Sydney Gamble, a member of the Procter and Gamble Soap Company family, believed that the depression was incurable because it was due to sun spots! He also agreed with the religionists who attributed bad times to God's punishment of the wicked. If both Nature and Nature's God were accepted as reasons for the economic malaise, accepted also were the equally simplistic, demagogical cures of Huey Long (divide the wealth equally), Dr. Francis Townsend (generous subsidization of senior citizens to stimulate the economy), and Father Charles Coughlin (retrogress to "the good old days").

Advice from many others across the land was perhaps much better, and they also recognized the imperative need for change. Norman Thomas, the Socialist, was welcomed by the bemused wealthy at lawn parties in Montclair, New Jersey, the plush bedroom of New York City. Franklin Roosevelt interviewed him at the White House to garner ideas. Upton Sinclair ran for governor of California on his EPIC (End Poverty in California) plan and almost won. His useful idea allowed the ill-clad unemployed to run the factories to make clothes for themselves. At

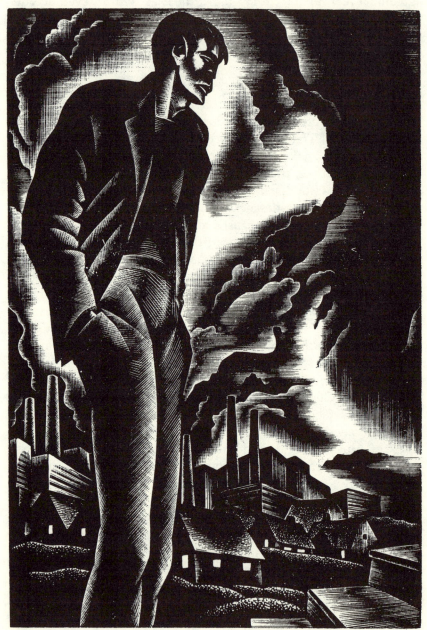

Figure 10.1 *From Lynd Ward's Wild Pilgrimage.*

Columbia University in 1932 George S. Counts, the educator, wrote *Dare the Schools Build a New Social Order?* at the same time that colleagues in the School of Engineering were saying that a moribund system must be replaced by Technocracy in which scientists would rule with the harsh objectivity of computers. John Dewey, as chairman of the League for Independent Political Action, had bold words for the abolition of capitalism, all in the context of an American setting. The league called for a second American Revolution in which the "magnificent audacity" of Sam Adams, Jefferson, Paine, and John Taylor of Caroline would be combined and repeated. Illustrious names appeared on the league's "United Action Campaign Committee": Stuart Chase, popularizer of economics; Ira Reid, black sociologist; Reinhold Niebuhr, philosopher of religion; and Fiorello La Guardia, mayor of New York City. Ideas were rife in the East and out into the farm belt on how to steady the shaking pillars of the social structure.

The direction of thinking that most appealed to Ward approximated Dewey's proposal with its expressed desire for a "Yankeefied" pattern of social change that used the slogans and ideas of the American tradition. However, Ward's plan was different in a basic way. He wanted patterns of organization and direct action to guide the people, more specific than the slogans, good as they were, generated by the Committees of Correspondence and Democratic Societies of the seventeen eighties and nineties. The masses would need modern organizational blueprints in order to guide change in fundamental ways. Their unions, their cooperatives, and other organizations must understand the direction and the goal of collective effort. This involvement of the people was a position largely foreign to the engineers who pushed Technocracy as they worked on the top floors of the Empire State Building in New York City, far above, in fact and in thought, the millions in the surrounding megalopolis. Ward raised the more-difficult question of just how the vast, generally ignored mass of people was to be organized and kept informed. Were leaders prepared and, in the trade-union sense, disciplined? Did they have clear and operable plans? (for socialists "must not come into office with half-baked plans"). With what social forces could they work? Questions like these were of paramount concern as he anticipated a possible transfer of political and economic power from, as the poor New England farmer William Manning stated in 1798, "the few to the many."

On December 6, 1933, a small group that included George Counts and Goodwin Watson, his colleague at Teachers College, Columbia University, met at the offices of *Common Sense* magazine to talk about a merger between the Forward America movement, a collection of liberals concerned over the economic situation, and an organization Ward was forming called New America. Ward, who could always combine bluntness and kindness, told his former student Goodwin Watson that Forward America tended to be naive and utopian. It lacked, he wrote to Watson, clear aims, methodology, historical perspective, and adequate economic analysis. Watson joined his former professor in the task of launching New America, which would appeal to the Declaration of Independence, the Bill of Rights, and other ideals of the nation's founding fathers. This Gideon's army of intelligent, realistic leaders was to be select and dedicated. Forward America never materialized.

The hour had come, Ward admonished, when liberals could no longer politically vacillate, but had to move to the left as socialists or to the right as capitalists. This was followed by the gloomy conclusion: "If the liberal thinks he can change the behavior of the reactionaries by persuasion, either as to profits or violence, let him observe the results of the appeal of Roosevelt on the matter of selling oil for the war in Ethiopia" (189). The reference was to American oil companies in 1936 supplying Mussolini for his attack on an independent African state. True liberals would move left because they saw the masses stirring, the farm-labor movement growing, and industrial unionism reviving. These winds promised a storm for which Ward urged preparation through careful organization. No more shilly-shallying, for a historical revolutionary movement was upon the nation. It seemed to him that organization should be quick and comprehensive. The Russian revolution of 1918 appeared to leap over a harsh fascist period, Ward theorized, because Lenin and other Bolshevik leaders were adequately prepared to move in the direction of a socialist society. The chief theoretician and guide for New America was the 135-pound, wiry man who taught ethics at Union Theological Seminary—who might have heard Gandhi's cry, "There go my people. I must catch up with them."

After spending more than a year quietly drawing up an overall plan, the leaders of the next American revolution were ready to announce their goals and procedures to a larger, carefully selected body of people. The basic assumption was that the purpose of New America would be to effect the transition from capitalism to a planned economy. Hence its members must organize to take over food supplies, public utilities, communications, and credit. At the same time they must suppress the counterrevolution before bloody civil war could arise. The organization had to be thoroughly active in carrying the revolutionary struggle to workmen, farmers, students, and teachers. With the rank and file organized they would gain from it further guidance in preparing a national plan. In the *New American*, March 15, 1936, the journal of the organization, are found some clearly stated purposes:

Our Purpose: *To record*, and explain the breakdown of the profit system, so that American people may get rid of it before it destroys them: *To prepare* the people of this country to put a planned and planning social economy in place of the profit system: *To unite* the American working people—industrial, agricultural, transport, commercial, professional, housewives—to the common task of taking and operating the political and economic power that belongs to them: *To enable* these New Americans, true to American tradition, to develop a society of free persons, democratically controlled, with equal access for all to health, education, and creative activity. (44)

The first steps toward achieving the grand goal had to be blueprinted. Personnel must be trained and prepared to start operations across the United States. Coordinated action must be speedy, democratic, and at all times peaceful. Then, as if to drive home certain points, these leaders who thought themselves to be twentieth-century Sons of Liberty listed what the essential characteristics of their organization would be:

1. The organization must be American in the use of words and in the appeal to American revolutionary heroes, precedents, and traditions. It would not look to Europe or Russia for advice or for a model.

2. It would be built upon the economic interests of workers, farmers, and professionals. These must be united to oppose a minority that would try to restore the old order.

3. It would reveal the main objectives, but it would "keep in its own inner circle the knowledge of some of the necessary measures to make this mandate effective, since these would arouse only unnecessary prejudice in certain groups." The leaders meant, for example, that the U.S. Constitution, but *not the Bill of Rights*, would be abolished and with it the whole legal and judicial system. The constitutional framework, more conservative in origin as Charles Beard argued in the thirties, would tend to block what the New America group wanted to achieve. "It will have to be opposed for there is no joyride," Ward explained, "into a new economic order." This bold suggestion may explain in part why the names of leaders and members of New America were somewhat difficult to discover.[1]

4. People would be given simple, honest directives built upon disillusionment for the old unjust order and enthusiasm for the new, more-cooperative one.

5. And finally, New America would observe the disciplinary policies that included frank criticism of one another's work and writing. "Democratic centralism" was to be practiced requiring unwavering loyalty to group decisions when confronting the opposition. The belief that people could learn the direction in which history was moving and let that direction discipline their action was a basic tenet of New America. Ward saw this as a certain means to a positive type of ethical behavior.[2]

In the numerous position papers Ward submitted for criticism and revision to his associates, he highlighted necessary *immediate* actions. New America must strive to win a national election;

then Congress must (1) nationalize natural resources, capital plants, banks, and communications; (2) provide a universal insurance system; (3) bring maximum and minimum income as close together as economic circumstances permit; (4) write a new constitution with courts to resemble people's tribunals; (5) liquidate state governments and have municipalities operated in a scientific way free from political rivalry; and (6) allow Socialists and Communists to run for office and to join the government providing they accept certain differences of outlook New America has with them. These necessary immediate actions were of considerable interest, especially since Ward was repeatedly and falsely charged with being a Communist.

New America literature used patriotic slogans at times; it quoted indigenous heroes and precedents; it was more national minded and less international minded in following the theory that a collectivistic economy must first become a reality at home before becoming too involved with the unity of the workers of the world.

George Coe had noted an article by Merle Curti in the progressive educational journal the *Social Frontier* (vol. 1, no. 3, Dec. 1934). The title, encircled by Coe, read "Our Revolutionary Tradition." It pointed out that even conservatives like Alexander Hamilton and John Adams believed revolutions might be necessary. James Madison, too, came even closer to Thomas Jefferson and Thomas Paine in affirming the right to revolt, but "not when property interests were in danger." In addition, Curti added to these names those of Abraham Lincoln, who reasserted the right to revolution, and the stolid Ulysses S. Grant, who wrote favorably of this principle in his memoirs. Coe sent the article to Ward as an aid to the Yankeefication goal.[3]

The organization did not advocate force and violence, nor did it exclude white-collar workers or middle-class people. It welcomed farmers, blue-collar workers, and the oppressed. Religious workers were not rejected if they cooperated in the common goal of ending a sinful economic order.

The purpose emphasized that New America was a revolutionary organization and not another political party. Analysis was necessary to its purpose, and it must be based upon a principle more fundamental, more dynamic than the traditions of revolutionary theory—the principle of the scientific method. The goal was not to be either dogmatic or dialectical, but scientific. Ward and his editors (names not given) of *New American* magazine explained further:

> New America thus approaches the problems of social change in this country on the basis of continuously developing analytical understanding. It sees a dynamic for social change, not in the clash of conflicts between classes more explicit in other nations, but in the contradiction between a declining profit system and the capacity for technical expansion for the benefit of all the people. It sees a revolutionary motive power not in the overthrow of one class society by another, but in the shift of the control over the means of production and the economic and political processes within society. (44)

As Ward continued writing out the guidelines for New America, which was one of the several organizations brooded by the large American League against War and Fascism, his philosophical pragmatism was even more apparent. New America, in contrast to the League of Women Shoppers, the China Aid Council, and Aid to Spain organization, was to be more of a study group, devoted to *method* rather than program.

> The means of arriving at this goal [the transfer of power] can be neither rigid or doctrinaire, but must take their character from the tendencies at work in American society. The understanding of these tendencies emerges from hypotheses, experience, analysis. Programs must be flexible, activity must be continuous and critical at the same time. The society which is to be built can be suggested by neither utopian or dogmatic concepts. It must be based on the continuous evaluation of the requirements of a new machine age checked against what is desirable. (44)

His paper ended by calling for a people's mobilization into a Peoples Front, a united front against capitalism, and saying that the forward-moving features in history must be followed.

The structure from the grass roots to the top of leadership reflected the intent of radical change. Residential groups, whose members were often referred to as "our Committees of Correspondence," formed the basic unit that would educate members by (1) raising issues, (2) freely debating them, (3) supplying facts through provided literature, (4) analyzing the facts, and (5) taking action. Action meant that revolutionary potential would arise from participation in local struggles such as protests, boycotts, and strikes. Members of the residential unit would be elected to a unit policy council, comprising a town or sections of a city, that would elect representatives to a district policy council. The district would elect to the state and so on up to the national policy council.

The discipline expected of members again was reflected in these councils. For instance, only after full and free discussion of an issue was democratic centralism expected after a majority vote decided the unity with all. Dues were expected to be paid monthly on an ability-to-pay basis, with those making $1,000 a year (this was in 1935) to give 1 percent of their salary, $2,000 to give 2 percent, 3,000 to give 3 percent, and so on up the income ladder.

Since Ward, Watson, Robert and Helen Lynd (the authors of *Middletown* and *Middletown in Transition*), Walter Rautenstrauch (the Columbia University engineering professor and more rational technocrat), and their associates believed that a revolutionary hour had come, they hoped to practice an impersonal group discipline of criticism, positive and negative, of one another's writings and actions.[4] They anticipated the Thermidorian problem of compromise that so far in history had troubled and frustrated most governments dedicated to a cooperative commonwealth. In 1798 it "teased the mind" of William Manning, the hard-working New England farmer who saw "the Concord fite" and later asked "why die for liberty and then in later years lose it."[5] To preserve liberty, if it can be done, seems to demand more than Jefferson's urging of vigilance, more than the once widely used Soviet group criticism, and more than China's Cultural Revolution requiring intellectuals, professionals, and top politicians to return regularly to the farms and to the common people for democratic inspiration and guidance. The university intellectuals and political leaders around Ward were going to attempt to gain and then to preserve the second American revolution. They were intent on the avoidance of *making* history, but rather they hoped they might participate in *changing* it.

The brunt of the socialist criticism fell on Ward himself, whose position papers, "Crisis" leaflets, and pamphlets sought to educate and to preserve gains. Thomas Wright, a Congregational minister and national organizer of New America, called some of Ward's rough drafts inartistic, badly written, "heavy, inert, too vague and general, and full of cliches."[6] Few, if any, leaflets were written by Wright, who preferred the freedom, as he called it, of spending his time beyond eight hours of work in eating, drinking, and making merry. Ward, then sixty-three years old, graciously admitted the truth of the objections and added "we must not be just negative in criticism, but explain exactly what we mean by 'too heavy' or 'absurd' or 'don't like ethical reference.'" But Wright, the armchair radical, was chosen to be national director probably because he was a good speaker, a young clergyman popular with youth. He was nonetheless unable to inspire the leadership New America needed and sought to prepare.

The hope had been to select leaders who would approximate the tested and dedicated Communist party members in the early days of the Soviet Union, about whom Sidney and Beatrice Webb wrote glowingly fifty years ago. The selection process was as follows: On recommendation of trusted friends a person could become a general member of New America. One could vote but not hold office. However, those who gave time and effort were identified as Actives, and they could hold office up to the national policy council. Those Actives who proved themselves most capable and disciplined were designated Leaders and could hold the highest offices. Thus the blue collars and open white collars with proved abilities could lead the organization.

The educational program of New America that considered seriously the needed reconstruction after the collapse of the old social order was impressive if for no other reasons than as an adult-education effort. Having followed Thomas Paine's use of "crisis leaflets" for his Methodist Federation, Ward continued the technique for New America. The organization issued an extensive series of broadsides and pamphlets on such subjects as the

"Concentration of Income," "Destruction of Markets," and "New America, Its Goal and Program."

The first ten leaflets put to use had already been written for the Federation. Both organizations circulated them. Congressman Thomas A. Amlie, a friend of Ward and Frank Lloyd Wright, wrote that the leaflets were "the best material in condensed form that I have ever seen." Progressives, he said, should send them out in a wholesale manner, but under the Methodist heading because they would be more acceptable. The name "New America" was new and a little suspect as compared with "Methodist."

Leaflet No. 10 stated that any member of the organization strong enough to wrest power or money from others would not be allowed to do so. He must agree not to do it. In one of his letters (July 19, 1934) Amlie questioned Ward about being so unrealistic, so favorable to complete equality. Rather he defended a period of transition toward an equal society.

However, on the issue of race, both leaders stood shoulder to shoulder. In a New America newsletter of June 25, 1934, it was written that no discrimination must exist, but instead they would agree to recruit actively black members who would join the whites in determining local issues and be represented on district, state, and national bodies.

Goodwin Watson, the educator at Columbia, was especially active in preparing leaflets and newsletters. Ward's other helpers were often members of his family, one of whom, Lynd, was gaining a national reputation as a wood engraver. The leaflets, usually 8-by-10-inch attractive brochures and pamphlets, were replete with clear charts, graphs, histograms, and drawings that carried an instant message to the viewer. All were designed to stimulate discussion. With each packet of study materials there were course outlines and instruction sheets for leaders. Each course in the series increased in difficulty. In free time, members were urged to familiarize themselves with the writings of Marx, Engels, and Lenin, but Amlie quickly added that "class struggle" or "dictatorship of the proletariat" be avoided as terms foreign to American soil. Marx knew nothing, wrote Amlie, about the western frontier. In any case, the life of New America was short and its ideological substance unfamiliar to many readers, despite excellent "grabbers," to use the modern word for enticements.

Ward and his associates found responses as far away as Chicago, several cities in Wisconsin, and on to the West Coast for the model revolutionary plan. In less than three years there were twenty units of New America functioning outside of New York City. Two paid national organizers traveled from coast to coast to rally still others. Toledo and Cleveland, Ohio, had units, as did Chicago, Illinois.[7] So did Iowa Falls, Iowa; Ann Arbor and Pontiac, Michigan; Denver and Boulder, Colorado; and Los Angeles and Berkeley, California, to mention a few stronger ones. Their delegates to the First National Congress in Lorraine, Ohio, in 1936 had an average age of thirty-five years. They were mostly union members—auto workers, steelworkers, railroad men, carpenters, laborers; but also represented were artists, doctors, ministers, engineers, and teachers. Sixty-five carefully selected (if the plan operated as hoped) and partially trained, dedicated leaders came to the only national congress called by New America.

To understand better this plan for change it may be helpful briefly to describe and analyze the denouement of New America. In the first place, its principal leader, Ward, was physically exhausted and financially drained in 1937 because he placed every ounce of energy he possessed plus much of his limited income, all at one time, into four organizations he had helped to establish. The American Civil Liberties Union, of which he was board chairman, was torn with strife and about to face a storm over a Communist board member; the American League for Peace and Democracy,[8] which he served as national chairman, was being falsely but effectively maligned as subversive. The Methodist Federation for Social Action demanded his constant attention; and New America because of financial exigencies had its informal headquarters in 1937 in his New Jersey home on the Palisades. The energetic man, even with the help of his family, was threatening the good health he so carefully cultivated throughout his life.[9]

In the second place, Ward noted the tensions that were increasing among the leaders of New America because of insufficient preparation and hurried discussions of working hypotheses. He spoke to Wright about this. They were in "a hopeless jam," he wrote, "working under impossible conditions when they tried to drag in the Soviets and Communist Party" while the leaders had not addressed themselves properly "to the issues of the country." As early as 1934, in answer to a question from the floor at a New America meeting, Ward made a more Dewey-like than Marxist statement. "The Communists belong to an international movement," he stated, "which is internationally controlled, and we are an American movement with all our controls within ourselves" (11). Even the title of his speech on that occasion used the famous instrumentalist words "New America and the *Present Situation*" [italics—EPL]. And two years later he explained to Wright in a letter the responsibilities of a national director as he saw them. Ward wrote, "It is certainly not enough for our director to think 'organizationally,' otherwise he will fall into the blunder of the Jesuits and the Communists. He must think dynamically, and recognize the instrumental nature and limitations of organizational procedure" (11). These elements of pragmatic procedure in Ward's thinking were probably a part of his larger Marxist orientation, but Wright seemed to use them out of context, resulting in New America's being pried from Ward's hope to establish an Americanized socialism. The movement was turned toward a kind of indigenous fascism.

Wright was complaining to Ward about finances and Ward's writings. Although little more than half Ward's age and with much less experience, he dared to say that his senior was writing in a too-popular vein, leading him to change Ward's editorials for the *New American* and give them a different slant.[10] The slant was, of course, the point of view—the paranoia over communism. In the financial aspect, Wright was making numerous demands on Ward to raise more money, and he requested more salary. He justified the increase as part of the discipline of the organization.

In the spring of 1938 Ward wrote long letters to Wright explaining his disagreements and warning him of paths that led into "dead ends." Again he admonished the young man to think carefully of the whole movement, to take the time from too much attention to a few local units and to use it to analyze and prepare national-level discussions.

Probably the middle-class acculturation of Tom Wright and others who worked with him in New America could be a third factor in the early demise of New America. He apparently was not aware of a straining for personal recognition and status, but it could have been the cause for his treatment of others in a condescending and often autocratic fashion, so that some described him as officious. "Tours of Inspection," Wright called his visits to New America locals, thereby appropriating for himself a position of authority. Armchair philosophizing appealed to him, causing him to fraternize in the Middle West in some locals of the American League for Peace and Democracy and some chapters of the Methodist Federation for Social Action as well as New America units. He would bed down among these congenial groups in which there would be Communists or sympathetic spirits who would spice the discussion by questioning him sharply about New America.

Little by little, instead of proceeding with difficult organizational work, Wright spent more time at sophomoric theorizing, turning his mind toward nationalism and anti-Sovietism and thereby widening the gulf between his thinking and the goals of New America. As a matter of fact, he saw New America as a rival to what he perceived as the Communist-inspired League Against War and Fascism and the Communist party. Apparently Ward and his associates had chosen the wrong person for the work they hoped he would accomplish.

Besides Ward's exertion and weariness in the critical Depression years, besides Tom Wright's perversity and path of deviance, New America seemed not to gain much from its indigenous, pro-American symbols and appeals. But pragmatist that Ward was, he had been willing to make a serious try. George Coe, his intellectual friend—who has been called America's most notable religious educator—was fully supportive. Hence to rid society of irreligious war and irreverent fascism, which was capitalism to them, Ward was willing (before the public at least) to avoid Marxist phrases and use Bellamy's "Yankeefied" socialism in preparations for the coming American Revolution.

The demise of New America was imminent, hastened by the resignation of Ward, who listed several reasons for his decision. For one thing, his physician advised that he cut his responsibilities by one-half; lack of physical strength made impossible the correction of difficulties. In addition, if he remained in the movement he would be held responsible for negative trends, such as (1) the growing inability to distinguish clearly the polar differences between fascism and communism; (2) a tendency toward rabid anticommunism; (3) a departure from the original purpose of New America, which was to show people, by education and action, that the "profit system" could never meet their needs; and (4) a drift toward intellectualism and false pride, which spurred a desire for a theoretical journal that Ward thought untimely and not the central task of a revolutionary group.[11]

What may be learned from this twentieth-century Committee of Correspondence, arising this time in the midst of the Great Depression of the nineteen thirties? Although it was more practical and possible than Technocracy, a Townsend Plan, Huey Long's Share the Wealth, or even Upton Sinclair's EPIC, because it had a broad-based approach of orderly involvement by workers, farmers, and professional people, nevertheless its light flickered and went out. The fact is that Ward blew it out as was his custom with dying organizations. One important conclusion, obviously, would be that neither the people nor their leaders, in and out of New America, were ready for fundamental change. Thrown into the billowing chaos of economic collapse, too many preferred to grasp the nearest panacea plank rather than be disciplined or forced to swim hard and painfully toward a distant lifeboat. Too many of the intellectuals involved affirmed socialist discipline in theory only. When it came to themselves, as history repeatedly illustrates, they failed to apply it, but instead thrust it upon those they hoped to lead.

Closely related to this as a reason for the death of New America was, as suggested previously, that too many of Ward's idealistic followers found it difficult, verging on the impossible, suddenly to "take the role of the other" as George Mead would explain, in sufficient measure to more closely identify with the poorer and oppressed classes. Wright thought he had achieved a workingman's outlook, but up to this time in his life, it was not in his cultural conditioning. He easily turned misleader. Ward, his students Watson and Lynd, if their life-styles and writings do not deceive us, achieved a downward identity; the others moved into the social strain for upward mobility. America's tiny "cultural revolution," like China's big one, could not yet survive in history.

The social milieu around New America, it must be remembered, also changed rather rapidly with the quick patching done by the New Deal. These palliatives, Ward thought, contributed to frustrating New America and the drift toward the coming American revolution foreseen by George Soule. The pall of fear of anything revolutionary spread by the House Committee on Un-American Activities (the Dies Committee) also helped to choke the voices of many social critics who spoke for economic democracy.

Certainly Ward would have said that both planning and acting for change as New America attempted were definitions of freedom, as Jeffersonian as inalienable rights. An experiential reservoir of trial and error was as essential for social as for scientific progress. The disinterment and study of New America and its central leader in this chapter will contribute to the many choices to be found in history and the revealed experimentalism will support Ward's reliance on the vista of history.

Although this attempt to lay down the guidelines and begin action for a new social order was short-lived, barely more than four years, it does tell us some important things about the substance of the prophet's vision. For example, he was convinced that something much like New America would come eventually. To prevent unnecessary sufferings and deaths, any new freedoms must be organized thoughtfully. Tired in body and mind, he nonetheless tried to look beyond rallies, petitions, protests, and strikes toward the grail of the actual functioning of a more-cooperative commonwealth. To have used the American revolutionary tradition with its ideal that inalienable rights make all persons kings and queens, but none dare wear a crown or wave a scepter, is of profound importance. Our American political democracy at its best has no rivals; but an economic democracy, as Ward would insist, does not yet exist. New America was a small attempt to bring the economic order out of feudalism just as had happened with the political order. Ward perceived that we could then with our technology become one of the all-around greatest among the nations of the earth.

Notes

1. Thomas A. Amlie, the radical congressman from Wisconsin in the thirties, urged that the Constitution be changed or abolished to

"allow a decent organization of our productive economy." He claimed he was quoting and agreeing with the New Dealer, A. A. Berle, adviser for the president of the United States of America (4).

2. From a memorandum of HFW, Nov. 25, 1933, "New America" file, Ward papers (11).

3. Charles Beard, considered by Richard Hofstadter and other scholars to be, with Frederick Jackson Turner and Vernon L. Parrington, one of our three most creative historians, was also an advocate of a type of Yankeefication.

4. "Organization of New America," Discussion 4 in a preparatory course for leaders. New America file, Ward Papers (11). An early issue of the *New American*, which survived only three years (1936–1939), mentions the involvement of the famous sociologists. How active and in what ways was hidden by the organization's attempt to protect its members from the Dies Committee in Congress.

5. William Manning, *The Key to Libberty*. The subtitle of this pertinent, though hardly literate, book reads, "showing the causes why a free government has always failed, and a remidy [sic] against it."

6. I knew Wright in those years. He was scintillating, outspoken, and a radical who seemed pleased to shock people and keep in the limelight. In 1937 some felt he introduced fascistic elements into New America.

7. Chicago was at first thought of as the national headquarters. Part of the reason for this was to tap the farmers in revolt, especially the Farmer-Labor Federation whose honorary chairman was John Dewey.

8. Tom Amlie was the one who suggested changing the League's name to "for Peace and Democracy" instead of "Against War and Fascism." Being "against," he argued, causes more strength for the opposition. Jews, he thought, should not fight anti-Semitism, named as such, for it only hardened the bigots.

9. Mrs. Ward was protecting and disbursing New America funds. Lynd and his wife, May, were producing the organization's journal *New American*. The Lynd Wards individually were becoming recognized in their respective fields and jointly were writing and illustrating children's books. Lynd received five distinguished citations, including two Caldecott medals (1950 and 1953) for his work on these books. Both have received other meritorious awards.

10. Wright later in 1938 changed the name the *New American* to *Social Change: Its Analysis and Control*. Gradually a group of intellectuals in the Chicago area joined him on the editorial board, people such as George Axtelle, the educator; Walter Lurie, vocational psychologist; John Teal Bobbitt, historian; and finally in 1941, an oil company executive who also wrote for *Fortune Magazine*. The issues from 1939

to 1941 speak of the USSR as a "menace" and of Dr. Ward as too "morally urgent" about the Soviets. The quarterly, it seems, became related to the Society for the Psychological Study of Social Issues.

11. Dr. Elizabeth Fackt wrote Ward asking why he and Goodwin Watson of Teachers College, Columbia, resigned. She was a professor of International Relations in the University of Denver and a member of New America. See her letter to Ward, Sept. 24, and his answer of Sept. 27, 1939, in New America file, Ward Papers (11).

11
The League
Against War
and Fascism

I had rather fail ninety-nine times with the people than
succeed once without them; for if I succeed without them
I should simply have to do it all over again.
—Henry Demarest Lloyd

"It can't happen here," said many in the thirties, referring to
fascism in the United States. "The hell it can't," responded
Sinclair Lewis as he started the 1935 novel *It Can't Happen Here.*
For the most part, Americans did not know what fascism was,
nor did they have a clear idea of the nature of capitalism or
socialism. Labor did not know it faced its most deadly enemy.
With no frames of reference taught in most of the high schools,
colleges, and certainly not seminaries that would help identify
and explain Hitler's and Mussolini's economic system, how could
Americans fear or rally to resist it? The only response was to
emote against the dictators as evil men per se. People had little
understanding of the socioeconomic nurture that fostered the
dictators and their beliefs and little realization of the necessity
to resist with vigor the soporific "it can't happen here."

The U.S. historian Charles Beard stated that one of the four
lessons he had learned from history was summarized in the
sentence "When it gets dark the stars come out." The dark of
the dictators was lowering. The stars began to appear in Europe,
because of nearness to Brownshirts and Blackshirts, but in less
than a year Ward also appeared. With a comprehensive sense
of what must be done and breathtaking organizational skill, he
brought together a broad-based united front for a grand effort
to stop fascism at once. History should not forget the man who
wrote and worked to imbed the Social Creed in our heritage,
who laid the foundation stones of the American Civil Liberties
Union, and who, by forming the League Against War and Fascism

194

(to be referred to as the League) did more than light a candle in the darkness.

The useful Peace Collection in the archives of Swarthmore College (2) helps to trace the origins and development of the League. The idea first was discussed with some Americans present at a meeting in May 1932 in Switzerland. This group issued the call for a World Congress Against War to be held in Amsterdam on August 27–29, 1932. Among its signers were Madame Sun Yat-sen, Maxim Gorky, Bernard Shaw, Theodore Dreiser, Albert Einstein, Romain Rolland, and Henri Barbusse.[1]

The Women's International League for Peace and Freedom has claimed the substance of the call to be the "greatest manifesto against war that has taken place in Europe" (3). Delegates numbering 2,244, representing fifty-seven countries, responded. Of the delegates, 1,856 were industrial workers, 291 were Social Democrats, and 830 were Communists. There were 412 unions and 683 so-called red unions from Communist states.

The United States responded by forming the American Committee for the World Congress, which organized a delegation that included—in addition to Drieser and Einstein—Sherwood Anderson, Bernhard J. Stern, Margaret Schlauch, Scott Nearing, and Israel Goldstein. Then this group in turn convened the U.S. Congress Against War to meet in New York City from September 29 to October 1, 1933. From this series of events sprang the American League Against War and Fascism.

It cannot be precisely ascertained when Ward became involved in the world peace movements, but when the American League was formed the organizational structure bore many features that clearly were his proposals. The national council was to have representatives from national organizations, with particular attention to labor bodies and to farmers. This would be a policy group. There was to be a national executive committee of twenty-five people living near New York City who could meet easily to elect officers, appoint committees, and deal with financial issues. This committee also would be charged with enlisting trade unions, "mass Negro organizations," the Socialist and Communist parties, seamen and harbor workers, artists, educators, and others. Each state was expected to form an organization led by a state chairman.

At the grass roots would be the city, town, and other local organizations.

The International Peace Campaign (IPC) had by 1937 involved Ward's attention and participation. In fact, as a member of the American national committee of the International Peace Campaign, he had been active in discussions of its procedures. The two international presidents were Lord Robert Cecil and Pierre Cot.[2] The USSR was included so this could also be "a united front" that had four main goals: (1) recognition of the sanctity of treaty obligations; (2) reductions and limitations of armaments; (3) strengthening of the League of Nations; and (4) establishing within the League machinery, ways to remedy by peaceful means international conditions moving toward war. As would be expected, Ward insisted that the IPC must involve farm and labor people. He volunteered to seek the support of John L. Lewis of the United Mine Workers.

The confluence of the IPC and the World Congress Against War provided inspiration for the American League Against War and Fascism. The IPC stood squarely for international collective security and the use of sanctions, as well as working with Communists. Throughout the life of the League the relationship with its international progenitors was preserved. By assuming the same policies, the League also inherited the same critics. The Council for Social Action of the Congregational Church, usually considered more progressive, shunned the united front. Other denominations followed, as did the Fellowship of Reconciliation (FOR), a somewhat Utopian kind of peace organization; the National Council for Prevention of War, a businessmen's peace group; and the Federal Council of Churches. The latter declared that such principles were "not in our policy." This did not prevent many individual preachers, priests, and rabbis from joining the effort.

Why could this tremendous organizational idea with such vast ramifications be considered the first and only united front in the United States?[3] Ward's answer is contained in the testimony he later addressed to the House Un-American Activities Committee. Rhea Whitley on the committee began by asking the usual question about Communist party membership. Ward provided the same answer consistently each of the many times he was asked. "No,

I am not a member of any political party and never have been"(11). This question could be considered an infraction of citizens' rights, since the government should not ask one's party affiliations.[4] Then he was asked to define "a united front organization." Though lengthy, his answer gave the heartbeat of the League. He had said to an associate, "I am out to tell those fellows a thing or two" about religion and its power among the people (11).

"Originally," Ward began, "the phrase meant a united front of left wing political parties," but with the formation of the French "Front Populaire" other groups than political parties participated. These were so-called people's movements, as represented by the League for the Rights of Man, corresponding to the American Civil Liberties Union and the French League Against War and Fascism. The American League began with the old view of being composed only of political parties, but Ward, when he assumed the leadership, took a wider view that would include "the middle classes, white-collar people, organized manual workers, industrial workers and farmers." Because the left and liberal parties were distrusting and fighting one another he felt there could be no effective power against war and fascism. To achieve unity all political-party identifications were eliminated by the League "in favor of a united front on a non-political basis." In other words, Ward saw the need not to stress political organizations, but to give prominence to trade unions, industrial unions, churches, whatever organizations were closest to representing a wider spectrum of the people. The whole labor movement was the essential element and the source of "living waters," as he saw it. The League must be a "Peoples' Program for Peace and Democracy."

The congressional inquisitor pressed another question that related to the inclusiveness of this united front. "Why does the League fight Fascism and not Communism, instead it includes Communists?" Ward had another opportunity to do some educating.

They [The Fascists] believe in war as one of the supreme expressions of mankind, not simply as a necessary instrument of policy. . . . Now the Communists do not believe in war for its own sake.

And they believe in it as a necessity of national defense. They regard it only as regrettable if it has to be used, but they will use it if necessary to defend their objectives. That is a very vital difference from our point-of-view, you see.

The other difference from our point of view is in regard to the attainment of democracy. The Fascist statements show over and over again that they believe in the complete abolition of democracy. They believe in it in principle as well as in practice. They believe that democracy is a bad thing for mankind and ought to be abolished.

Now the Communists believe in the extension of democracy. They say it might be necessary to suspend democratic civil rights during a period of transition, but only to suspend them. That is their belief, and they say, "we are practical about this—we may not be able to give people their civil rights during the period of struggle for power, but that is only temporary." In other words, they believe in political democracy, which must be extended to economic democracy and then to social democracy which is exactly the opposite of the Fascist position. (11)

The central faith Ward stated here was the underpinning for the inclusive and comprehensive social movement he led for approximately six years. Could it have turned the country into a new American revolution had not the military-industrial complex, as Charles Beard thought, turned it toward war with all its threats against the growth of democracy?

The person who would soon become the special investigator for the House Un-American Activities Committee was the first chairman of the American League Against War and Fascism— Joseph B. Matthews. His tenure in the office was not long. He seemed to be subject to intellectual confusions and dilettante radicalism. For example, he said to me while serving as executive secretary of the Fellowship of Reconciliation, "Hell, I don't believe in fellowship or in reconciliation." Again, when asked about participating in a nudist club each week at the Park Central (now the New York Sheraton Hotel), he blurted to me, "No, I don't go for health reasons as most people say they do. I go to look." Coming out of a southern "hard-shell Baptist" background into the radicalism of the Great Depression, he did not understand his divided self. Now he was for a united front, "but not this one." He was opposed to anticommunist hysteria, but not the kind he aroused as a well-paid informer on his old friends as he served the Dies Committee. Ward succeeded Matthews as chairman of the League Against War and Fascism, and the League was off to introduce impressive pages in the story of people's history.

Members of the League should be mentioned and the many organizations either started or supported by it. They were important, coming from various walks of life to join the move to create a mass movement. The national council members included Robert Morss Lovett, University of Chicago scholar in literature; journalist Lincoln Steffens and Earl Browder, general secretary of the Communist party, as vice-presidents; Anna Davis as treasurer; and Ada Dailes as secretary. Board members were Roger Baldwin; Columbia University professor Margaret Forsyth; Channing Tobias, black leader; William Spofford, Episcopal social-action advocate; and Walter Rautenstrauch, professor of Engineering at Columbia.[5]

The extent of the influence of the League was also reflected in the variety of organizations associated with it. The councils, societies, conferences, unions, and committees listed below are representative and were largely activist, some even militantly so. Those marked by an asterisk were initiated by or directly related to the League. They might be thought of as satellites.

American Civil Liberties Union
American Committee to Aid Spanish Democracy
American Student Union
B'nai B'rith
*China Aid Council
Churches
    Baptist
    Congregational
    Episcopalian
    Methodist
    Presbyterian
    Unitarian
Committee for Defense of Political Prisoners
Committee on Militarism in Education

Consumer's Union
Farmer-Labor Party of Minnesota (a section)
Farmer's Union (Minnesota)
*Friends of the Soviet Union
*International Women's Congress Against War and Fascism
Labor Unions:
    American Federation of Teachers
    United Auto Workers (UAW)
    Brotherhood of Railway Trainmen
    Amalgamated Clothing Workers
    Hotel and Restaurant Workers
    International Ladies Garment Workers
    Pontiac, Michigan, Central of UAW
    Detroit, Michigan, Central of UAW
    Longshoremen
    Chicago Central Labor Council
    Painters' (Cleveland)
    Streetcarmen (Cleveland)
    Silk Workers (Patterson, N.J.)
    San Francisco Central Labor Council
    Toledo, Ohio, Central Labor Council
    Kenosha, Wisconsin, Central Labor Council
    United Mine Workers of America
*League of Women Shoppers
Methodist Federation for Social Action
National Association for Advancement of Colored People
*National Farmers Holiday Association
National Negro Congress
Negro Elks
New America
New York Teachers Anti-War Committee
Philadelphia Citizens Anti-Nazi Committee
Southern Conference for Human Welfare
*United Citizens Committee
United Farmers League
*Women's Commission
Women's International League for Peace and Freedom
Young Peoples League of United Synagogues
*Youth Congress of League Against War and Fascism (Detroit)

YMCA
YWCA

To understand the broad influence of the League, it may be useful to outline the efforts of several satellite organizations. Each had a special mission complementing the goals of the entire movement. Members of these groups were automatically enrolled in the American League.

The story of the China Aid Council, its origin, and Ward's part in it—traced in Chapter 7—may be extended here. This council and the American Committee to Aid Spanish Democracy (another member of the League but not a satellite) set about to resist fascism at two critical places, Spain and China. The League initiated a medical bureau to serve in each country and raised money for an ambulance service in Spain to be headed by a capable young surgeon, Edward Barsky, of New York City.

Ward had gone to Montreal in 1936 to help the Reverend A. A. MacLeod start a Canadian League against War and Fascism. This league sponsored a medical bureau that supported the skillful thoracic surgeon, Norman Bethune, in Spain. After his scalpel aided the sword against Nazism there, this humanitarian then volunteered to help repel fascism in China. With dictator Franco winning, the struggle in Spain seemed lost to Bethune, but China's Red Army was holding out against Japan's invading forces. The China Aid Council cooperated with its Canadian counterpart in support of Bethune with money, supplies, and personnel.

In these undertakings, cold-war writers not withstanding, the China Aid Council received support from both the political right and left. Physicians whose names are readily recognized, like Charles Mayo, Leona Baumgartner, Walter Cannon, and Wilder Penfield (Canada), became sponsors or board members. The League for Peace and Democracy (the League Against War and Fascism up to 1936), with Ward as national chairman, encouraged and implemented the China Aid Council's money raising. Teas, tag days, collections, and benefits involving actors, artists, and other professional people abounded. The etchings of Hendrick Van Loon, writer of attractive geography books, were auctioned, and Eugene Ormandy offered special concerts by the Philadelphia Symphony.[6]

Another broad-based membership group, formed on April 14, 1936, was the United Citizens Committee. Its chairman was Quincy Howe, a news analyst of the day. His colleagues were other noted writers and commentators. Playwrights Sidney Howard and Elmer Rice, along with Eleanor Brannon, Bennett Cerf, Max Lerner, and Robert Morss Lovett, to mention a few, formed what they called "an all-partisan organization opposed to war and fascism." People were urged to "buy an anti-war certificate" to raise funds for the League. "It Must Not Happen Here" was their motto.

The young people of the country were not overlooked by the solidarity process of Harry F. Ward. The Youth Congress League Against War and Fascism adopted a manifesto in 1934 at its first meeting, which proclaimed that:

1. It must fight efforts to militarize our generation.
2. The Civilian Conservation Corps is part of the war machine.
3. All forms of military training in high schools and colleges must be abolished. ROTC money must be used for free lunch and school supplies for daughters and sons of workers.
4. Citizens military training camps must be abolished; the money to be used for unemployment relief.
5. Support youth in colonial countries; Liberate Cuba and China.
6. Munitions production must be stopped.
7. The peace policies of the USSR must be supported. Stop the barrage of lies against the USSR.
8. Support the youth of Germany who are being crushed under fascism.
9. Push an energetic struggle against growing oppression of Negro youth; abolish persecution, lynchings, Jim Crowism.
10. Youth Committees against War must be set up in all shops, youth organization, neighborhoods and schools. (37)

Two years after the circulation of this manifesto sixty-one youth organizations with 25,000 members could be rallied on Memorial Day 1936 by the Eastern Pennsylvania Youth Congress meeting in Philadelphia. One of their leaders was Joseph Lash, who later wrote books on President Franklin Roosevelt and Eleanor Roosevelt. By 1939 the youth were advancing a program to: (1) seek the best way to preserve peace; (2) resume trade with the Spanish democratic government and extend commercial credits; (3) feed the war victims from Spain and China; (4) stop sending arms to Germany, Italy, and Japan; (5) open doors to refugees escaping dictators; and (6) establish "good-neighbor policy" with Latin America.

There were a number of commissions as a part of the corpus of the League. One that was supported by Daisy Ward was the Commission on Women, inspired by the International Women's Congress Against War and Fascism that met in Paris, July 28–30, 1934. An American committee was formed whose chairperson was Elesa Addis, the wife of Dr. Thomas Addis, a noted kidney-disease specialist at Stanford University. The medical bureau to aid Republican Spain was supported actively by this physician; his wife was a leader of the Commission on Women. On her national executive committee were, among others, Mary Beard, Ella Reeve Bloor, Dorothy Chertak, Mrs. Walter Rautenstrauch, Mary Van Kleeck, and, of course, Daisy Ward.

The League's *Amplifier* (vol. 2, no. 2, Jan. 15, 1936)[7] reveals that the Wards' son Lynd made wood engravings for this publication and also for the *Fight*, the national paper of the League. The *Amplifier* reported how the Commission on Women was opposing laws injurious to working women, how women were the last to be hired and the first to be fired, and how they were called into factories and there subjected to the "speed up." The commission also opposed the ROTC on all university campuses. The Italian invasion of Ethiopia was condemned as well as the harsh treatment of the "Scottsboro boys" in Alabama. The *Amplifier* kept all the commissions and organizations working in the League informed of each other's activities. The women were fortunate in having the writing skill of Dorothy McConnell, daughter of the bishop who was president of the Methodist Federation. Her column in the *Fight* was headed "As to Women," with nearly every issue pointing out their work for peace at home and in various countries.

The Commission on Women seemed to stress the study of an economic system that they felt created war and fascism. This effort led them into studying the effect jingoism had on children. They decided to encourage peace education with dramatic and pictorial studies, to help children under fourteen understand the nature of these two social diseases. As if these goals were not sufficient, the women called a conference of office secretaries to help them with labor-union strategy sessions, community appeals, demonstrations, parades, membership drives, and affiliations. Ward's methodology surfaced again with the women issuing broadsides called *Critical Issues* and a press service called *Facts and Figures*. The latter carried short paragraphs on "Fascism in the Movies" and "Lynching as Fascism."

Another parallel organization to this commission was one in which Daisy Ward starred even more—The League of Women Shoppers. This group tended to draw direct actionists as members, in contrast to the educational approach of the commission members. The main idea started by Mrs. Ward was the unselfish purpose to see justice done. Since 90 percent of all buying was done by women, the members saw they could use their buying power to better living standards for workers. Their spears were leveled against exhorbitant prices and bad labor practices. They organized boycotts against the silk from Japan and the firms at home with unjust working conditions. When strikes occurred, they were ready to picket with the workers.

To recruit members for the League of Women Shoppers, Daisy joined her husband in late 1937 on a trip to the Pacific Coast. She wrote about it in the official newsheet called the *Woman Shopper*. She reported little success in Detroit, only a modicum in California, but in Oregon "things began to happen." Seattle, she observed, gave good response, and in Chicago things were excellent. "Imagine a membership of fifty-five sending out five hundred invitations for monthly meetings with speakers supplied." That was reliable dedication, Mrs. Ward thought, in the effort to encourage "buying power for justice"—a slogan of her league (11.1).

Leading figures in the women's campaigns were Helen Lynd, a coauthor with her husband, Robert Lynd, of *Middletown* and *Middletown in Transition*; playwright Lillian Hellman; Evelyn Preston, wife of Roger Baldwin; Florence Eldridge, the actress married to Frederick March; Mary Dublin, economics professor; Muriel Draper of the dance family; and Aline David Hayes, who founded the first local of the League of Women Shoppers and was president of the national in 1939.

The League of Women Shoppers recruited and seemed to be gaining strength in 1939–1940. Firms that practiced poor labor policy—such famous stores as Gimbels, Woolworths, and the May Company—were named, picketed, and boycotted. Rockwell Kent came by one day when the women were marching in front of a supply house for artists. He remarked, "I'd paint with soot and yellow clay on shirt tails before I'd buy from that company."

The League of Women Shoppers' second national convention was held in Washington, D.C., in 1939, where they announced that good wages to workers created buying power and prosperity. Mr. and Mrs. John L. Lewis invited the members to the Lewis home for tea.

Two years later (1941) Daisy Ward and her sisters were still active. Besides picketing Helena Rubenstein's plant for its nonunion policies, they circulated a questionnaire entitled "Consider the Household Worker." This latter action raised questions about wages paid, hours worked, size of the house, and the duties of house cleaners. This questionnaire, preserved in the New York Public Library, was the last in the sparse file of the League of Women Shoppers.

Daisy was the only member of the family ever to have been arrested and hauled in a paddy wagon. Evelyn Preston and she stepped from an auto to greet two of the organization's pickets in front of the May Company. For a few minutes the two of them made four picketers on the sidewalk, and by law that was two too many. The police found the chance to arrest "for creating a crowd and blocking the sidewalk." The Irish cop seemed to dislike arresting the white-haired, proper little Daisy. He spluttered, "Mama, I shouldn't be taking you to jail." The Wards were quietly proud of "Mama" and enjoyed repeating this, one of their many religion-labor stories.

The League Against War and Fascism fanned out in all directions and touched almost every corner of the country. The programs and conferences of the entire organization sparkled with ideas of great variety. Probably because the League was a united front—a cultural pluralism, a kind of heterosis or hybrid vigor was created as the ethnic and class groups mingled and interacted. The policy insisted that affiliates must retain their identity as organizations. Carl Sandburg wrote that "the people are a poly-chrome." The League seemed to have been a verification.

As for activities of the national organization, a "Manifesto and Program of the American League Against War and Fascism" was issued. As noted earlier in this chapter, the World Congress Against War continued on the Western world scene. Americans Sherwood Anderson, John dos Passos, and Harry Ward served on the international executive board. With this support the American manifesto spoke to national as well as world issues and indicated important interrelationships. The goals of the first united-front conference in 1933 were to: (1) stop the sale and manufacturing of munitions; (2) expose war preparations under the guise of national recovery; (3) give war funds to relieve poverty; (4) oppose U.S. imperialism in Latin America and Asia; (5) support the peace policies of the Soviets and their proposal of universal disarmament; (6) oppose fascism and its encroach-ments on civil liberites; (7) win over the armed forces to the side of workers, farmers, Negroes; (8) enlist women and youth in the united-front effort; (9) aid workers in foreign lands who are opposing imperialism; and (10) form action committees against fascism and war. After the adoption of this social decalogue the congress of the League resolved to set the principles in motion.

As stated previously, the first chairman was Joseph B. Matthews, who was at that time the director of the Fellowship of Recon-ciliation. J.B.'s lack of dedication and genuine interest led him to neglect the infant League. Roger Baldwin telegraphed him in February 1934 and asked him to withdraw as chairman. Then work was begun in earnest on the Second Congress of the League Against War and Fascism to be held in the Chicago Coliseum the next September.

Divisive efforts were appearing. Baldwin was being pressured by Norman Thomas, his Socialist friends, and others to "get the communists out" at the upcoming conference. They demanded that more noncommunist literature should be available and more noncommunist speakers such as the LaFollettes, Jane Addams, George Coe, Sherwood Eddy, and Colonel Raymond Robbins. Of course, Norman Thomas wished to be included. The League board approved these suggestions and asked Baldwin to invite the speakers, beginning with Thomas. Though Baldwin continued to plead by letters and in person not to create a split, he failed to get Thomas's support in the antifascist cause. Ward, a moving spirit of the League, seemed to be a personal threat to Thomas, giving rise to emotional resistance to most of Ward's organizational work. When one ponders this, one wonders if the scintillating graduate of Princeton Theological Seminary, an ordained Presbyterian minister (a denomination that predominated at Union Theological Seminary), did not feel he should have been the first to hold the chair of Christian ethics on Morningside Heights rather than Ward. Whatever the reason, there must have been more than one argument used to explain why Thomas, a person with humanitarian impulses, would express petty excuses for not joining the resistance to a deadly threat to mankind.

Baldwin presided in 1934 at the opening of the second national congress and introduced Harry Ward, the next chairman, as the keynote speaker. Ward talked of building a broad base, of getting educational materials arranged, and of uniting more securely the forces that had been rallied. The unified movement must be strong as it confronted the owning class with its pervasive power. The left wing must be encouraged to cooperate, he urged, but one political party must not be allowed to dominate.

The second congress rallied 3,332 delegates, compared to 2,700 at the first. The second represented thirty-five states, together with Canada, Brazil, and Cuba. Delegates were sent by 434 fraternal organizations; 343 youth groups, 154 unemployed workers, 105 Communists, and 44 professional organizations were represented. There were 26 church groups as well as 11 Socialist party activists who defied Thomas's boycott. Next to Illinois and New York, Michigan had the largest state delegation and had already formed a Detroit Youth Commission Against War and Fascism. The Philadelphia group grew like September mushrooms, soon claiming seventy affiliated bodies. It was the first to follow the national lead by sending a letter to Arno Mowitz, German counsul in the city, protesting the treatment of Jews, the Socialists, and the Communists in Germany. Each Sunday afternoon the Philadelphians held forums to discuss the problems of war and peace and to keep the people informed.

All of this was reported at the Chicago sessions in the printed *Proceedings of the Youth Congress, Second U.S. Congress Against*

War and Fascism (37). The Youth Congress met separately, elected James Lerner as national chairman, welcomed Peter Hunter and the 250 delegates from Canada, and chose a presiding national committee formed of delegates from member organizations. They pledged to stir antiwar demonstrations, to strike against attending classes, and to protest against militarism on the campus.

At the plenary sessions of the League itself on the second day, Chairman Ward opened with some informal remarks. Nazism was a united front of free enterprise, he said and this congress was the response. He urged that it be remembered there was a united front much like the one in the United States in the prisons and concentration camps of the Third Reich! The capitalists always had and always would tremble before a united front, and their response was to spawn a "red scare" to divide the people. This he almost shouted as he struck the podium with his fist.

Other items of business at this session were the election of George S. Counts, George Coe, Malcolm Cowley, Earl Browder, Langston Hughes, and Adam Clayton Powell to the national steering committee. Greetings to the congress were read from Maxim Gorky and from the "Friends of the Chinese People." Before Ward adjourned the morning conclave he reported that the youth group had discovered a nearby restaurant that refused to serve blacks. Just as the ERA[8] advocates know which states are not to be patronized today, the youth delegates knew which food shop to avoid for a lunch.

At the closing session of the third and last day a series of dramatic actions took place. Lucy Parsons, wife of the martyred Albert Parsons—executed for the false charge of inciting the Haymarket Riot—was introduced and was paid tribute by Ward. Straightforward resolutions were passed to uphold the Scottsboro Blacks, Mooney and Billings, and to condemn the terror in Germany and Austria. "It was all a great success, very fair and democratic," wrote Joseph Goldman to his fellow anarchist, Roger Baldwin. "The Soviets oppress just like other governments. We cannot support them. We will, however, support unity with all who love liberty and independence." Then the lights in the Coliseum started to dim as the chairman introduced an officer of the National Guard and a lieutenant in the U.S. Army who were to make short speeches expressing unity and loyalty to "the fight." To preserve their anonymity and freedom from court martial, they wore masks as they walked to the rostrum in the lowered lights.

This second session of the unique League was about to close when Donald Henderson, formerly economics teacher at Columbia and now in 1934 a union leader, stepped forward to say:

> This Congress has proved that the work during the past year has realized on the promise of the First Congress. At one time we had a desertion from our ranks. Leading fighters whose words in the First Congress promised undying devotion and support, deserted our organization as a result of an incident in which this organization had no part and had no responsibility.[9]
>
> A man came forward, a man to whom more than anyone else the success of this Congress and the success of this work during the past year is due. That man is your chairman, Dr. Harry F. Ward. He has been no chairman who has merely lent his name; week by week he has conscientiously taken on his already burdened shoulders the concrete work of giving weekly guidance to the work of the League, has helped to work out the policies. I think the delegates to the Congress should give Dr. Ward three rousing cheers. (all delegates arose and cheered) (37)

Ward's reply to this recognition was characteristic: "Fellow workers, this movement does not depend upon personalities. It doesn't matter who individually enters or drops out. Of greater importance is that top rulers are manufacturing death and the greatest force against them is that of the undeveloped capacities of the mass of mankind. As they are seeking to mobilize every resource of the American nation, so we must match them by mobilizing an equal resource to defeat them. . . . " "They have the money to do it with, but we have the people" (37).

Before asking that all stand and sing "Solidarity Forever," he added:

> As one who has been in this fight now for almost thirty years, I say to you it is important to be found on the firing line every day. It is one thing to be found in the dramatic moments of the

struggle. It is another thing to do the spadework, the dirty work day by day without which the dramatic moments and crises cannot be won. (37)

The loyal spadeworkers responded in implementing the directives of this congress and moved to call and plan the third national session. That session convened in Cleveland, Ohio, Jan. 3–5, 1936, as one of thirty-three such leagues (France, England, Spain, and elsewhere) in the world movement. Two thousand seventy delegates, representing 1,840 organizations in the United States, heard greetings from Romain Rolland, famous French writer and the international president. Seventeen conferences in the United States had been at work for the past eighteen months preparing for this national conclave. Ward was reelected general chairman with cheers. He read a welcome from the mayor of the city, then went into his opening address, another call "to defend our lives and liberties."

European aggressors like Hitler and Mussolini must be resisted, Ward declared again, not by going to war, but by using "peaceful" means such as boycotts and other "quarantines." Please note that Ward was apparently alerting the delegates to Hitler's aggression against the Soviets. The capitalists everywhere wanted the panoplied Reich, he observed, to destroy the socialist state, but—and here his confirmed pragmatic philosophy again asserted itself—"our position is only for the present situation. It will have to be adjusted to future emergencies, to combinations of circumstances that cannot be foreseen." The "living present" was the arena of decision making as George H. Mead had believed. This philosophy aids in explaining Ward here, as well as it does his decision on the Nazi-Soviet Pact and his acceptance of World War II.

The American League Against War and Fascism—was it anticapitalistic? Ward answered his own question by "of course it is, for how otherwise could it stop war? Fascism is capitalism and we must point this out to people. War and fascism are rooted in the profit system," he stated bluntly.[10] The familiar call to action followed: "Write letters to Congress to kill the gag bill (the Kramer sedition act), broaden the base of the League in inclusiveness, develop a more adequate propaganda, and

increase the militant defense of workers' and farmers' rights"
(38).

Nine commissions met during the three days. The Trade Union
Commission of course commanded Ward's and Chappell's special
attention. Ward spoke as a member of the Columbia University
Teachers Union and stated that labor unions would lead against
war and fascism, therefore it was important to bring in as many
as possible. The Farm Commission, with delegates from nine
states, was composed chiefly of farmers from the upper Middle
West. The other six commissions were Religion (Rev. Herman
Reissig presided and Rev. Charles Webber spoke); Education (led
by LeRoy Bowman); National and Racial Minorities; Veterans;
War and Fascism (led by Roger Baldwin); Children's, which dealt
especially with the effects of Nazism on the youth; and Literature,
which was to distribute "the truth" in as many ways as possible.
The organizers planned to carry the activities of the League to
the grass roots. People were urged to write letters to editors and
to encourage clergymen to speak against war. The schools were
to be kept from disseminating war propaganda. Movies that
glorified war were to be exposed. League books were to be put
into libraries and antifascist posters should be put up wherever
possible.

The ambitious program and the encouragement of the League
Against War and Fascism prompted activities from coast to coast.
Pittsburgh and the New Jersey League committees produced
monthly letters. Minnesota citizens led by Governor Elmer Benson
and Wisconsin people led by Thomas Amlie were peace marching,
while Baltimore was striving to block arms shipments to dictators—the seamen's and longshoremen's unions stayed away
from ships. Formats for radio talks were sent out, and they were
aired extensively. Among the titles were "Democracy in Danger,"
"Answering Father Coughlin,"[11] and "Dangers of Anti-Semitism."
In Denver, League members were rehearsing the drama *Peace
on Earth,* to be presented in that city as well as in Boulder,
Colorado Springs, Pueblo, and Fort Morgan. In St. Louis the
women, wearing black veils, organized a protest march and urged
people to boycott Japanese silk.

These activities could be expanded upon, but only a Garrick
Theatre program in Philadelphia will be noted. It was called

"The Public Trial of German Fascism." Participants were Kurt Rosenfeld, a former minister of justice in Germany; Aneurin Bevan, a member of Parliament and leader of the British Labour party; Mrs. William Ellis, English author who had visited Ernst Thaelmann, German Communist leader, just before he was tortured and killed at Buchenwald concentration camp; and Dr. Mildred Fairchild of Bryn Mawr, who acted as chairperson. Seats and standing room were filled to capacity.

It is obvious now how busy Dr. Ward was on the home front. But before moving to the fourth national conference of the League, it is necessary to highlight an international experience in 1936 in which Ward played a significant role. He was chairman of the American delegation of twenty-two to the World Committee Against War and Fascism meeting held in Brussels, Sept. 4–6, afterward referred to as the Brussels Peace Congress. He spoke before the congress and gave a position paper he composed especially for the U.S. delegation (38).

After his address he met his friend the Rev. A. A. MacCleod from Canada, and the two, using Ward's speech, drew up The Peoples' Peace Pact. Nehru and Chou En-lai could have patterned their famous Panchshila (Hindi meaning "five basic principles"), drawn up at Bandung in 1955, on the Ward-MacCleod Peoples' Pact announced in 1936. However that may be, the pact inspired leagues in Canada and the United States to organize. Since the records of dissent history are not preserved too well and since the proposals have remained timely and significant, The Peoples' Peace Pact is reprinted here in full:

Preamble:

The people of the world want peace. The governments are preparing for war and making war; some against their will, others with aggressive intent. At this moment, in violation of their pledged word, the troops of two great nations are upon the soil of others, imposing their will. The governments have failed to secure peace. They have failed to protect freedom. It is time for the peoples of the world to talk directly to one another; to unite; to act.

Therefore, the following national organizations, representing millions who seek to escape the terrible fate of unwillingly destroying each other, and desire that all peoples should have peace and freedom, unite in the PEOPLES' PEACE PACT.

They join in declaring that they will:

1. Inform their governments whenever the occasion requires that they will not take part in, or in any way support its invasion of or attack upon any other nation in violation of the covenant of the League of Nations, the Paris Pact or the Rio de Janeiro Treaty.

2. Demand of their governments that the armed forces and armaments shall not exceed the amount required for actual defence of its borders and coasts from invasion; this amount to be determined in each case by a national Peoples' Commission after hearing the judgment of experts; this to be but a first step toward universal, complete disarmament.

3. Proclaim the invader of another nation the enemy of mankind; demand that their government order the cessation of all commercial, financial and diplomatic relations with the invader until the invading forces are withdrawn, organize to stop, by peoples' action any war supplies, loans or credits going from or through their country to the invader.

4. Initiate and support measures designated to secure equal access for all nations to all things needed for their development, realizing that this can only be accomplished through world-wide agreement and mutual exchange between free peoples.

5. Resist all attempts to prevent or stop the people from expressing and organizing themselves on behalf of these or any other measures that seek to secure peace and freedom throughout the world. (38)

The world vision expressed in this document is inspiring, but any extensive peoples-to-peoples program, involving interaction between the poorer and the working classes, would seem some distance in the future. Nonetheless, George Mead and his Chicago pragmatists affirmed the "it ought to be possible" philosophy, and Harry Ward made the idea a part of his active faith.

The fourth congress of the American League met in Pittsburgh on November 26–28, 1937. Delegates numbering 1,416 arrived, with 413 coming from labor unions (39). Seven thousand gathered for the opening mass meeting to hear Dr. Fernando de los Rios, ambassador from democratic Spain. Reinhold Niebuhr gave a short talk followed by Harry Ward's reelection as congress chairman. His thoughts and guidelines were as down-to-earth as ever. One delegate had noticed also how seldom Ward used "I," but rather chose "we" and "our" along with "action," "concerned action," and "what we must do."

The emphasis at this congress was clearly to be the defense of the democratic government of Spain, which was suffering invasion by the direct aid of the forces of Hitler and Mussolini. A Gallup poll had indicated, according to Chairman Ward, that three-fourths of U.S. citizens were sympathetic toward the duly elected government. Therefore, the embargo on arms placed on Spain by the United States should be lifted, and the embargo should be placed upon Germany, Italy, and Japan instead, asserted Ward. This position-paper type of speech praised labor's Magna Charta, the Wagner Act, and said it should be defended to prevent homegrown authoritarianism. In addition the chairman emphasized the need for the umemployed to get work immediately.

The American League, with the cooperation of the Canadians, had brought a Spanish delegation to the United States to attend this meeting. The visitors went on tour in the two countries and laid the groundwork for the North American committee to Aid Spanish Democracy. In his speech Ward warned that democratic forces had acted too late in the cases of Germany and Italy and now in Spain. Only France, he noted, united in time to disarm its fascists and drive them off the streets. Behind this action was the French League Against War and Fascism, which alerted and prepared the people. On occasions, the chairman stressed, democracy had to assume a military defense.

The fourth session also organized The American Friends of the Chinese People to gain and then distribute information on movements of the Japanese totalitarians in Asia. What was occurring in German concentration camps and Italian prisons troubled Ward because it was generally not known in the late thirties, nor did many Americans know of the cold-blooded cruelty taking place in Chinese villages. Norman Bethune, the Canadian surgeon aided by both the Canadian and the American leagues, was one of the first to report the barbarities of the fascists in Spain. Later his letters from China told of the horrors the Japanese military committed in Chinese villages. Ward searched extensively for supportive facts. Aid funds were then collected, and messages and telegrams were sent to President Roosevelt that read, "Our organizations will eagerly support legislation to prevent any of our economic resources from being used by the invaders of China and Spain." The convention was strongly in favor of "quarantining the aggressor."

The League leader suggested members do everything possible to get more union affiliations, more worker members; in fact— and this is of special significance—the conference was urged to employ a trade-union organizer for League growth. This is another example of Ward's religious conviction that the staying power for permanent change was imbedded in the lives of working men and women. If the League was to survive a roller-coaster tendency of effective organizations being up today and down tomorrow, if it was to remain active, it would not be egoists, frustrated social workers, writers in search of a remunerative story, or anarchistic intellectuals that would keep the car steady on the track. Those whose toes were pinched, as C. Wright Mills, the sociologist, exclaimed in the same vein as Ward, only they could be relied upon, only they were the steadying force.

From its inception the League Against War and Fascism was criticized for including the Communists. Did Norman Thomas have much to do with this fault finding? The accusations grew more jolting from the Socialists, who soon withdrew their membership, but continued criticism of the League for being "dominated by the Party." To meet this attack and prevent divisiveness, Ward brought the statements to the entire body of delegates. The announcement was made that the board suggested that no political parties hereafter be permitted to affiliate. The only one that remained affiliated at this point was the Communist party, so Ward asked Earl Browder, party leader, to comment. He stood, addressed the chair, and officially withdrew his party. The Communists, always a minority among the general membership, remained active as individual members.

This incident was both dramatic and momentous. A silence fell over the assembly as Browder made this gesture to preserve solidarity and the united front. After the applause subsided Chairman Ward spoke so that all heard his crisp sentences: "I have worked for many years in public life in relation with all sorts of people and particularly in the religious world. I have never worked with people who have played squarer or fairer then the Communist Party dealing in the work of the American League" (39). Take this incident home with you, he added, to refute those who say a party runs us. Robert Morss Lovett, the literary critic from the University of Chicago and vice-president of the League, agreed with Ward and added the Communist delegates were the first to notice that a nearby restaurant in Pittsburgh was still another one refusing to serve blacks.

Some members felt better to be "for " rather than "against" something and resented words like "fight" and "against" in the name of the organization. They pressed for a positive approach and preferred the adoption of the name The League for Peace and Democracy. To others the change seemed more evasive, more wrapped in an aura of utopianism. However, the new name was adopted.

A "tumultuous ovation" for Ward burst out at the end of the congress, after the Rev. Herman Reissig presented the following resolution: "This Congress, deeply appreciative of the wise and untiring leadership which Dr. Harry F. Ward has given to the American League and appreciating particularly his genius as a presiding officer of this Congress, expresses to Dr. Ward its deep thanks and the hope that we may have him as our leader until the fight for democracy and peace is won" (39). By acclamation he was reelected as chairman for the next congress. After this he replied: "Well, that was worth living for. (applause) When I got back from Europe in 1932 I decided to dedicate my life to the cause of fighting war and fascism. Now I feel we have a genuine chance to stop it in this country" (39). Then he repeated with slightly different words his own theme for all these congresses. Was it his intention to add emphasis? Here is what he said: "The future of the world is not with the people who now control it. It is with the undeveloped resources of the common people and that is why we cannot be beaten" (39). Reverend Edward L. Peet, a former student and longtime disciple of Ward, calls this "the dynamism of the good end." The delegates reacted as though they were inspired by the words of the irrepressible prophet.

While leagues were forming as far away as Australia and New Zealand, a march and mass meeting called "Save Czechoslovakia" was activated largely by the League in 1938. With the encouragement of Dr. Voyja Benes, brother of President Edward Benes, and Dorothy Thompson, columnist whose husband was Sinclair Lewis, the rally protested Hitler's invasion. About the same time Elmer Rice's play *Judgment Day* was sponsored by the Washington, D.C., League, and Ward—speaking for the League—affirmed its position supporting the independence of Ethiopia and joined with the National Negro Congress and the International Committee of African Affairs to cable the Chamberlain government of England criticizing its do-nothing policy toward the invasion by Mussolini.

Invitations to radio speeches and mass meetings came one after another to Dr. Ward. He traveled to Terre Haute, Indiana, to address 2,500 citizens in the home city of Eugene V. Debs. His effort was strengthened by the fact that the rally was called by the Protestant Ministers' Alliance and the Central Trades and Labor Council. How could he decline this? A big Armistice Day rally (1938) was at Carnegie Hall in New York City. "No Munich for Spain and China" was Ward's topic. He must have been encouraged by those who appeared with him: Bishop George A. Paddock, Maxwell Anderson, Van Wyck Brooks, Rabbi Stephen S. Wise, and Rockwell Kent.

Later in November 1938 the League for Peace and Democracy, as now called, learned more of the plight of the Jewish people and was determined to publicize it as widely as possible. Historians have indicated that the Pope knew of the persecutions, but tended—as others in high places did—toward silence. Instead, Ward made a hard-hitting proposal to the national executive board of the League. The president of the United States should call a conference of all democratic nations to provide homes for Jews now in Germany. The cost should be charged to the German government. If Germany refused, she would get no loans, credits, or exports from the cooperating countries. Should these countries fail to help, then the United States should withdraw its ambassador from Germany, cancel trade agreements with her, and refuse to buy Nazi products. The League board recommended the circulation of this proposal and agreed to give some of its scarce funds to four committees for the aid of refugees from Germany. One was the Greater New York Coordinating Committee, a Jewish body; another was an anti-Hitler German group; the third was the American Christian Committee; and the fourth the Non-Sectarian Committee for Political Refugees, operated by the International Labor Defense.

The united-front spirit of the League was much alive in the South also, where the Social Creed earlier, and the New Deal now, stirred new democratic movements. A Birmingham, Alabama, convention of 1938 was similar to the American League in its organizational efforts to include labor unions, the blacks, youth, and all political parties. Ward was not present, but his influence seemed to prevail. Some church denominations and the YMCA and YWCA were advancing social reforms. All these forces combined, according to historian Thomas Krueger in his carefully prepared study entitled *And Promises to Keep* (288), became "the first bold emergence of the liberal South as a self conscious group." The convention adopted the name the Southern Conference for Human Welfare. One of its early chairmen was John B. Thompson, at one time a Ward student and later a prominent American clergyman. James Dombrowski followed as chairman.[12] Behind Jim's quick smile, friendliness, and sharp mind there was the same burning ardor for justice and fair play and a "happening religion" that consumed his professor. He was inspired to do all he could in his native Southland to bring interracial understanding and equality and to organize both black and white poor together, as a way to advance democracy. The South, with vestiges of Social Christianity observable among other positive forces, joined the programs of the League. The Southern Conference for Human Welfare and its successor, the Southern Conference Educational Fund, was led by Dombrowski for nearly thirty years.

The National Council of American-Soviet Friendship was another of the burgeoning organizations founded at this time. If not struck from the mind of Ward, it certainly bore many of his imprints. Corliss Lamont, as noted elsewhere, was an associate and defender of Ward. Active in the ACLU and now the American League for Peace and Democracy, this naturalistic Humanist was instrumental in efforts to educate people about the Soviet Union and in work to preserve the natural response of Americans to maintain friendship with their anti-Nazi ally. The National Council of American-Soviet Friendship grew in the fertile soil of the League for Peace and Democracy and flowered with distinguished members like Harold Ickes, Karl Compton, and Dwight D. Eisenhower. Both these organizations suffered from the wilt of the "red scare" days to follow. Some historians now pay a belated tribute to Paul Robeson, Elizabeth Gurley Flynn, Franz Boas, and Rockwell Kent. Surely Clio, the grace of History, will in time touch James Dombrowski of the southern conference and Richard Morford of the friendship council, who learned from Harry F. Ward.

The fifth and final national conclave of the League for Peace and Democracy was held in Washington, D.C., on January 6–8, 1939. The propaganda of the House Un-American Activities Committee, together with that of the radio priest, Charles Coughlin, was taking its toll on the number of delegates. There were 1,274 registered, presenting 388 from labor, 107 from youth groups and 63 from educational and cultural bodies. The League had 19,800 members at this time, reported Chairman Ward (40).

In his opening remarks the leader focused on the attacks by Dies and Coughlin. They and their minions feared a united democratic front, he explained, and they intended to destroy it by false charges. He spoke plainly, and as if to cheer the gathering, he read greetings from well-known persons like Harold Ickes, secretary of the interior, who said he had hoped to attend. Then the "Congress," the name used for this session, passed a resolution condemning the groundless indictments made by Father Coughlin and Martin Dies.

As in previous years, commissions were formed to implement goals. One was the Civil Rights Commission, with the black leader Max Yergan as chairman and Roger Baldwin as secretary. The congress advised cooperation with the new Southern Conference for Human Welfare. Ruth Benedict, Boas's student in anthropology, was chairperson of the Latin American Commission;[13] Henry L. Bibby, pediatrician, headed the China Commission; Thyra Edwards, black leader, cochaired the Spanish group with the Reverend Herman Reissig. Ward's friend and helpful benefactor was Dorothy Chertak. Dorothy, who in 1937 headed the speakers' bureau, was the chairperson of the Anti-Nazi Commission. There were others, for example, the Labor Commission, this time chaired by Richard Frankensteen of the United Auto Workers.

The publications of the League were outstanding features of the program and had wide distribution and influence. The principal media organ was the *Fight Against War and Fascism,* changed in 1936 to the *Fight for Peace and Democracy.* It appeared monthly under the editorship of Joseph Pass. The banner line was "The Fight" and beneath in smaller letters "Against War and Fascism." The cover was arresting, often using color and a dramatic cartoon to command attention. Pictures were used and well spaced throughout the journal, but not at the expense of elucidating text. The print tended to be large. Authors were notable people who represented various nations. To those already mentioned in this chapter it might be instructive to add Jennie Lee, England;[14] Clark Eichelberger, director of the League of Nations Association; Langston Hughes; Louis Fisher; James T. Farrell; Norman Bethune; Romain Rolland; Sir Norman Angell; and individuals from Spain, Germany, China, Mexico, and elsewhere. Some of the art work was done by Lynd Ward and William Gropper; some prints were by Goya or Käthe Kollwitz. There was, of course, a department headed "In Step With Labor," where the HFW initials were most often signed.

However, Ward wrote much more than this single column. After he gave an important speech, the essence of it would appear in the *Fight.* Many of these were then printed and circulated as pamphlets issued by the League. It seemed there was a veritable snowstorm of pamphlets written by prominent leaders around the world. For a nonprofit organization dependent upon only a few advertisers, inexpensive subscriptions, and minimal membership dues, it was an impressive effort. Nine pamphlets, a distinctive art calendar, and eight leaflets largely composed the output that averaged a distribution of 32,000 per month. In 1937 twenty-three different pamphlets and twenty-six leaflets were circulated for a total distribution of 621,000.

Added to this was the previously mentioned monthly paper called the *Amplifier,* which Ward identified as "the organizational bulletin." It seems to have contained suggestions for programs and activities. Another, called the *Distributor*, was a guide for literature committees in locals on ways to circulate broadly the various publications.[15]

In addition to these, there were a number of other bulletins. It appears the offical one of the League was to be called the *Headlight*. Only one is known to be extant; it is dated June 1938. Others were called educational bulletins. Number one dealt with "War Budgets and Armaments"—a scathing analysis of war costs. Number two was an exposé of the dangers to democracy in the Sheppard-May bill, which advocated an "industrial mobilization plan" under which virtually dictatorial powers would be given to the president in wartime. John L. Lewis opposed it, even though he later became something of a dictator in the miners' unions. Lynd Ward of the American Artists Congress, Dorothy Detzer, A. Philip Randolph, and in fact most of the labor movement opposed the Sheppard-May bill. The third bulletin told of the money raised to build a home for the children of democratic Spain forced to flee from the fascists. One home, according to this bulletin, had sixty children, and forty of them were cared for by American League money. Observers were impressed by the program at a home where the children participated in the work-learn process of helping in poultry and rabbit breeding. Bulletin number four argued for the nationalization of all the munitions and war-implement–making factories and for prohibition of the export of their products except when ordered by Congress and then only when a country was being invaded.

During the peak days of the *Fight* in the year 1938 it produced a special issue on women, another on Spain, one on youth, and one on trade unionism. All were well written and illustrated, but if one were chosen from among all the writings of the League over five-years time as most pertinent, an essay by Ward might well be chosen. Called "The Development of Fascism in the United States," it was first published in *The Annals of the American Academy of Political and Social Science* (182) then reprinted by the League.

Ward's essay indicated the way in which unchecked capitalistic dictatorship would undermine American democracy. In some respects, it might rival the literary effort of Sinclair Lewis to do the same in his *It Can't Happen Here,* but was a more penetrating analysis. Some of the main points were: there will be scapegoats, but they will be blacks, not Jews. The European fascist patterns were not popular in the United States, so they would come in a "Yankeefied" guise. Five of these have almost a modern ring:

1. Unconstitutional actions by the federal government, justified at first by political oratory. The centralized bureaucracy of Franklin Roosevelt was the beginning.

2. A greater concentration of political power by the use of loans and grants.

3. A tendency toward a one-party system. Though two may exist as a facade, both will be dominated by the same economic interests.

4. The use of the "democratic" state to secure markets abroad. This would centralize the state and violate democratic rights at home and abroad.

5. A continuing drive to destroy the labor movement.

These, he went on, were emergents on the American scene and would intensify until any dissent was banned and there would be increasingly harsh repression. Because violence seemed so indigenous to the United States with its frontier conditioning, repression would be more violent. Effective opposition to this gloomy outlook would be to stop war, since it has always intensified the dictatorial patterns. Further, he urged rallying people to seek understanding of the underlying causes of war and unemployment and to build resistance. The League saw that this pamphlet was reprinted and widely distributed.

The backlash against the League for Peace and Democracy grew more extensive as free-enterprise groups, state "loyalty" committees, FBI agents, and congressional bodies increased subtle, insinuating propaganda in all the media channels, in churches, schools, and colleges. They were so intense they almost obliterated an important expression of popular democracy from the pages of the first fifty years of this century. Efforts like New America and the united-front League were not fanciful passing events of little importance to history, otherwise why was the establishment actively opposed, especially to the League? Statements from those who wished to destroy the movement unintentionally testify to its significance and potential. J. B. Matthews, described earlier as the paid "investigator" for the House Un-American Activities Committee, said "This [American League] is the most ambitious and influential of all the communist united fronts launched in this country. . . . It numbers among its supporters in one way or another personages whose names I prefer not to mention." Of course it was important enough so that "Moscow gold," as falsely rumored, provided about one-fourth of its income.

Even segments of the Methodist church attacked the League and its chairman. The Conference of Methodist Laymen, formed in 1935, was ready to bring before the general conference in Columbus, Ohio, in 1936 a frontal criticism. The purpose of the church was to build Christian character; it should not be concerned with subsistence. The laymen, according to Donald Meyer (298, p. 334) were men from big banks, bond houses, railroads, and insurance companies, as well as utility investors.

Of course the most damaging charge brought against the united front was that it was controlled by the Communist party. As pointed out earlier, Ward spent five hours before the Dies Committee in Washington in 1939 to make clear, resounding defense of the idea that no political party was represented or had undue influence. Judiciously, he volunteered to appear before this un-American committee. He was never subpoenaed. The first countercharge Ward made against the Un-American Activities Committee was the gross unfairness of the hearings. The members had never contacted or interviewed a League officer nor had the League been called upon to present its facts; instead only its enemies were heard. The second part of his defense involved the purpose and activities of the organization. "I challenge your committee to find anything in the activities of the League that is 'un-American' or 'subversive,' anything that should not command the support of loyal American citizens. . . . We reject throwing Communists out of the League as an act against the rights of citizens to be members of any party," he went on, "your next move, will be to attack the unions as subversive, then the churches, just as Hitler is doing" (200). Within the next decade the congressional un-American committees in both the House and Senate were emasculating labor unions and indicting the clergy as "reds."

When the investigating committees "posted" (a word used in early America for public charges printed on posters or broadsides and placed on fences and walls by a citizen or group attacking another) someone as a subversive, it almost always meant loss of one's job. Therefore many drifted from the League because of people's need for their wages in order to live. At this point the ACLU story told in Chapter 6 may be related to that of the League. Ward was pressed to choose between board chairmanship of the ACLU and the leadership of the American League. How could anyone be objective about civil liberties asked, first, Norman Thomas, then John Haynes Holmes and finally Roger Baldwin, if that person serves an organization that is "Communist dominated?" Yet nearly twenty years later (July 6, 1961) in a letter to his erstwhile friend Harry Ward, Baldwin declared the League was not communist controlled in either policy or program. One year after that (July 6, 1962) he wrote to Lee Ball, Ward's "good and faithful servant," then executive secretary of the MFSA, to assert that the League (with which he was associated from its beginning) was not Communist-party controlled (14). Had it been so, added Baldwin, that fact would have destroyed the organization straight off.[16] However the charge in 1939 did much damage.

After Baldwin resigned from the League on October 25, 1939, his machinations to push Ward aside were more clearly evident. Two letters in the Baldwin papers (1) are enlightening. Henry L. Mencken, the former editor of the *American Mercury,* wrote Baldwin on October 27, praising him for withdrawing. He asked why Baldwin had not followed Mencken's advice to withdraw eighteen months ago. "Hearty congratulations." The other letter from a good friend of Ward's took the very opposite view to the Baltimore fatalist. William Spofford, the director of the Church League for Industrial Democracy (Episcopal), urged Baldwin to "Hold off, Roger, in your quick judgment on what the Soviet-Nazi Pact might mean. It may have smashed the Axis." Continuing, he wrote:

Better bide your time and not turn anti so fast. We would join the Eugene Lyons, Norman Thomas's, Louis Waldman's and the Father Coughlins. We haven't enough information to condemn the USSR.

I think Norman Thomas is a rat and I think he is wrong. What right has any decent guy got to use such a situation (clash between ACLU and the American League) to blast at communists in trade unions, etc. . . . The more I see the actions of some of my old friends here the easier it is for me to understand the purges in Russia. I'm going out for a drink. (11)

The American League for Peace and Democracy was dissolved on May 31, 1940, upon Harry F. Ward's motion and the vote of his loyal friends. World War II was at the door. Truth is the first casualty of war, as Charles Beard wrote. Ward was not a man to keep a mordant organization going. The *Fight* ended in July 1939, but be it observed that in the May issue the column "Building the League" announced new branches in Birmingham, Michigan, and in Richmond, Virginia, and noted the growing interest of the clergy.

Down, but not out, the League was still repeatedly "posted" by those who feared expressions of collectivism and solidarity. Some members of the executive board were "outraged" that the League "hadn't paid the help." Ward said "false" and had to use affidavits from union staff to prove it. The action to dissolve was made legal on June 25, 1940, when with the aid of an attorney all debts and finances were officially brought to a close.

Sinclair Lewis never allowed Doremus Jessup, the independent newspaper editor in his *It Can't Happen Here*, to die though he suffered the acme of physical cruelty. The American League was like Jessup and Joe Hill, deathless, because it was part of a long process of citizens learning, in a painfully slow way, to control undemocratic forces. The emergence of the League as part of the course of history came from similar forerunners like the Anti-Imperialist League at the turn of the century. This league was, according to Daniel B. Schirmer, a "coalition" against monopolies and composed "of laborers, farmers, middle class, blacks, whites, native and foreign born, all political parties, radicals, liberals, conservatives."[17]

George Boutwell, who was a friend of Abraham Lincoln and had the support of William James, believed that only labor could halt imperialism and monopoly: "The final effort for the salvation of the republic is to be made by the laboring and producing classes." Boutwell saw the continuity of history as did Ward.[18]

True to paths of history, the American League for Peace and Democracy was ended legally, but within a year many of its basic ideals were carried on by the organizing of the American Peace Mobilization. Jack McMichael, Ward's understudy, was active with persons of stature who once aided the League, familiar names such as Franz Boas, Langston Hughes, John Thompson, Theodore Dreiser, and Paul Robeson. When Hitler raided Britain and the Soviet Union, the group changed its name to the American Peoples Mobilization, with emphasis upon the slogan "Squash Hitler." The war marched on, and the people's movement faded into a temporary oblivion. Religion and Labor, hand in hand, would return in the next decade.

Notes

1. Other famous world-minded citizens involved in subsequent years were Gandhi, Sir Rabindranath Tagore, Aldous Huxley, and Bertrand Russell.

2. Cot was the Air Minister of France in the Blum cabinet. He was tried for treason by the Vichy government established by Hitler.

3. Solidarity Day, September 19, 1981, gave only a suggestion of being a united front. With some common agreement on issues it would have come closer.

4. This issue was somewhat clarified by the U.S. Supreme Court in *Watkins* v. *U.S.* (1957) and *Barenblath* v. *U.S.* (1959). The court ruled that citizens could refuse to respond to congressional inquiries regarding their political affiliations if such questions were not related to a legitimate legislative purpose. This clarification was made by Dr. Jon Gottschall, my friend in the Political Science Department at SUNY-Plattsburg.

5. No definitive list of the 17,135 members in 1937 has been found. Besides those mentioned in the text of this chapter there were other prominent men and women whose membership marked the caliber and variety in the League: Amlie, Thomas (congressman, Wisc.); Balch, Emily (professor); Bethune, Mary M. (black educator); Bosch, Richard (farm organizer); Bridges, Harry (labor leader); Davis, Jerome (Yale

professor); DeKruif, Paul (scientist); DuBois, W.E.B. (international black scholar); Fisher, Dorothy Canfield (novelist); Imes, William L. (black churchman); Jones, E. Stanley (Quaker philosopher); Kallet, Arthur (Consumer's Research); Kirchway, Freda (writer, editor); Mather, Kirkley (scientist); Marcantonio, Vito (congressman); O'Connell, Jerry (congressman, Montana); Parker, Dorothy (poet); Parodneck, Meyer (cooperatives); Polakoff, Dorothy (social services); Sigerist, Henry (medical historian); Sinclair, Upton (writer); Warne, Colston (Consumer's Union); Watson, Goodwin (professor, Columbia); and Watson, Morris (labor leader).

6. This was the first symphony from the United States invited to give concerts in the People's Republic of China.

7. This social document is extremely rare. Except for one or two issues in the Ward papers at Union only one issue is to be found in the archives of the Hoover Institute on War, Revolution, and Peace at Stanford University.

8. Equal Rights Amendment.

9. Socialists had accused a group of Communists of disrupting a meeting.

10. These kinds of statements may seem strange to younger readers and to those older ones who have forgotten that in the thirties a large group of persons believed that profits (especially large ones) were unjust, even immoral. Modern economics, on the whole, has led people to accept private profits as not only necessary but fair and just.

11. Charles Coughlin was the radio priest of the day who started out in support of the New Deal, but turned quickly to defend an American-type fascism.

12. A recent issue of *Southern Exposure* (July/August 1982) is largely devoted to Jim Dombrowski, with a color reproduction of one of his paintings on the front cover. The title of the article about him is "American Heretic, Portrait of Jim Dombrowski, artist and activist. . . ." The articles are written by Frank Adams and Margaret Rigg.

Two other students of Ward, Malcolm Dobbs and Jack McMichael, took vigorous leadership in this upsurge. The latter was to become executive secretary of the Methodist Federation for Social Action.

13. Benedict was one of several successful women anthropologists trained by Boas. The others were Gene Weltfish, Margaret Mead, and Ruth Underhill. Benedict and Weltfish wrote a pamphlet in 1943 called *The Races of Mankind*, which was distributed to the armed forces by the CIO (Congress of Industrial Organizations) to counteract racial prejudice. Because it combined simplicity of statement with scientific backup, it was widely read and discussed.

14. Jennie Lee was a young Member of Parliament from Scotland's mining districts, who married Aneurin Bevan. Together they led in bringing national health insurance to the British Isles.

15. The *Amplifier*, the *Distributor*, and the *Headlight* are almost nonexistent except for a single copy or two in the archives. What little is extant on the League is so shabbily cared for in the New York Public Library, as an example, that the rare documents literally fell apart in the hands, another indication of the fate of the people's-movement history.

16. What elicited these conscience letters from Baldwin was the efforts of Ward and Ball to prove to the McCarthy Senate Committee that clergymen who belonged to the League were free of "red" charges. This was the only attention Ward ever paid to Baldwin after 1940.

17. *Republic or Empire: American Resistance to the Philippine War.* (Cambridge, Mass.: Schenkman, 1972), p. 258. Rev. William H. Scott, a black man, was vice-president of the Anti-Imperialist League. Two Social-Gospel members were Charles F. Dole and Rabbi Charles Fleischer, both from Boston. Intellectuals were James and Charles Norton. Labor was represented by George E. McNeill.

18. Frank L. Grubbs (280), pp. 141–143, describes still another attempt, somewhat like the League, taking place in 1917 and called the Peoples' Council of America. Louis Lochner was a leader. It fell before the patriotic outburst of World War I.

12
Union Seminary Days:
Theology or
Moral Action?

We are in for a fight on the social question.
—Arthur Cushman McGiffert
President, Union Seminary

One cannot be alone with God.
—George A. Coe

Before Ward came to Union Theological Seminary there were influential clergymen who had strong feelings about the social question. The Congregational minister, Jesse H. Jones, preached "Our business system is pagan in origin, selfish in nature, and the deadly foe of Christianity." A Methodist lay preacher, Edward H. Rogers, stated the same sentiments. Both men felt Christian communism was a way to bring equality among people. In Union, itself, the broadly and fearlessly progressive Roswell D. Hitchcock wrote a book in 1879, which he called *Socialism*, presenting the concept as religious.

The issue with these clergymen and Ward's immediate predecessor at Union, Thomas C. Hall, was not whether the social question existed, but how its implicit needs were to be met and its goals achieved. These churchmen, with the exception of Ward, were social gospelers. They were dualistic in their philosophical point of view, accepting the premise that religion had two drives, one toward personal salvation and the other toward social reconstruction. The latter, however, was secondary to personal salvation. Ward was unique in wishing to follow the scripture that read to make the love of neighbors *like unto* the love of God. Social reconstruction and the divine were one drive for him.

George Albert Coe, the first professor of Religious Education at Union, in 1916 invited the maturing Harry Ward from Boston University School of Theology to give a series of lectures. Coe also was a monist who felt that the social surroundings were internalized to become human nature. Coe knew from two decades of regular contact and friendship that Ward felt the economic order was an unethical and mechanized structure that was creating individuals who could only be released from being culture bound by participating in social reconstruction. Could Coe have felt that if his friend came to Union, as professor of Christian Ethics, his activism would reach more young clergy rather than religious-education people and could measure the effectiveness of Coe's educational theory? While these churchmen were discussing such social questions, John Dewey was formulating similar ideas concerning the extent to which a democratized industrial system could release human potential and prevent the mental as well as the physical enslavement of workers and others.

President Arthur McGiffert was caught in the winds of the philosophic pragmatism of the day and tended to accept the scientific study of the Bible, using natural as opposed to supernatural guides for study. He seems to have been impressed with Harry Ward's initial lectures even though Ward criticized the materialistic incentive of private profit and upheld the principle of labor organization. McGiffert appointed Ward to the chair of Christian ethics two years later in 1918.

An agreement was reached, much like the one at Boston, that allowed the new ethicist freedom from full-time teaching. The Methodist Federation, again, was a part of his appointment, because in his involvement with community groups it would be possible for him to reach many kinds of people. A memorandum sent early in his tenure to President McGiffert stated some of these understandings and reported his activities. He spoke outside his seminary classes only once a week to conserve his energies for seminary work, even though requests were three times the number he could accept. "My addresses to labor and radical audiences are only a very small proportion of the total," he reported, "I think this year it was five out of some forty or fifty engagements" (11). Reasons for speaking to the leftist groups were to discover methods to get the Christian message beyond its present limitations and to come into contact with firsthand sources, which alone can enable a sound ethical judgment to be passed upon these various movements and forces. He always insisted on this standard for his students, therefore he, too, must continue to break from the cloisters and identify with the sustaining community.

In this memorandum to McGiffert Ward went on to establish other basic ethical principles. Dealing with the vital present in the larger community, he warned, would of necessity give rise to controversial subjects. William Hazlitt's writing that "if a subject is not controversial it is not worth discussing" would encapsulate Ward's position. His own words about teaching are worthy of longer quotation:

> Realizing that the subjects which I discuss are matters of acute controversy, it is my rule in public speaking concerning them to stress verifiable facts and to practice restraint concerning moral judgments, believing that perhaps the most important function is to get the facts ascertained, made known. It has seemed to me a part of my obligations to the seminary to endeavor to prevent the public, and particularly the public of the churches, from being misled into making unsound moral judgments because of misinformation when the real facts in the case have come into my possession in connection with the work in my department. (11)

In assuming the chairmanship of the new American Civil Liberties Union, Ward wrote that he accepted for two social interactionist reasons. One was his acquaintance with various groups, both radical and conservative, that he hoped to unite in a common effort. The other was an attempt to avoid force in democratizing economics by the enhancement of freedom of opinion, assemblage, and speech. These principles for guiding his work and teaching at the seminary were, Ward thought, in harmony with the liberal tradition of the institution.

The annual report for the department for 1918-1919 indicated that Ward had taught Christian Ethics, a two-hour course (CE 11-12) "The Development of Christian Ideals," each semester. CE 21 and 22 were called "Modern Social Movements" and "Social Christianity." CE 31 and 32 were entitled "Industrial Conditions and Relations" and "Social Reconstruction." These last two were given at Teachers College, Columbia University (T.C.) and attracted a large enrollment of 111 and 147 students respectively. Administrative necessity was the reason for cancellation of the T.C. courses the next year. The response from the instructor was sorrowful because "the Seminary will lose and especially the extension of its message and spirit." Ward seemed sometimes to want to reach the Columbia campus where he thought too much antiquarianism, scientism, and cynicism prevailed among those who were confident they knew how superstitious religious behavior was. Continuing numbers of Columbia students heard of this unusual professor who often was rewarded with applause at the end of a lecture. They swelled his classes beyond the hundred or more formerly at T.C.

Added to class preparations, which he always planned with care, were articles, an essay, and a book that came from his pen during 1919. He spoke on the average of once a week, sometimes as far away as Iowa, and still never missed a class.[1] At the end of the year and during the upcoming summer at Lonely Lake, he planned two other courses. The one-hour course called "Ethical Interpretations of Current Events" was to become popular and long-standing in the curriculum. Students attended who were not majors in Christian Ethics, with many dropping in from outside the marbled foyer of the sedate seminary. Requirements were that a student each week must select at least two issues from the news and apply Dr. Ward's three famous questions: What are the facts? (Does the news story give the facts needed, and if not, try to get them.) What do they mean? (Give their social causes and consequences.) What should be done? (Form a judgment or evaluation and, if possible, act upon it.) The class became so large a student assistant was requested. The second course contemplated in 1919 was a seminar that explored "The Ethics of Property."[2] Later the Ethics professor offered a "History of Revolt and Revolution," a well-known and recognized class at Union with academic credit given by social-science departments in Columbia University. Merle Curti in the late thirties introduced the study of revolts and revolutions in American history at Columbia. But many continued to go across the street to Union to hear its professor explain world patterns of protest and social change.

The powerful influence of informal education, the interaction of teacher and student outside of class, was used regularly. The tea the Wards provided in his office each week, with Daisy coming all the way from the Palisades to help, was of a social issue–centered nature. It could not be compared with the light talk at a tea in a faculty apartment in Hasting's Hall, where a starched maid did the serving. These formal teas seemed to express a professor's intent to train young men to preserve the gentlemanly tradition of the clergy. But sometimes at the Wards' tea a social critic or a labor organizer was present. Again, unlike the after-dinner informal education in the lounge of the refectory with Reinhold Niebuhr present, Ward quietly permitted the students to talk over a burning question. At appropriate times he would interject facts or raise a Socratic kind of question. Niebuhr, in contrast, usually held center stage, tossing out wit and polysyllabic nouns. Or as the Reverend Edward Peet remarked, he flashed "the juxtapositions of undefined nouns." Dr. and Mrs. Ward went on from week to week as well as holiday to holiday. As if to create more opportunities to converse, students often visited their home across the Hudson River on Sunday evenings and at Thanksgiving and Christmas.

If modern religion had, as Ward believed, two emphases, the Christianizing of the social order and the movement to promote religious (social) education in all ways, then his teaching, formal or informal, must "manifest the interpenetration and the inter-dependence of ends and means." He wrote for the Rauschenbusch memorial issue of *Religious Education* (1929), in a manner loyal to this interactionism, that "education at Union must be used as the continuous revaluation and transformation of life."

Of the thousands of students who heard Ward's scientific faith during his lifetime some spat it out at once; others, if the Baconian categories may be used, tasted and tossed it around in their mouths largely for academic reasons and then expelled it; still others found that the professor's words carried nutritious food to be carefully chewed and digested.

In the first category of quick expectorators may be included those who were early warned to avoid the radical professor because he had no religion, or if he had, it was only a veneer to cover his wish to advance socialism. Some Divinity School faculty at the University of Chicago warned students to avoid the classes of the stimulating humanist Alfred Eustace Hayden until they had been properly indoctrinated by the Christian ethicist Shailer Matthews, who spent much class time discussing the morality of smoking and card playing. Though caution regarding Ward was prevalent at Union, exploring minds registered for one or more of his courses.

Reinhold Niebuhr tended to bring more and more defection from the Wardian orientation. He caused students who had no background in what George Mead called "sociality" thinking, to taste Ward guardedly and then return to a theology devoted to the mysticisms of nouns and the theological will-o'-the-wisps outside of history. Niebuhr was comforting in those trying social and economic years of the thirties. He relieved the pressures to work for basic change in a harsh economic order by administering to troubled minds a charming array of cleverly turned theologisms, alluring Biblical anecdotes, and daring intellectual gymnastics. For example, one can take an illustration from one of Niebuhr's morning worship services in James Memorial Chapel when he gave the sermonette. "The trouble with the Pharisees," Niebuhr remarked, "was that they stank. In their hot country, wanting sufficient baths, washing only up to their wrists caused much dried sweat and that stunk," he explained. Then giving a slap, heard over the chapel, to an upturned tuft on the rim of his balding head, he added, "the Pharisees were not bathed in grace!" Histrionics combined with a ready smile charmed students, swelled his classes, and set hearers to discussing his often opaque meanings. Introduced into such presentations was the ever-present stinkiness of mankind standing in need of grace from a deity far removed from history. Ward's well-researched and clear presentations of a vital present issue, tracing where it had come from and what it demanded in action, was a style declared to be simplistic and romantic by the neoorthodox Thomists. His methods and guidelines went unmasticated by many students under the force of the so-called new realism—one must accept the reality and permanence of sin—pressed by Niebuhr. Ward was not asked to lead the worship service often.

There were, however, always those who were nourished by Ward's down-to-earth religious thought and action. The foreign students from Europe and Asia kept their teacher abreast of the social situation in their home countries and widened Ward's sensitivity. The following are representative of exchanges between Ward and some of his Japanese students in the nineteen twenties.

After thanking Ward for the Christmas dinner invitation, Jutaro Yoki wrote:

> It is better not that I accept your invitation for the Christmas dinner, after I heard your chapel address this morning. I am in full sympathy with you. What you said this morning moved me very deeply. I shall visit your home some other ordinary time. . . . [Christmas Day] I shall either visit the Lower East side [the slums] of New York City or shall spend the day at home quietly.

And Ward responded on December 19, 1927:

> I am much troubled. . . . We celebrate Monday, December 26th. Spend Christmas as you suggest and join us December 26 with other Japanese students. We try to set what would be called a simple Christmas meal, such a meal as is served to the poor people by religious and charitable organizations, and of course we see to it that as many poor people are fed at our expense as are our guests, and in the same way. So please come and share this with us. (11)

Another Japanese student wrote asking for a list of books to prepare himself to teach Christian Ethics, and Ward mentioned three sociology texts, including Cooley's *Social Process* (published in 1918, and four economics books that included Veblen, Hobson, and Bliss's 1879 *Encyclopedia of Social Reform*. He added: "You and your friends have our sympathy and prayers. . . . I am glad to learn that some of your friends are contemplating organizing a body to propagate the principles and plans of the Christian social order. You need this for your own stimulus and development as well as for the purpose of making effective your beliefs and ideals" (11). One former Boston student translated *The Labor Movement* into Japanese for publication.

Letters, whether from France or England or the Soviet Union, varied little in spirit from those coming from Japan. Only the environs of the writers differed. James Dombrowski, at this time one of Ward's students, was in England in 1931 debating whether or not to accept an invitation from Sherwood Eddy, the international YMCA leader, to act as his aide in leading tours to the Soviet Union. Jim was advised to leave "piddling jobs like tours to those who cannot do creative work." Daisy also put in some advice to this student who had become almost an intimate of the family. She urged him "to break away from the seductive comforts of Mrs. [Roger] Baldwin's menage." Her advice was for him to stay in Russia, "teach English for a year and not let side issues interrupt your goal" (19).

Clearly—though perhaps at times unwittingly—Ward and to some extent Daisy pressured members of the family as well as the students who were his closest followers. For example, Ward wrote Dombrowski not to get involved with Patrick M. Malin, another courier for Eddy tours who became an executive with the ACLU. To Ward and others the ACLU had begun after 1940 to lower its banner. So there were more important things to do, he urged, and "you can and you should get on with it."

Occasionally students at Union complained that they could not get enough classes with their ethics guru. John Darr, Jr., a student friend of both Coe and Ward, said that at a conference at Harvard in 1941, Ward had remarked that he would give a course "out of college" at his home each week. At once Darr and Jack McMichael signed up, so they could learn something more about Ward's prophetic religion. They felt Union was absorbed by institutional religion. It sought to preserve the status quo, which would insure the protection of the property on which its livelihood depended. Prophetic religion was, to use Darr's words, "one that sought the truth and ever spoke the truth as he found it." Self-preservation of an individual or the institution was not the aim. It was instead "To fight ever for the welfare of mankind and for society in which all men would have a chance to live creatively. Union Seminary lays emphasis on institutional religion because Dr. Coffin [the president] wants his young men to get jobs and he finds that contemporary churches are preaching institutional religion" (6). President Coffin did indeed worry over the number of students who went into social work and reform movements rather than into the pulpit.

One example of this would be James Dombrowski, who decided in the thirties to work in the South, with its one-third ill-housed,

ill-clothed, and ill-fed, and to establish the Southern Conference
for Human Welfare. Another was Myles Horton,[3] who introduced
Bishop N.F.S. Grundtwig's Danish Folk School into the communities of the poor in the South. Also there was Arnold Johnson,
who cast off all ecclesiasticism in order to give his energies to
building the American Communist party. Had not his mentor
explained that enlightened and militant unions would be the
force for bringing about a more cooperative commonwealth?

Ward's students who tried to preach or teach his religion found
themselves for the most part threatened by being unable to earn
adequate food, clothing, and shelter.[4] These threats in our "free
society" have often broken the spirit or induced intellectual
dishonesty among men and women. In their letters, former
students wrote of the torturous choice before them. "My great
fear," confessed the minister of the First Presbyterian Church in
Utica, N.Y. (1923), "is that in the midst of a rather rich church,
I shall lose something of the vision which I think I truly caught
under your leadership. The Ward home will always remain an
ideal toward which we shall strive."

"Harry Ward influenced me as much or more than anyone,"
Arnold Johnson recalls. Harlan County was a fearsome place in
1932 when he consulted his teacher about summer work. "If
you got guts," Ward is quoted as saying to him, "go to Kentucky."
Reinhold Niebuhr took the young seminarian as far as the Niebuhr
summer cottage in Black Mountain, North Carolina. Two days
later Johnson went over to the Harlan coal-mine area alone. "So
many lads at Union debated as I did," Johnson said to me in
1981, "between staying to the 'right' or going 'left'!" While most
stayed at the right, the Harlan experience changed Johnson's
mind toward going into the labor movement instead of the church.
To learn by direct experience was the guideline for better living.
To find prophetic religion among the miners who went down in
the dark, the dust, and the damp to face against the black walls
of the coal mine would be one of many places where the author
of the Social Creed found a viable religion. But he advised his
students to stay in the church if they possibly could. Many of
them discovered the religious road and some walked straight
down it, some staying in the church and some leaving it.[5]

Whatever the rationale for actionist religion, Johnson's decision indicated he understood what his teacher was talking about, even though he may not have read *The Labor Movement From the Standpoint of Religious Values* (64) or *Our Economic Morality and the Ethics of Jesus* (156). However, to act upon what he had learned took courage, especially to identify with the communist wing of workers' organizations. A few faculty members were disturbed by the action. President Henry Sloane Coffin, the remarkably tolerant father figure for the young men, in a half-jocund manner said to Johnson at a reception for the graduates in 1946, "You have to admit Union Theological is still liberal. It has given three persons who are communists degrees; the student from Holland, the one from Germany and you."

Johnson served a term in federal prison on the false charge of advocating force and violence. Reinhold Niebuhr composed a letter to the president of the United States, to be signed by others also, that asked amnesty for Johnson and the other Communist prisoners. The Rev. Marion Frenyear, who stayed in the church—giving generous praise to Ward for directing and encouraging her religious thinking—gave savings from her meager salary, the sum of two hundred dollars, toward bail for her seminary mate, Johnson. After Johnson came out of prison, he attended an alumni luncheon at Union with another former student of Ward's, John Darr. They were late and the refectory seats were occupied. As they were searching for a seat, President Henry Pitney Van Duesen, who had known both young men in their seminary days, noticed Johnson, arose and walked back to him, shook his hand, and said, "Come down in front with me." Though Pitt, as the students called him, had no tinge of radicalism, he was perpetuating the gallantry and open-mindedness of his predecessor, "Uncle Henry" Coffin toward Ward and his followers.

One other experience from those days was a pleasure for Johnson to recall. In 1939 Ward visited Arnold and Aurelia Johnson when he addressed a large public rally organized by the League for Peace and Democracy in Ohio. The Johnsons told me in 1981 that Ward's opening remark included the statement, "I am happy to be here because one of my students, Arnold Johnson, is the leader of the Communist Party."

In the Ward papers (11) are letters from former students and others who sought his opinions on ethical matters. The replies that exist are marked also by his incisive teaching. Letters from Francis B. Sayre, a well-known Episcopal priest; Robert Bruere, writer for the magazine *World Outlook*; and Robert Russell Wickes, dean of the University Chapel at Princeton, were among these. Dean Wickes requested Ward's views on the proper counseling of a seminary senior who had wealth inherited from his father and wished to devote his life to some form of social service, but worried it would bring little income for his family. Should he go into the bond business and "make all the money he can as soon as he can" and then devote himself to public service? Any social interactionist would know the essence of Ward's rather detailed answer. Moreover history, if the young Princetonian was taught to read and respect it, was about to give him a jolting answer. The date was November 1929!

From Bern, Switzerland, in 1923 came still another student letter seeking advice on ways to circumvent a decision of the Bundesrat banning ministers who were conscientious objectors from preaching in the national church. Ward answered, "Will you not start a popular movement to change the decision made by the legislative body?" A pastor of the University First Methodist Church in Morgantown, West Virginia, wrote, "We can't get reliable information on the coal miners situation. Can you help us?" Another former student, pastor of the First Methodist Church in Lynn, Massachusetts, wrote "Did me good to hear your name applauded at a meeting of the striking United Shoe Machinists in Salem recently." A member on the international committee of the YMCA appreciated the scholarly skills Ward developed in him and added that he cherished having the historical viewpoint more than any other contribution to his education. Finally, a testimonial from Bridgeport, Connecticut, detailed the values of studying with Ward. This student learned (1) "really to read newspapers," not one but several of contrasting views; (2) the content of magazines new to him, such as the *Nation*, the *New Republic*, and the *New Masses* (he had never heard of these before); (3) a new interpretation of Christianity; (4) the value of group participation in the search for truth; and (5) "your simple prayers are perfect," giving a new idea about down-to-earth action-prayer.

President Coffin in his *A Half Century of Union Theological Seminary* (272) included a letter from a student who praised Ward. For Dr. Coffin to bring it to light, even though Ward brought more protests to the administration than all other faculty combined, revealed a president of grace and nobleness. The letter read in part: "In the course that I enjoyed with Professor Ward I was never at ease. His slow, low-voiced manner . . . focused attention and made us plough deeper than our *status quo* minds had been wont to do. He was ruthlessly honest and painfully probing. That he was a prophet I never had any doubt."

The prophetic teacher had been on Morningside Heights only a short time before his challenge to traditional views of religion and society awakened condemnation among the faculties of Columbia, Teachers College, and Union. As an example David Snedden, who could be called a "house" sociologist at Teachers College, took issue with the use of the words "radical reconstruction" and "revolution." Holding to the views of William McDougall and Herbert Spencer, Snedden stated that Ward was resisting basic forces and laws by his teaching and speaking and in time would create sorrow and folly, destroying all the fine things we have. He added the caveat written so often on the pages of history by those who fear change and defend things as they are, "you shouldn't stir up the students." On January 30, 1919, Ward mailed a one-page answer to Snedden's five pages: "The objective of my life work is two-fold 1) to promote those social changes which I conceive to be required by the needs of humanity and Christian Ethics; and 2) to promote these on the basis of scientific knowledge and by orderly processes of political and social evolution. The second part I pursue no less strenuously than the first" (11).

But Dr. Snedden, with his trust in instincts, elites, and fixed laws, was not mollified. He had the aggressive instinct to drive him to show the correspondence to Dean William Russell and other faculty members. Then Snedden approached Ward for an interview. Ward, in a brief but gracious way, repeated how busy he was and suggested Snedden might like to read the views of younger economists like Simon Patten, Thorstein Veblen, and J.

A. Hobson. He would discover these political economists did not believe that economic laws were absolute, but instead believed that they dealt with human relationships where social will can control economic activities in the direction of the common ethical ideals of mankind. Ward accepted no absolutes in economics. Instead he wrote: "Economics as inexorable economic laws have become justifications of the existing order and of the predilections of those who taught it" (156).

On the other hand James C. Bonbright of Columbia Faculty of Economics, a close friend of both Ward and Coe but a defender of private enterprise, was the constant critic of his collectivist friends. He battled often with them during excursions into the wilderness, at camp-fire discussions, and in exchange of letters. The respect for one another was mutual; the exchange of ideas stimulating. Ward, as has been stressed, welcomed honest disagreements and had great patience in exploring ideas that differed from his.

Of course to question the existence of "absolutes" at that time would indeed have brought rejoinders from the larger faculty in the seminary quadrangle. Coe had begun this in the thirteen years he was there by questioning any Rock of Ages concept in which one might hide. Instead he and Ward offered to their respective fields the idea that participation in ongoing social problems led to the call of God to the students. Thought, action, and adaptation were of the essence; there were no incontrovertible absolutes. As John Dewey distinguished between rote learning and activity, so Coe deplored a transmissive religion of assertions in contrast to religious creativity. This shift in emphasis, major as it was, introduced a disturbance among church people that partly explained Coe's leaving Union in 1922 to join the education faculty at Teachers College.[6]

In a review of Coe's 1929 book *What is Christian Education?* President Henry Sloane Coffin doubted a hiatus existed between transmissive and creative religious education. A dilemma did not need to exist, Coffin pointed out, for the task was to pass on religion, as well as to create a new world. This position would indicate he believed in the Social Gospel as opposed to Social Christianity. Coffin, who came from an affluent family and took no salary as minister of the fashionable Madison Avenue Presbyterian Church, gave aid to Charles Stelzle, minister of the denomination's working-people's church, the Labor Temple. This church pressed for social reform rather than giving much time to otherworldly types of worship and religion.

Coffin stated that for Union he wanted the traditional liberal theology to prevail, and he tried to balance his faculty, which seemed to him to be overweighted with the intellectualism of some and the social emphasis of others. Ward agreed with him on the amount of time given to exegetical intellectualism with its seeming pedantry, but he disagreed that any restraint be applied to the social outlook. Coffin's liberal theology brought this response from Ward. "I told him," he confided to Coe, "that I wasn't interested in it. And that in twenty years or so he would find it was done" (6). In the Great Depression years, Ward did think drastic change was just around the corner, and not prosperity. His prediction was about as accurate as President Thomas Jefferson's, that two hundred years would be needed for his country to colonize as far as the Mississippi River! Coffin's liberal theology recognizing both the prophetic and the priestly would seem to have prevailed at the great seminary.

In his autobiography Coffin wrote that Ward's commitment to extreme radical views and his disbelief in liberalism made him difficult to defend. Yet Coffin did it with stubborn grace, with an admixture of jocularity about how his radicals at the seminary had counterparts to be found in the Bible. One Union trustee wrote to Ward saying he had admirers not known to him. About the same time Coffin received an anonymous note deriding his ethics professor as "a cross between a yellow dog and a pole cat." The two chuckled over that one. The president talked or exchanged letters with "Harry" on international affairs dealing with controversial areas such as Nicaragua, the Soviet Union, and China. Coffin respected Ward for his concern, his information, and his accuracy in fact finding, but sharply rejected his professor's neglect of "the Fellowship with the living God in Christ," the Pauline Christology, and other theological positions.

When his stormy Ward arrived at age sixty-five he could have been retired, but he was urged by the president, with the endorsement of the trustees, to extend his teaching for another three years. The New York Teachers Union noted the seminary's firm stand for academic freedom. A resolution passed by that union praising the action was sent to administrators in colleges and universities around the state. When Ward received the letter that extended his teaching years, he replied to thank President Coffin, adding that this was "the only educational institution in the country that had shown such forbearance and freedom for teaching" (11).

In the years at Union, Coe had founded with John Dewey The Religious Education Association, which was active from the beginning in the progressive-education movement. Coe was involved in the Student Christian Movement and its nationwide conferences, but not so deeply as Ward. Like Ward, Coe had numerous international admirers, resulting in his books being published in Spanish, Japanese, and Chinese. A Danish translation of one of Coe's books influenced Bishop Grundtwig in starting his folk schools in Denmark.

The informal teamwork of the two friends that began in their Chicago days, as they assimilated the views of James, Mead, and Dewey, is worthy of note.[7] In the Coe papers at Yale (6) are exchanges in 1924 and 1925 between the two on the idea of "selfhood" and its social nature. "For we cannot accept," Ward commented, "that society is merely an arrangement between persons." Coe agreed, stating that the unremitting pressure of environment must be considered the Christianizing influence, not separate from action and life, but in and of the surroundings. "Christianity (or any form of truly religious expression) must become the presupposition of our family and community life, as pervasive as the atmosphere, as natural as conscience or as love. One cannot be alone with God."

A letter Coe wrote in 1941 to a student of both men would express their sentiments. The student, John Darr, was being guided toward religious creativity: "If our dependence upon Jesus is of the sort that commonly is assumed, then what we have to do is not to create anything but rather to be conduits of a power that is not original to us. In this case either personality is not finality or else depravity is the clue to history" (6).

When lifelong friend Coe retired, Ward was indisposed and could not attend his farewell to the classroom. Instead, he wrote "School's Out for George A. Coe," which was published in 1927 in *Religious Education*. This salute highlighted the results of the dynamic faith the two held in common; it read in part:

> Others can estimate better than I what you have done for religious education, and as well as I what you have put into the development of religion in general.
>
> What I should have stressed had I been present, aside from my personal obligation, is your value as a citizen. Your unfailing support of every cause, movement or protest where an issue of freedom or injustice arises has been and is a constant inspiration and stimulus to those who are younger. (214)

Niebuhr, whom Ward supported strongly for an appointment to the seminary faculty in the Christian Ethics Department, was in the late thirties allowing his "imperative toward Marx" to fade as he found the German Thomist theologian, Karl Barth, more to his liking with his stress on "the impossibility of love in full practice." Among the Coffin papers (7) is a letter dated December 1, 1954, from Niebuhr to Mrs. Coffin, written just after her husband's death. The letter refers to the young Niebuhr's early years at the seminary when "my youthful political indiscretions were handled in such a fatherly way" by Dr. Coffin. One may wonder why he held to these "indiscretions" so long beyond age thirty-eight and then suddenly made a major turn in his life that severed his close relations with Ward.

Ward and Coe would feel that the reason was buried in the economic system when a great depression held scholars and others in its power. Positions were lost by firing and threatened by name calling. Dean William Russell at Teachers College was disturbed with the *Social Frontier* editors and other writers who advocated the building of a new social order. The dean felt these editors and their Teachers Union were infected with communism, which caused him to issue threats of dismissal, of no salary raises, no promotions. Dewey's philosophy was questioned, and the shadows of the congressional committees on un-American activities were beginning to darken the sun of free speech and writing.

Whatever the reasons for Niebuhr's reversal, Ward was not one to compromise his principles nor to renounce one life view for another. The rift between the two men grew wider. In moving toward neo-Thomism, the younger man inadvertently made clear that the differences between them were deep and permanent. "God is doing," proclaimed Professor Ward to his students. "He is in and of the social process. He is found in change itself." The new professor of Applied Christianity, Niebuhr, said "No." God stands above and beyond history. His revelations came as "relative absolutes." Ward taught there were no finished revelations of the God of ongoing process. Yet Ward was accused by Niebuhr and others of defending the Soviet Union in an absolute way, as the Kingdom on earth, a type of Utopian society.[8] The continuing search for the better day by the use of the scientific method of fact finding, hypothesizing, and action comprised for Coe and Ward the religious scientific method: God functioning and creating.

The transcendent God of Niebuhr was rather like gods over the centuries in all lands, who demanded submission and subjection to their feudalistic majesties. As he admitted, his God "touched history but never became immersed in it." Religion was essentially the same dualism that involved a *personal* moral climb on man's part, his only possible aid "a dispensation of grace by which heaven descends." The democratic god of Ward meant that the people participate in all that affects them; that participation and its sociality would provide a more-confident faith for living in a world of hope where the values of justice and love could and would continue to emerge.

As for Jesus, Ward thought of him not as above history but as a part of history also, the product of the great prophets and of social experience. Jesus was a representative of the highest morality of mutual aid, expressed well in the Sermon on the Mount, which according to Mahatma Gandhi was the greatest sermon ever preached. Jesus was not a moral absolutist, nor was much of what developed into Christianity, his religion. Pauline theology combined with mystery cults like Mithraism and others to compose much of Christianity. When the propertyless unfortunates revolted against the church, temple, or skyscraper, Ward would say they were following the Jesus of history—a revolutionary figure who believed in the possibilities of all men and women, including the poor and deprived.

Niebuhr must have found it relatively easy to depart from Ward because the Thomist could and did accept much of the Pauline Christ idea. Christianity became for Niebuhr a religion of redemption that stood high above rational day-to-day moral struggles. Once he quipped that pragmatic religion was romantic partly because it put "man on the Throne of God" and he added, "hot dawg." Jesus to him revealed the absolute in history, and his religion transcended the ethical. Christ was one who had always everywhere revealed the divine will and plan.

Ward with his religious sociality could not uphold a discrete salvation, one soul seeking to be ushered through the pearly gates displaying narcissistic holiness before St. Peter. Rather the self, being social, could find salvation only with others and find redemption only in service to the beloved community. Inextricably man and God are one and work as a force for change. Sin was situational or—as has been stated—"holding to an outworn good."

For Niebuhr, in contrast, sin was a powerful innate reality. In fact, to recognize its potency was what he termed "realism," thus confusing the concept with the sociological and naturalistic meanings of Ward. To accept Jesus as the divine forgiver of inborn sin, "condones man's inability to do what he ought to do."[9] Those who believed that man's nature was potentially good—not sinful, not bound by instincts—usually were labeled as "romantics" by philosophers such as those who came to dominate the University of Chicago with the arrival in 1930 of Robert M. Hutchins, neoorthodox advocate and educator, as president of the university.

With persistence, Niebuhr was widening the gap between Ward and himself by writing the book *Moral Man and Immoral Society* (305). It was reviewed in the *Christian Century* of March 15, 1933, by George Coe. This philosopher of religious education dealt Niebuhr some telling blows as he retreated toward the safety of mysticism. First, said Coe, Niebuhr dealt inadequately with human nature, leaving the impression that society—because of it—was unjust and would remain so. Second, he posited a dualism of man versus society that anthropology and social psychology have not found much evidence to support. Third, imagination and conscience came from the social matrix, Coe pointed out, and not from any vague natural gift. Fourth, a scientific method was woefully lacking in Niebuhr because of his easy generalizations about human nature. Fifth, he seemed to be much attracted emotionally and intellectually to absolutes, as illustrated by treating Jesus's love of yourself as entirely separate from love of your neighbor as yourself. "Christian love Niebuhr identifies with absolute disinterestedness—a process that would spoil any voluntary beneficiaries of it. Love ends in a contentless emotion, an emotional absolute." Sixth, Coe continued, Niebuhr confesses that such love has no ethical punch for "the religious ideal has nothing to do with social justice." Then Coe strikes at the heart of Niebuhr's assertions:

> But this brings him up smack against the ethical necessity of transcending this kind of religious ideal. It should be transcended by forthrightly saying that "love" that he mistakenly calls Christian, if it existed, would be a nuisance. But he thinks it sublime, and therefore he regards as inescapable tragedy the fact that it won't work. Instead of ethically revolting against the religious emptiness that he takes to be absoluteness, he subjects himself to the tortures of a divided loyalty. Thereupon the attraction of sharp antitheses and emotional absolutes leads him to turn our ethical finiteness with its uncertainties into an anti-ethical absolute. The inevitable and everlasting ruthlessness that he attributes to human nature is not a fact, it is an experience of relativity that is being turned out of house and home by a pseudo-experience of the absolute.

This lengthy quotation from George Coe's criticism is offered because it cogently expresses Ward's views, helping the reader better understand Niebuhr's loss of drive for social reconstruction in his later years and his apparent abandonment of Ward. A year after Coe's review, in a letter to his former student Professor Adelaide Case, Coe indicated where Niebuhr's theology would lead him. He wrote bluntly that the neoorthodoxist philosopher had apotheosized the benevolent man of wealth, the capitalist, who by giving freely represented absolute Love. Forgetting the origin of his wealth, Niebuhr awarded him "Love," the highest in his hierarchy of contentless absolute nouns, with "Justice" ranked lower. This moved Niebuhr, as Professor Arthur Swift commented, "out of the game of Life and on to the sidelines, where his God is."

Of all the differences of opinion that existed among faculty members at Union, the most predominate in the thirties was this one between Ward and Niebuhr. The two grew wider apart on Marxism and the Soviet Union. In his last year of teaching Ward replied to an article by Niebuhr, writing that he felt Niebuhr's conclusions on Russia were "unstable and unethical." Such views, he wrote, left little chance for reconciliation or understanding, instead making war possible (11). Karl Barth, Niebuhr's mentor in Switzerland, was unsympathetic toward Niebuhr's extreme stand against the Soviet Union making peace efforts difficult. Pope Pius XII, after World War II, had challenged the U.S. government to disarm and accept the Soviet's offer to do likewise. This bold suggestion by the Soviets and its endorsement by the Roman prelate Ward observed in 1946 and added that in comparison "we drive on in our imperialism and policy of 'containment,' using our bomb, and our support of a cruel dictatorship in Greece." He turned then to criticize the obfuscation of word meanings around the seminary, which tended to freeze effective moral action. There is no such thing as "consistent collectivism" to be contrasted with "consistent laissez faire" except "in the minds of writers who work too much with ideas and too little with facts and moving forces" (11).

By amiability and humor President Coffin helped to prevent serious eruptions. One or two examples may be of interest. Niebuhr was a Socialist candidate for Congress in 1932. One day at a faculty luncheon Dr. Coffin walked in with an eight-inch-wide heavy cardboard button pinned over his heart. It read "Vote for Niebuhr and an Empty Dinner Pail." Both Ward and Niebuhr possessed a sense of humor that at times ameliorated the tenseness. One evening in 1932 we students heard Niebuhr shout across the lounge at Harry Emerson Fosdick, after the Riverside preacher had teased him about his socialism. "Harry," spurted Niebuhr, "you lack consistency, pulpit chameleon that you are, you are going to crawl across a patchwork quilt one of these days and burst."

An example of Harry Ward's ironic type of humor may be perceived in the following incident. At a faculty meeting in 1927 he made a motion that the portfolio of Union Seminary's stocks be examined to dispose of those companies that were exploiting China and the "banana republics" of South America with support for ruthless dictatorships. The motion was sent to the chairman of the board of directors, who responded quickly to the faculty in the vein of you do your research and teaching and leave the finances of the Seminary to us. Several years later at the nadir of the depression, the board asked the faculty to cut salaries voluntarily by 15 percent. Ward, with that famous twinkle in his eyes, arose to read a statement he had prepared as an answer. The reply stated that this faculty had been clearly told to tend to their assignments of writing and teaching and leave financial issues to the august body of trustees, and they had resolved to do just that. Though taken to be humorous by many, this repartee had a serious element in it for the professor of Ethics.

In the busy days at the seminary Ward wrote much, not in a compulsive way for money or self-expression but to guide his reform movements, to inform people, and to compensate for restrictions of his message to fewer and fewer platforms. Therefore he composed or edited a blizzard of fliers, tracts, articles, and pamphlets during the days of the thirties and forties. At the same time he wrote five more books. Many of these warned of the growing American type of fascism, disguised in red, white, and blue and named Silver Shirts, Vigilantes, the Order of Seventy Six, the Ku Klux Klan, and other "patriotic profiteers."

*   *   *

Many people have testified to Ward's masterful skill at organization during the apex of his activities on Morningside Heights, and it went right on after his retirement, as will be noted in the next chapter. One of the unprinted, undated articles found in his papers at Union (11) written as a speech for a conference of the Teachers Union at Hudson Guild Farm, New Jersey, was a testimony to his faith in organization for effective resistance. Get organized, was his plea, and stop bowing to the idol Freedom. Instead teach social-mindedness—a serving of the community and its citizens. Inspire children to unite in working for humanitarian goals, he encouraged, and do it by introducing realistic material from current life. He advocated the extension of facilities that would insert more organizationally formed social values by and for people. New moral values should be taught with the new social values as their goals. Tear down the old, but not without a plan for the new. This mental and moral effort could prevent the coming of violent revolution by clearing the way peacefully for building a better order. This call for organized thought and action of, by, and for the people appeared also in his reprinted and widely circulated article in the *Annals of the American Academy of Political and Social Science* mentioned in Chapter 11.

Organizer that Ward was, he maintained his teaching at Union, got the many-faceted League Against War and Fascism in movement, both near and far, and assumed leadership in the thirties for the formation of the United Christian Council for Democracy (UCCD), the first religious radical united front in Protestantism. How much Ward favored coalitions, federations, and leagues was affirmed again in the UCCD where all denominations were urged to cooperate. The first body to respond was the more fundamentalist Conference of Southern Churchmen. This assemblage expressed the latent populism of the old South. It was represented at a preliminary conference of radical Christians, which met at Union in 1933. Northern denominations present were the Methodist Federation (represented by Ward), the Evangelical and Reformed Council for Social Reconstruction (Niebuhr), the Presbyterian Fellowship for Social Action (Morford), Episcopal Church League for Industrial Democracy (Spofford), the Unitarian Fellowship for Social Justice (DeWitt), the Christian Church, and the Rauschenbusch Fellowship of Baptists (delegates unknown).

At a meeting on May 20–21, 1936, a "Call for a Conference" was sent out to clergy and church laymen nationwide. A corrected typescript copy may be found in the "UCCD" file of the Ward papers (11) in which he stated what the participants in conclave needed to do: (1) explain the breakdown of the economic machine, and (2) consider the social imperatives of the Christian religion. The economy, he explained, had doomed millions to unemployment, lack of food, and the danger of war. As for his imperatives, religion must turn its back on capitalism and turn instead toward "the redemptive forces of God, the prophets of love and justice, and the teachings of Jesus." The new organization would be a federation representing all the denominations that would organize and support concrete actions on the local and national scene. The first national meeting was held in Columbus, Ohio, on November 17–18, 1936, at the Indianola Methodist Church. Eighteen leaders signed "The Call," including those mentioned and Herman Reissig representing the Congregational Church for Social Action.

Six months later the first UCCD national conference assembled. After Niebuhr had been chosen as its chairman and Richard Morford as secretary, Ward, who declined an office, volunteered his services, as was often his way. He would serve on the "strategy and policy" committee, which quickly drew up for discussion and action a guideline paper, characteristically entitled "The Task Before Us." Some Catholic leaders raised the need to form a religious front against communism, but the majority expressed regrets for the anti-Christian bias of communism as well as the dogmatic antireligion of some labor leaders who were invited. Most participants in this first give-and-take of the council admitted that the church had been tied too closely to reaction.

It was again Ward who used terse sentences and clear explanations to capture attention and induce wide reading to alert and rally Christians this time. Crisis leaflets appeared every few days. "Six Battles for Peace" were drawn up for the UCCD and distributed to reach seventy-one denominations. The substance of each could be useful today: (1) stop inflation, (2) secure full employment, (3) defeat free enterprise, (4) destroy cartels [now trilaterals and transnationals], (5) eliminate discrimination, and (6) extend democracy. At the end of each one of these fact-packed condensations he wrote, "On Which Side Are You?"

A closer look at "Eliminate Discrimination" reminds again that the unfounded criticism of Ward for overlooking the racial issue was simply a product of inadequate, perhaps even red-baiting, research.[10] The blacks' burdens were always considered in Ward's organizational efforts reaching back to the Social Creed he scribbled on the yellow telegraph blank. The very first sentence read "For equal rights and complete justice for all men in all stations of life."

The UCCD in 1934 was active in opposing the poll tax that denied most southern blacks the right to vote. It took up racial problems in several cities, especially Detroit, asking the ministers there to lead out in opposing antiblack, anti-Semite, antiforeign-born injustices. The advice was "Get on the Mayor's Interracial Commission. Use the facts and suggestions the UCCD will send you, in every possible way" (11). Secretary Morford was guided by Ward. The exchange of letters between the two confirms this interchange with requests for guidance from one and suggestions from the other. Ward's work in finding financial gifts from well-to-do people was again undertaken, as seemed to be an additional task in all his crusades. Not many knew of his quiet efforts along this line. The New York fountainhead of the national UCCD met usually at Union Theological Seminary.

This professor-activist seemed thoroughly to relish his classes and teaching. But equally he must validate his teachings by putting them to work on the highway and in the hedges. He liked a combination of teaching and practical work. Ward often remarked, "I reach a few who become a multiplying factor." Half jokingly he asked Richard Morford, who for most of his life was director of the National Council of American-Soviet Friendship, "How did you become a radical? You never took one of my courses." The reply was an example of the multiplying factor. Morford learned Wardian concepts at meetings of organizations the teacher guided and at the serious discussions that went on at the Ward home (26). Here friends and students in and out of the seminary heard of Sacco and Vanzetti and of calls to action such as writing letters and other acts of protest.

These informal educational sessions were stirred by the sincerity of the leader in his comments as well as in his writings. On the Sacco-Vanzetti case Ward combined the anger of the writer Upton Sinclair in his 1928 novel *Boston*, with the emotional shock created by the artist Rockwell Kent when he painted, in somber colors, the gory heads of a fish peddler and a cobbler on a tray dripping with the blood of the innocents.[11] Oh, Salome, what have you done? Ward seemed to address King Herod as well as his demented dancing voluptuary:

Figure 12.1 *"Rising Storm," by Lynd Ward.*

You will feel often enough the primitive blood hunger of man the killer aroused from his well fed good nature because someone seems to threaten his meat, intensified by imagined danger to cherished institutions and standardized by propaganda. Those who seek to save civilization and the soul of man from the fatal willingness to kill in defense of vested or imagined interests will need to remember how often the followers of Him who was this way put to death, have done it to defend their religion, thinking it was His. The destructive capacities of the human animal are always ready to be unleashed in behalf of the false religion of prosperity. (11)

The same multiplying factor among preachers and religious editors, Ward believed, made them the vocational group that did most in efforts to save Sacco and Vanzetti.

The civil-rights revisionism of the ACLU in 1940 turned Ward toward its more militant successor, the Civil Rights Congress. As a cochairman he soon discovered that a majority of cases were those involving the rights and liberties of blacks. Little wonder that the few Afro-American students in the seminary, people like Shelby Rooks (later to be husband of the operatic singer Dorothy Maynor) and James Robinson, majored in Christian Ethics.

An early recognition of Ward's efforts came in 1927 in a letter from friends of Jane Addams, who invited him to participate in a program honoring her. He responded by writing directly to Addams expressing the valuable contributions she had made "to what, for the lack of a better term I will call the spiritual fibre and tone of these United States." The letter closed with an acknowledgment of his deep appreciation for the contributions she had made to his thinking (11).

In 1941, the year of retirement from Union, Ward in a farewell speech at the seminary drew attention to certain points that "stood out" during his tenure there, "rising like mountain peaks above the mists that obscure the way" (211). Because of their fundamental quality they would appear appropriate as a summary of this chapter.[12] "One of them," he began, "is the inseparable connection between the individual and society." George Mead would have called it "the self" arising in experience. One self, not two. But all the writers seemed to have missed, Ward continued, that "the very term social gospel is an unconscious confession of error. . . . It expresses a reaction from an impossible individualistic type of religion and it fails to recognize that the Gospel, like man whose redemption it seeks, is neither social nor individual but inseparably both."

Then Ward attacked the deficiencies of the social-gospel movement again as stressing too much church worship and theology, saying these were escapes that have prevented the proclaiming of a social message in this tragic moment of history. Instead, one gospel—in contrast with a personal and in addition a social one—forces the recognition that redemption of a person requires the redemption of the social environment.

Another point that stood out was the insistence that the religious approach in life can and must be scientific. Really the two are as one when the compulsions of science move in the same social direction as the religious ideal. As the hand functions in relation to the arm so humanized science and socialized religion had to function together. Likewise, "if the future of mankind depends upon religion becoming scientific and therefore social, it equally depends upon science becoming social and therefore religious."

A third peak above the mist was that the economic base of societal interaction is fundamental. An increasing judgment has been forming in the scientific world concerning the technical inefficiency of our present economy in its later stages. The spiritualizing, in the way Ward used that word, of the economic system is the main task before those who are called to seek a scientifically efficient organization of human affairs.

Finally, the last sentences of this summary stated his purpose for a seminary:

> Plainly, it is not mere education in theology. Neither can ethical religion be taught effectively in a department dedicated to that purpose. If Christianity is an ethical religion, then the whole Seminary exists to promulgate it, and effectiveness in that task becomes the test of every department. To paraphrase an historic phrase, the Seminary exists not to explain religion, but to change life.

Notes

1. A request came to speak at the national convention of the Religious Education Association in 1919 with the assigned topic, "What can the Modern Church do to Interpret Democracy to the World of Labor?" Ward declined and suggested that the socialist writer Scott Nearing be asked to speak on "What the World of Labor can do to Interpret Democracy to the Modern Church" (11).

2. Evidently this seminar was not ready until 1921 when he wrote to Johnston Ross "Somebody has yet to work out the effect of economic interests upon our religious life. I think I shall have a seminar on that next year. Certainly the issue which Christianity is now facing is whether capitalism, the modern form of imperialism, will do to it something similar to that which the ancient Roman Empire accomplished in subjecting the organization of the Christian faith to its own spirit and purpose" (11).

3. Horton was never in one of Ward's classes, but was considered a student of his in the broad sense of consultations and the reading of Ward's books.

4. Two outstanding exceptions were Alfred Swan, minister of the First Congregational Church of Madison, Wisconsin, and John Thomp-

son, who became minister of the chapel at the University of Chicago. Both men, however, confronted charges from investigating committees.

5. See Appendix B for Ward's advice on this.

6. Harrison Elliott, a Coe protégé, continued Coe's position at Union. Two other former students of Coe and Elliott, Adelaide Case at Teachers College and Sophia L. Fahs at Union, joined the new emphasis. Case and Fahs both were appreciative of Ward's outlook.

7. In fact, a biography of George Coe should be written. He is in no way a dated philosopher.

8. Donald B. Meyer, *The Protestant Search for Political Realism* (298), charges that Ward was "utopian," "absolutistic," in fact "a pure mystic." While he honors Ward by giving him considerable attention and a nod of approval, the result is to praise Niebuhr and denigrate Ward. Though Meyer writes in Niebuhr's style and appears scientific, he fails to define his terms, viz., *social gospel* which he does not distinguish from *social Christianity* as Ward did. Moreover, he asserts that Ward is "rigid," "dogmatic," and held to "the great leader" theory or personality cult. Meyer's central weakness is that he is not well informed about a nondualistic religious outlook. Buried in a footnote on p. 431 is the only reference to George H. Mead, where Meyer writes "the genesis of the 'self' exclusively in social experience was not at stake in the differences between the social and neo-orthodoxy." Since Mead, James, and the molding experiences on Ward in Chicago (Chap. 3) are ignored, Meyer's conclusions are inadequate.

9. Arnold L. Mobbs's thesis, "Some Aspects of the Contemporaneous Social Christianity in the U.S.A." (333), was used to help set up the contrasts in these paragraphs.

10. The *Union Seminary Quarterly Review* (vol. 28, no. 2, winter 1973) carried an article "Social Gospel Christianity and Racism," by Glenn R. Bucher, which claimed that the Social Gospel preachers ignored racism. The statement is generally true, but Ward was not in the Social Gospel category and rejected many of the views of its adherents. Bucher and Professor James Cone of Union Seminary not only missed this critical distinction, but also overlooked Ward's antiracism activities.

11. This painting was only recently "discovered" in the then incompletely cataloged art works of the indefatigable creator Kent. Sally Kent Gorton, Rockwell's spouse, showed it to me in 1979. She then, as owner of the "Kent Legacies," seemed to want to hide it again as if the memories of injustice it raised were too horrible to contemplate.

12. A companion piece to this "Christianity, an Ethical Religion" was his equally important paper read to the alumni and faculty in

June 1941. Entitled "What I Have Learned While Teaching," it appeared in the Union Theological Seminary *Alumni Bulletin*, vol. 16, no. 3. Both essays are well worth reading because of their candor, clarity, and timeliness. In fact, Ward's book *Our Economic Morality* is just as pertinent to our day as the philosophers and sociologists have found George Herbert Mead to be.

13
On the
Firing Line
Every Day

Everything present is pregnant with the future,
Everything future comes from the past.
Have hope, struggle for it,
Bear these on your shoulders.
—Shu Ting
Chinese poet

Even though the statements for industrial justice found in the Social Creed had been used to help give Franklin Roosevelt's years a liberal justification, even though the American Civil Liberties Union had turned from stressing the basic rights of working people and their organizations toward defense of tangential and anarchic freedoms, and even though Harry Ward and his friends had to liquidate a people's united front whose purpose was to uphold peace and democracy, still in his late seventies and into his eighties Ward would be found "on the firing line every day." Leaders in religion and in public life came to Arcadian Way to consult. Several came regularly each week to check the movement of history and to probe with Ward its meanings for action.

The visitors noted a growing change in freedom of thinking and feeling in the political and economic arena. The financial groups in the United States seemed, especially since the turn of the century, to use every possible means to discourage any kind of socialistic discussion. The public school was accepted and strengthened; the great national parks system was established just in time to avert the threat of being leased to private groups; the Post Office was flourishing and was in its Golden Age; police and fire companies and the coming municipal and rural electrification projects were forming—all successful public institutions. On the other hand, socialism was being derided and condemned seemingly at all times and in all places in favor of free enterprise. A few years after the Russian Revolution (even to present times), the word *communism* also became an anathema stirring anger and anxiety. It had become to most people a monolithic system of gross evil representing the devil to atheists and liberal religionists as well. It was beyond reason or logic or the understanding of its origins. Confessions of ex-Communists poured from the media and tended to set the tone of the era.

The United States, as most readers know—but sometimes forget—was a country rich in resources and geographic protection from the wars and poverty elsewhere in the world and so became a bastion of extensive private economic power. Since the Great Depression this free-enterprise system had been on the defensive in many circles where the last of the corporate "robber barons" were fighting to survive and expand. In the defense of this financial system around the world the face of America changed slowly in the direction of accepting private enterprise as the final definition of freedom. Private profit making, an unethical "sin" for Ward as well as for many noted and "common" people, was made more sacred, to be accepted unexamined on pain of social ostracism and sometimes imprisonment and even death if resisted.

In this social atmosphere everything Ward had advocated seemed to be denied. The economy was so powerful that any advocacy of a cooperative commonwealth with rights for the poor, the blacks, the women, or the trade unionists was radical, socialistic, or communistic—was unacceptable. Opponents of socialism of any variety were in command. In 1924 in the *Christian Century* a survey of the "outstanding preachers" indicated one-half preached the Social Gospel. About the same time Kirby Page, editor of the *World Tomorrow*, a liberal journal of religious opinion, with the cooperation of distinguished church leaders sent a questionnaire to 100,499 clergy asking whether they preferred capitalism to a "cooperative commonwealth." Only 5 percent of the 21,000 returned replies voted for status quo capitalism. In response to the query as to which political system they thought would bring a more-cooperative society, 51 percent voted for a reformed capitalism and 28 percent said socialism. Eighty-seven percent were quite willing to reveal publicly their choices, including those among the socialist group. In all, 6,000

Figure 13.1 *From Lynd Ward's Wild Pilgrimage.*

Protestant ministers declared for socialism and spoke for its candidate, Norman Thomas. Some joined Reinhold Niebuhr in running for public office on the Thomas ticket in 1932.

Back when the Dies period arrived, the House Un-American Activities Committee attacked first labor leaders, then black leaders and professional people—especially artists, writers, and actors—as Communists or as persons who were "fellow travellers" defending Communists. Then it turned on the clergy. The war intervened, and Hitler was for a time the target. Socialists were allies. In the Truman years Joseph McCarthy, through his Senate Internal Security Committee, renewed the drive to eliminate Communists and socialists everywhere and all those suspected of subversion. Taking up where Dies left off, McCarthy agreed with Stanley High, an editor of a Methodist journal, that there were 6,000 card-carrying Communists among the preachers of the land. John A. Mackay, moderator of the Presbyterian church, also sensed danger and took a position toward Communists that recalled Cotton Mather's toward witches. In a general letter to the Presbyterian church in 1953 Mackay warned that communist witches were a menace, but that they should not be named or in any way abused. James Fifield, a Congregational minister in a large Los Angeles church, joined the name calling of the congressional committees. John Dewey and Harry Ward, he preached, were subverters of youth and peddlers of socialistic creeds. J. B. Matthews, ill-famed "investigator" for Dies and later McCarthy, wrote a sensational article in the *American Mercury* called "Reds and Our Churches."

This was only a small part of the bombardment that Ward and his Social Christianity followers were subjected to; the intent was to discredit and destroy the movement. The National Association of Manufacturers (NAM) joined the campaign to eliminate socialistic thought by arranging a series of sumptuous dinners and inviting selected clergymen to discuss social issues. Ward's letter declining this invitation may be found in his papers in the "Church and Industry" file (11). Spofford, the Episcopal social-action leader, also refused to attend, writing instead to Ward saying that only he could adequately confound the NAM people.

This total assault on a free pulpit brought forth the last major battle plan of Harry F. Ward. The formation of a Religious Freedom Committee was suggested by one of Ward's faithful friends, Lee H. Ball, a pastor who spoke the truth as he saw it, without fear, and followed it with actions that brought him much social persecution.[1] From 1960 to 1973 he and his wife, Mae, kept the Methodist Federation for Social Action going in their home in Ardsley, N.Y. It was Ball who contacted Guy Emery Shipler, editor of the Episcopal *Churchman,* in 1952 and asked what could be done to counter this free firing at America's ministers. Shipler's response was more than noteworthy: "Let's go see Dr. Ward." A national steering committee was formed that included two other friends of Ward and his family—Richard Morford,[2] who has for many years headed the National Council of American-Soviet Friendship, and William Howard Melish, an Episcopal priest who has suffered opprobrium because of preaching Christian ethics and acting upon them. Their lawyer was Royal France, whose wife, Ruth, was an active admirer of Ward (11.2).

This core group met regularly each week. Lee Ball drove down the Hudson River to pick up Ward at his Palisades' home and take him to New York City. If Ball was not available, the elderly Ward set out on his own, boarded a ferry, then a bus, and finally a subway for a tiring trip to keep his promise to attend. The long day usually meant that Ward needed a nap, which he got at the comfortable apartment of his friends and financial contributors to his projects, Mr. and Mrs. William Manealoff, on Central Park South.

The Religious Freedom Committee had a national membership of lay people and clergy pledged to work to maintain free exercise of religion as granted by the Bill of Rights. The national executive committee consisted of thirty-five and an administrative committee of seventeen persons. There were black as well as Jewish, Catholic, and Protestant members on the national committees, and their paper "Religious Freedom News" was published regularly.

One of the first chapters was organized in Los Angeles by such persons as Linus Pauling and Carey McWilliams. The chapter resisted an attempt to impose a loyalty oath on clergy in California.

With the Unitarians, the American Friends, and the Methodists it circulated a flyer with a headline: "Congress shall make no law respecting the establishment of religion or the free exercise thereof."

The guiding figure in the national organization, though in the wings, was again Ward, who avoided the stage lights and any assertion of himself. Instead he worked intensively writing letters, petitions, press releases, and leaflets. He identified himself as "consultant" to the committee, thus playing a role somewhat like Mohandas K. Gandhi, who refused public office and remained the adviser and guide to Jawaharlal Nehru, first prime minister of free India. As previously explained, Ward had made no public claim to the writing out of the principles of the Social Creed nor of laying the groundwork for the American Civil Liberties Union. He was urged to become the national chairman of the League for Peace and Democracy in order to save it from the showman, Joseph B. Matthews. So in his last crusade he worked behind the scenes, advising Lee Ball, Richard Morford, Howard Melish, and others. Admirable though this modest behavior might be, it tended to lessen the credit he deserved.

After the Religious Freedom Committee began its defense of the Social Gospel ministers by circulating facts, defending constitutional rights, and providing aid, considerable acrimony was directed toward it. Ward was writing daily in those years in defense of Carl and Anne Braden, ministers to the forgotten poor of the South. He defended the gentle Willard Uphaus, pacifist and advocate of world understanding, and the Rev. Claude Williams as he built a southern people's church. Corrected and recorrected notes in Ward's papers at Union attest to his carefully written defenses for clergy called before either the Velde or the Eastland Congressional committees. The secretarial notes taken at meetings of the Religious Freedom Committee contain sentences such as "Dr. Ward to draft letter" or "Dr. Ward to write a letter to" a congressman, senator, or other leader. If an important meeting of the committee was to take place in any state where he could not attend, he often wrote and sent a kind of position paper to set the tone. Later this paper would become a pamphlet for mailing to the membership.

In 1954 it was agreed that he should tour the country to gain numbers and support. In preparation he wrote fliers to send ahead. Their titles read "Congress and Religion, Who is Lying" and "Has the Un-American Activities Committee Investigated Religion?" He also wrote a defense of the work of the Religious Freedom Committee for the Methodist general conference and sent a copy to the board members of the committee for comments. Dean Robert Wicks of Princeton wrote to request materials on the social and economic thought of the Methodist church from John Wesley to the present.[3]

Senator James O. Eastland and his investigating committee claimed that the Supreme Court had handed down its decision against segregation because of brainwashing by the communists in the National Association for the Advancement of Colored People (NAACP) and the National Council of Churches. The committee planned to publish "A Handbook for Americans" in which it named the Methodist Federation and the American Jewish Labor Council as communist controlled. This brought out two responses from the Religious Freedom Committee, one an injunction against publishing the handbook and the other a pamphlet entitled "Congress and Religion," again primarily Ward's work (251).

There were other serious cases of repression of those who believed in a free pulpit. Time will permit the mention of only a few. William Howard Melish and his son, both ministers in the Episcopal church, became close friends of the Wards. Dr. Ward and the Religious Freedom Committee defended them against many false accusations from the government committees as well as from charges made by the Episcopal hierarchy. The son's high crimes included the packing of his church each Sunday with political followers and not true Christian adherents. For such nebulous reasons he was removed from his pastorate.

Another case grew from a 1959 printing of a manual by the U.S. Air Force containing the statement that the Chinese People's Republic revolution of 1949 and its leader Mao-tse Tung murdered 30 million people. The manual expressed shock that Protestant church groups were asking for mutual understanding with these "barbarians," pleading for their admission to the United Nations as well as recognition by the United States. Equally absurd was the charge that out of ninety-five scholars who worked on the Revised Standard Version of the Bible, thirty were procommunist. Ward, of course, was one of these along with other men like Mackay of Princeton and E. Stanley Jones, the Quaker leader. It was said they were "communist infiltrators."

The Religious Freedom Committee worked assiduously to counter the continuing barrage of this kind of propaganda. Interesting facts were uncovered. The Air Force derived its information from evangelist Billy James Hargis, one of the perennial "Contemporary Bunk Shooters" that Sandburg castigated in his poem, and from a group of Methodist laymen who called themselves "Circuit Riders." The Circuit Riders were started in 1951 to rid the Methodists of integrationists, NAACP influence, and liberal clergy. The executive director was Myers G. Lowman, a public relations man in Cincinnati who was paid $10,000 a year, a good sum at that time, to ferret out the "reds" in the church. According to the York, Pennsylvania, *Gazette and Daily*, March 19, 1960, wealthy laymen representing bankers and southern oil and gas interests, many of them members of White Citizens Councils, were financing the project. Using the statements of the since-discredited Louis Budenz, the Circuit Riders spread widely the charge that Ward was a Communist, as were 2,109 Methodist ministers and 614 Presbyterians!

After the Religious Freedom Committee discovered the sources of this material used by the Air Force manual, the committee published a memorial in April 1960, addressed to the General Conference of the Methodist Church. It then learned that the Air Force had already withdrawn its manual. Few people ever learned of this victory. Ward's repeated requests to the Air Force for specific information to be offered in a response by letter or in the press were ignored (11.2).

Guiding the civil rights defenses was enervating for a person entering his eighties, especially when accusations were circulated by colleagues in the seminary from which he retired. He suffered this fate when a student, Ralph L. Roy, wrote a book called *Apostles of Discord* (1953). The first half of the book was devoted to exposure and criticism of the fiery evangelists who spread anti-Catholicism and anti-Semitism in the name of religion and, as today, collected millions of dollars from Americans. Although this section of the book lacked careful scholarship and analysis, the second section could be criticized in this respect even more, for the author admitted it was "thrown together."[4] This second half was called "the Ministry of Disruption." It launched abuse on every church person found to be preaching about a political economy of social betterment. The Ward type of undiluted Social Christianity was too much for Roy and his advisers, who believed that Ward should have, for example, condemned the Soviet Union at every point. The fact that he did not caused Roy to present unsubstantiated charges and damaging innuendos.

Some of the better known Social Gospel faculty at Union Theological Seminary accepted Roy's innuendos and careless research. The contents of the book were sponsored first as a dissertation written with the guidance of John C. Bennett, who later became dean and then president. Bennett wrote to Ward on Oct. 20, 1953, defending Roy as a fine young man who wanted to be fair; even though Ward had pointed out to Roy and his adviser two unethical errors appearing in the book's methodology. One was the "labeling" of his fellow ministers as reds, and the second was the use of "guilt by association." Bennett's letter ignored these criticisms except to state that he was very sorry if his student had "smeared" anyone.

After the book circulated, doing serious harm to Ward and friends, Bennett wrote again (Nov. 16, 1953) trying to justify the book. He said that Ward must know that the peace movements of the churches were often communist controlled. It reminded one of southern leaders who were certain that black freedom movements had the same control. The conscience of Dean Bennett, trained as he was in Christian Ethics, prompted him to say that Roy did not mean that people named in the book were consciously involved. "Some may be, but Roy doesn't think you are" (11).

Reinhold Niebuhr, too, endorsed the book because he thought the author was, as he wrote, generally fair. His letter to his elderly associate, who seemed to expect some support from the seminary faculty, expressed the view that the left groups let the party dictate rather than their Christian faith. He insisted Roy did right to accuse these groups and to have done so in an unbiased way. (Niebuhr to Ward, Oct. 8, 1953.) In closing he added that he was sorry to hear Ward was to be called before the Un-American Activities Committee. "You should be spared this ordeal." As a matter of fact, Ward was never called, but he did volunteer to appear.

What forces were behind these charges? Ward always attempted to probe and often uncovered the motives and their tactics. The Religious Freedom Committee had discovered that Clyde R. Miller (an outspoken professor at Teachers College who required his students each day to read the *New York Times* and the *Daily Worker*, the Communist paper, to get contrasting points of view) had been offered a promotion and a side job totaling the munificent sum of $50,000 a year if he would identify as "reds" Ward and some others who upheld the social gospel. The terms included the liquidation of the Institute of Propaganda Analysis,[5] whose purpose was to uncover and publicize the sources and intentions of public information; further, to denounce the Progressive Education Association, which represented John Dewey's philosophy, and to resign from its board. These requests came from an official of the Chase National Bank, whose name Dr. Miller sent to J. Edgar Hoover for further investigation. The threat to Miller was, in case of noncompliance, a congressional committee with "a dossier a foot thick" with which he would have to deal.[6]

At the same time that the Religious Freedom Committee was bringing forth these facts it was seeking further the impetus behind *Apostles of Discord* and its author. The first clue was that The Fund for the Republic was involved. The chief executive of the fund was Robert M. Hutchins, former president of the University of Chicago, where he had introduced Thomist theories, similar to those of Niebuhr, into higher education. Hutchins assumed a liberal stance on some questions, but he was instrumental in the total change of the Philosophy Department at Chicago and the loss of George Herbert Mead, one of the noted philosophers in the history of the university. The Fund for the Republic had been mentioned here and there as a bit radical, even communistic, because of some studies it had compiled.

Suddenly Hutchins announced a grant of $300,000 for a study of "Communist Influence in American Life," to be guided by the historian Clinton Rossiter at Cornell University, usually identified as a conservative. The Reverend Ralph Roy was to be financed from funds to revise and expand his dissertation. The

Religious Freedom Committee protested at once. The fund responded by inviting cooperation in the endeavor. The administrative staff of the Religious Freedom Committee first declined unless the policies of "name calling" and "guilt by association" were dropped, but then it offered to consider cooperation if the Religious Freedom Committee could share in the choice of Rossiter's staff. Hutchins, however, insisted Professor Rossiter was a competent scholar and could choose whom he wished. Undaunted, the committee suggested a discussion among the three principals, Rossiter, Roy, and Ward. "No," answered Rossiter, "you will have to have faith in my scholarship." These exchanges continued for more than a year with both Hutchins and Rossiter adamant. The last appeal of the Religious Freedom Committee was to Paul Hoffman, chairman of the board of the Fund for the Republic. The committee's letter was not answered; so it took the firm position to ask its members to refuse cooperation with the fund's study of communism (11.2).

To have the book published by the respected Beacon Press of Boston was another attempt to clothe bias with the role of liberalism. One of the editors, Melvin Arnold, was considered a red-baiter by the nationally known Unitarian minister, Stephen Fritchman. For several years Arnold had been determined to discredit Fritchman because he was a social critic and a minister who joined Ward in the defense of a free pulpit. One way to disgrace the clergyman was to publish and circulate the Roy book because of the sensational charges directed at Fritchman.

Hutchins too was criticized for getting involved in this ignoble deal, as was Beacon Press for printing the book. Professor Jerome Davis of Yale Divinity School spoke up about these involvements, as did Kenneth Leslie, Canadian poet and editor of the *Protestant Digest*; Guy Emery Shipler of the *Churchman*; and others. One of the most dignified rejoinders came from the able, soft-spoken religious-education philosopher and director of religious education at the famous Riverside Church in New York City, Sophia L. Fahs. In a letter to Ward (Sept. 14, 1953) (11) she speaks of being disturbed over the Unitarian Beacon Press's stooping to circulate the Roy book. The press had published all of her books on better methods and new contents in the spiritual growth of children. The seminary should not in the first place, she wrote, have accepted such an inadequate thesis.

Ward continued on the firing line with his friends and former students beside him, and he fought with the vigor of ideas and leadership worthy of a man half his eighty-four years. He asked Roy to permit a supplement to be added at the end of the book and received evasive replies written at first on Union Theological Seminary stationery and a little later on paper of the Fund for the Republic. Denied this, Ward wrote out a twelve-page supplement. It was offered to editor Arnold, who vacillated, then finally advised that he would accept one page. On March 12, 1956, Ward received a letter from Albert Taylor Bledsoe of the Beacon Press stating that all consideration of supplementation had been abandoned.

After the smog of the Roy book settled, another attack on Dr. Ward came in the *Union Seminary Quarterly Review* (311) written by June Bingham. Her article did less damage because it was printed in a seminary journal and not widely circulated. However, it was quoted and reprinted. Entitled "Theologian in the Making," the article characterized Ward as one who spellbound the naive and simple people, a thorough-going Marxist who saw only "catastrophism at home and idealism abroad." She quoted students who called Ward a prophet of gloom—a morose person—and mentioned encountering a student who gave up his faith in God and left the seminary.

Ward objected again to what he felt were unfair statements; so he prepared one of his famous defenses and sent it to the editor of the *Quarterly Review*. The editor answered on October 30, 1961, stating the objections were not valid and could not be printed. Ward, now in his eighty-eighth year, had no opportunity to defend himself.

However, he did not relent, but continued to fight back whenever he felt wronged. During all this turmoil he continued defending the rights of religious and political freedom. For example, the peace-loving, internationalist Willard Uphaus sought Ward's counsel when his "World Fellowship" camp in New Hampshire was attacked as subversive and Uphaus was imprisoned for his refusal to give the names of his campers to the investigators. His struggling organization, in appreciation, presented Ward with a recognition

for his distinctive service in the cause of international understanding.

The black leaders Paul Robeson and W.E.B. DuBois gained
Ward's support through cooperative journals in which he wrote.
"The Case of Dr. DuBois" appeared in *Jewish Life* (246). Ward
wrote that DuBois's "crime" was his leadership in the World
Peace Council. The *Jewish Life* article described the treatment of
DuBois in the court. Probably the most outstanding Black scholar
in U.S. history stood while the cases of a white man accused
of manslaughter and two other white men, one charged with
gambling and the other with nonsupport of his child, were heard.
The aging DuBois, unlike the white men, was fingerprinted,
frisked for weapons, and handcuffed.

A French progressive publisher in Paris in 1951 requested
Ward to write on how "A Christian Looks at the World" and
to include in the contents, "U.S. Policies with Regard to China"
(11). This came the same year Ward had submitted several articles
to explain his faith to editor Paul Hutchinson of the *Christian
Century*. However, by this time Ward was so generally persona
non grata that editors avoided his writings. Hutchinson wrote
in response to a submitted article: "I'm busy, and your article
would be out of date by the time I got to it" (June 26, 1951).[7]

With determination and continued optimism Ward planned a
book and finished another. His social evangelism never flagged
as he persisted in his hope to gain more attention for his work-
place Christianity. "Jesus and Marx" was the completed book,
which will be discussed in Chapter 14. In 1954 he sent to a
friend, Guy Brown at Macmillan, abstracts of a book entitled
"Congress and Religion," which would deal with the question
of the interference of government in the practice of religion.
Should ministers be reprimanded by the state, for advocating
The Social Creed? The Religious Freedom Committee was the
answer. But this time Ward wanted to emphasize the relation
of social and economic questions to religion as a religious fact,
upholding the right of the clergy to participate more directly in
the political process. No encouragement for him to write this
book was forthcoming.

The last published writing was a brief explanation to a minister
who believed Marx argued that in the final analysis the only

determining factor in society was the economic system. Ward's rejoinder appeared in the April 4, 1963, issue of the *Witness*, journal of the Episcopal church, where he quoted Engels extensively and ended with his statement: "Marx and I are partly to blame for the fact that younger writers sometimes lay more strain upon the economic side than is due it. We had to emphasize this principle in opposition to our adversaries who denied it and we had not always the time, the place, or the opportunity to allow other elements in the interaction to come into their rights" (260). Ward must have enjoyed quoting this interactionist statement from Engels for it recalled ideas he heard in Chicago before he had studied Marx in depth. Now it was useful to him in opposing those who labeled with nouns and were dogmatists.

With all this effort to remain on the firing line every day, still a people's prophet has almost been pushed into an undeserved oblivion. A friend in 1952 asked him why he was not listed in *Who's Who*?[8] "I hadn't noticed the omission," was his reply, "I will write to find out." He appears in few of the religious biographical books, except as his name is dropped here and there. The *Dictionary of American Biography*, in which he wrote so well and magnanimously of Walter Rauschenbusch, does not include him, nor does the extensive *Biographical Dictionaries Master Index*. Only Upton Sinclair in his *Goose Step*, as I mentioned earlier, gives some recognition to the youthful minister helping to organize the packinghouse workers in Chicago.[9] Regardless of the misrepresentation of him and the lack of recognition for so much of his work, Ward remained loyal to a philosophy of life expressed in his words: "There is no final victory, only sometimes the winning that is never really won, and mostly the losing that is never lost."

Notes

1. Not all was persecution by professionally patriotic groups. Ball filled a pulpit in Mahopac, N.Y., for ten years, where his down-to-earth ethical preaching captured the loyalty of Jewish neighbors. Some attended his services, and still more helped in putting new shingles on the Methodist parsonage.

2. According to Lee Ball, it was Morford's hard work that prevented a witch-hunt against the clergy.

3. See Appendix C.

4. This remarkable admission was made in a letter from Roy to Ward, April 12, 1954, in the Ward papers (11). It suggests that the student could have been a "puppet."

5. An active sponsor of the institute was historian Charles A. Beard.

6. Letters from Miller to John S. Wood, Committee on Un-American Activities, April 17, 1952, and Miller to Ward, July 23, 1953, are in the "Velde" folder, Ward papers (11).

7. In the Ward papers (11) are letters dated Aug. 8, 17, and 27, Nov. 4, and Dec. 1, 1951, from Hutchinson. Other excuses are of considerable interest, such as, his "staff didn't know Ward and therefore must have rejected and returned his article." Another stated that Ward followed "the party line" in his articles on atomic morality.

8. A very brief and incomplete biography did appear in one edition of *Who's Who*.

9. My attention has been called to the autobiography of writer and poet George Abbe, a former student of Ward. For Abbe's respect for his teacher, see *The Non-Conformist* (262).

14
The Outrageous Assumption: Jesus and Marx

*I speak truth, not so much as I would, but as much as I dare;
and I dare a little the more as I grow older.*
—Montaigne

Reason in man is rather like God in the world.
—Aquinas

"Jesus and Marx," Ward's last manuscript (261), was a book that resulted from the drive of his ever-active life to inform and inspire people on the lands enclosed by the seven seas. Instead of memoirs or diaries or an autobiography he spoke to his own famous question, "What needs now to be done?" The final writing was a supreme effort of his unflagging faith in the social institution of religion, if it remained true to its history by following the social ethics of the Judeo-Christian prophets and Jesus, the carpenter of Nazareth.

In the manuscript he advocated that Marx be observed as another Jewish leader influenced by the prophets of Judaism and their passion for a peaceful land and social justice. In fact, he would dare to include him in the succession. This outlook, because its bottom line was social in nature, encompassed other religions of the world as well who had prophets and teachers proclaiming humanitarianism. No doubt, among other experiences, Ward's visit to China had helped him draw this conclusion. At that time the student followers of Dr. Sun Yat-sen had rallied around this unusual missionary from America as he spoke to them of what was a universal faith in social justice. Without using the western names of Amos, Micah, Jeremiah, or Jesus, he drew crowds and often traveled at night to avoid the police. The modern Chinese, especially during the Cultural Revolution, pointed out to visitors the degradation they had suffered under the old corrupt order. Disorganized, they were too weak to resist their children being

276

taken away before they were twelve to work for and serve landlords in every way. They bore the disgrace on large signs at park entrances "No Chinese or dogs allowed in this park." The farmers were beaten for not giving up their grain as taxes while their children followed a few ducks to gather fresh dung for food. If E. P. Thompson, the respected contemporary English historian, as an agnostic can speak of those who contrive for a nuclear holocaust as belonging to "The Kingdom of Satan," could Harry Ward not feel the same revulsion toward satanic prerevolutionary China? The cry for justice breaches national borders, as he discovered, to include people whose cries are to the same God under different names and whose kingdom of Satan is just as real though labeled by unfamiliar words.

For both Ward and Thompson the injustice was worldwide and included the masses of the East who were struggling to feed, clothe, and shelter themselves. Theology was not for Ward the religious basis for action leading to creative living. It was rather in working with people and with nature that God was to be found. If Thompson's call is heard urging worldwide unity against Satan's forces in the hall of haughty power, note that Ward had been shouting it since the beginning of this century. The worldwide religion of this teacher could not be contained in one Bible or in the walls of a seminary.

The life of Karl Marx, according to Ward, was absorbed in how workaday living could be organized to bring into reality a "love of neighbor" social system. The prophets and Jesus had declared for better ways, tracing the high goals of lamb and lion lying down together, of studying war no more, and of justice rolling down. The method by which to bring these goals into living action was the contribution coming from the research and writing of the poverty-stricken Karl Marx and his collaborating disciples. Marx became Ward's hero, just as Kipling and "Chinese" Gordon had been in his youth.

This startling idea of mixing Marx and Jesus was not born suddenly from the head of the prophetic Ward. It was germinating when Graham Taylor and he were trying to induce stockyard workers in Chicago to support the church. It grew when he drew crowds of militant workers to hear his Ford Hall noon lectures in Boston, afterwards published as *The Labor Movement from the*

Standpoint of Religious Values (64). It matured in the constant intellectual interaction between Ward and his companion, George Albert Coe. Ward, to repeat, saw the labor movements as religious. Coe agreed, but directed the discussion away from Utopian tendencies and toward the fact that human institutions were malleable. Folkways, he suggested, were subject to change— aggravatingly slow at times, and human nature was not an innateness combining both "good" and "bad." Coe considered Marxism to be a workable plan, a way to achieve the better, not the Utopian "best," society. The interchange of thoughts between the two professors went on for hours by letter and by discussions, mostly at Lonely Lake.

In the Coe papers at Yale (6) there is a letter to Ward (Jan. 23, 1946) in which Coe stated that he was not as well read on Marx, so that the questions he raised might seem naive or recondite. For example, "If a communist society is created, will a non-communist society then appear for dialectic reasons?" But then Coe added that he was reading commentaries on aspects of Marxism written by scholars such as Dirk Struik and Howard Selsam, some of which Ward had sent him. Coe wrote "dialectical materialism in no way denies either the existence or the priceless importance of ideas and moral values. It does not hold that ideas can be reduced to matter." He was calling for Ward's rejoinder.

The path to truth was the scientific method, by which Ward meant inductive procedure, experimentalism, in essence the philosophy of Coe, Dewey, and Mead. Marxism, with its emphasis on historical process involving social classes, the masses of people versus the few, and ways of organizing to "alter or abolish" an unjust social order, now also became a scientific method for Ward. It is doubtful that Coe was ever able to read and criticize "Jesus and Marx." With Coe's retirement to California and his declining health in the late forties, letters between the two philosophers were more infrequent. Ward had practically completed the book when Coe died.

Inevitably, however, the question of a workers' or people's revolution had arisen between them. Coe's last letters always dealt with the subject and endorsed the general idea. "The church and its social message are one," wrote this unusual religious educator, "only a social revolution of vast process can make the modern church more like life in the large" (6). After Coe's death in 1951 Ward, his friend of fifty years, wrote a poignant essay for *Religious Education* (Mar. 1952) entitled "We Were Friends." It ended by pointing out that in their last days together they contemplated the "sickness" of our acquisitive society and its "unethical consequences":

> "I have known only a few of my Christian friends to recognize the truth that what is splitting the world is the ethical core of Marxism and the political system that has developed in Russia." "May I quote you?" [Ward asked.] "Quote as much as you like," came the reply, "for we are not done with Marxism when we weigh the merits and demerits of the Soviet government, nor when we choose between the communist and the anticommunist ideology. Marx raised the fundamental ethical question whether it is humane or just that a man's sustenance should depend upon his contributing by his labor to the private profit of another. This ethical core of Marxism is being ignored by both the political and the ecclesiastical thought that is most characteristic of the United States today." (249)

Out of this substantive interplay of two searching minds came "Jesus and Marx" by the one who was to live another fourteen years.

At least six publishing houses returned the "Jesus and Marx" manuscript with a variety of reasons for doing so. Conservative establishments like the Macmillan Book Company generally found it too radical, advancing as it did "the outrageous assumption"[1] that a faithful follower of the Nazarene could also be faithful to Marxian tenets. The leftist press seemed generally as uninterested in Jesus as the rightists were in Marx; the latter rejected the manuscript for fear it might introduce "you'll eat pie in the sky when you die."

Incredibly, the day after Ward himself died in 1966 a letter arrived from President John Bennett of Union Theological Seminary saying that the seminary had just employed Roger Garaudy, a Marxist professor from France. Jesus and Marx, their ideas and teachings, were now going to be considered just as prophet Ward had foreseen. This development has been called Liberation Theology by another of its exponents, Gustavo Guttierrez, who advocates it for guidance of the priests and sisters who work among the wretched poor of Latin America. In this spirit, some clergy have even taken up arms to aid guerrilla fighters in resisting exploitation. Catholic nuns who were serving schools and hospitals for the suffering Indians of South America have been molested and shot by the junta government kept in power by some large corporations. An archbishop in San Salvador was riddled with bullets as he was offering a mass for the poor in the city's largest cathedral. He had been pleading their cause. Jesus and Marx had meaning for all these martyrs.

During the sixties the revolutions of rising expectations had become more a reality, not only in Latin America but also in Asia and Africa. A billion people in China, one-fourth of the earth's population, by using the name and ideas of Marx had abolished an oppressive social order and established a new one. The United States, a citadel against the growth of collectivism, has preserved a religion about Jesus in the glass temples of evangelistic priests. Neither the teachings of Jesus nor of Marx, Harry F. Ward felt, were understood. Some English and French clergy, like Garaudy at Union Seminary, have found it possible to relate the prophets and Jesus with the revolutionary upsurge so that "liberation theology" expressed the new trend.

Publishing "Jesus and Marx" today would seem justified on several grounds. First, it is not parochial theology. It is the expression of an idea that Paulo Freire, an influential educator in modern Latin America, has called "conscientization." The meaning of this term may be summarized quickly as referring to a long, largely Judeo-Christian process of a body of ethical teaching and behavior emerging to become a part of our collective conscience. Marx in this era has given it organized and written expression, Ward argued. The "conscientized" or "critically aware" groups and persons, those most alert to the ethical sweep of history as Ward saw it, have internalized this ethical drive that gives a person the patience, strength, and courage to pursue struggles for freedom. A sense of divine power pervades all efforts for justice. This was God incarnate for Ward, now called "conscientization" by Freire. It is not exclusive of non-Christians, as might be indicated by some liberationists who use the word "Christ," a term, incidentally, seldom used by Harry Ward.

In the second place, it sometimes appears that the manuscript "Jesus and Marx" goes beyond liberationist thinking because of its extended explanation of the involvement of capitalist economics with the profit motive—an involvement that will, Ward insisted, destroy humanity one of these days and humaneness between now and then. The inordinate craving for profits, which has been called a cardinal sin, was the central issue for Ward. Yet it is hardly mentioned in Guttierrez's *A Theology of Liberation*, published in 1973. The unearned increment, as Marx specified it, was the primary reason for the need and for the inevitability of revolutionary change.

A student once asked Ward, "How can you judge whether the Soviet Union is still socialist?" His answer was that capitalism had returned to power if the USSR ever allowed the means of production to be used for private profit leading to the loss of public control. A current debate in the United States has raised the question of whether liberation theology can organize tightly to bring a transfer of power in the Latin American states. Must it place more emphasis on Marx, the organization of a strong labor movement, and the abolition of personal profit, as Ward advocated? Or will the theology of liberation tend to blunt the sword of a more-militant labor movement, a movement more experienced in its understanding of the difficulties to overcome, in order to establish a socialist system?[2]

Third, a liberationist has written that "God is close to man. He is a God of communion with and commitment to man." Such assertions would seem again dualistic, much like "Christ the supernatural" versus the "Jesus of history." The more monistic Ward saw God and people as one, so that participation among the oppressed was the way to commune (as in a community) and the only way to find commitment. The theologians of liberation seem to juxtapose God and people. "Jesus and Marx" tried to avoid this. This unified view of life, as we have noted, caused Ward to reject the Social Gospel. His last book, therefore, is of merit, because he begins and ends his philosophy with Life

282 The Outrageous Assumption: Jesus and Marx

and Action in the vivid, creative present. All things are in the vital present; God, selfhood, commitment, and communion.

No doubt Ward would have been pleased with President Bennett's letter to him announcing a new faculty member who was an acknowledged Marxist. Anathema that it was in Ward's day, he had seen the need for a dialogue between Christians and Marxists at the great seminary on 120th Street, New York City. He wished to stimulate the dialogue with his daring book of six rather long chapters (290 pages of typing). In Chapter one "By Way of Introduction," he traced the "uniting threads" between the teachings of Marx and Jesus. Chapter two he called "The Classless Society"; the third is entitled "The Economic Factor in History"; the fourth, "Guiding Philosophy"; the fifth, "What is Life For?" In Chapter six, "A Look Ahead," he read the direction of history and again became prophetic. His last writing effort should be better known.

Coe's last book was published in 1943. *What Is Religion Doing to Our Consciences?* was praised for its "incisive rejection of the lazy distinction between sacred and secular" and its "Marxian drift in ethical theory." Ward always stated similar views, but stressed labor in factories and fields even more than his friend; it was the common religious ground among all peoples of the earth. And all people, including the workers, would have to resist evil: "I am not defending the labor class. There is as much possibility of predatory instincts dominating in the working classes as in the wealthy class. It is as necessary to fight greed among poorer groups as those with millions back of them" (11). On all his travels in the United States and abroad he invariably contacted labor federations and tried to talk with working people. If some unions are infiltrated and corrupted, still the large body of organized and unorganized workers, as C. Wright Mills pointed out, arises to correct these profiteering deviations.

And the real cause of the predatory instincts in the poorer or the wealthier classes was the capitalistic society, according to Ward:

There is not sufficient purchasing power in the masses of population to consume the products of the capital plant created by the desire for investment returns no matter how much the products may be needed by them, either on the score of social health or personal development. Thus what our orthodox economists proclaim as the only sound way to create needed capital plant also creates idleness of the plant and the unemployment of the workers. It is a self-defeating system. God is not mocked. Inequality and injustice are socially destructive. (130)

That this may not be an analysis of the situation for all time and places, Ward as an interactionist and dialectician would be among the first to agree. Nothing could be stated for eternity.

Organized labor was the vanguard in social change, and Ward hoped for a peaceful transfer of power. Striking by working people, he believed, would lead to better living conditions and eventually would help in the moral imperative of throttling nuclear-bomb proliferation. At age ninety he was writing to scientists at Brookhaven about the nuclear holocaust. On his desk at his death was "the latest material on the subject" (Dennis Puleston to Ward, April 22, 1963) (11). That same year he signed an open letter to President Kennedy, circulated by a labor group, to end the war in Vietnam because of its horrors and threat to world peace.

Though Ward doubtless knew the phrase of George E. McNeill, AFL[3] trade-union leader, who said at the turn of this century that "the order of God may light the torch of revolution," did he read a few years later that blacks in the more-militant United Mine Workers spoke of revolution in religious terms in the way McNeill did? He was doubtless aware that the early unions condemned stratification, saying "God does not assign stations in life, for it is preposterous, repulsive, and degrading to God and man."

Ward paid a price in the closing years of his life because of the history he presented and the stance he took in his writing and speaking. He was ostracized. It is arresting to read today of German theologians, such as Oscar Arnal: "The German Democratic Republic's Marxist historians have been meeting with their Christian counterparts to discuss such issues as the importance of personality and ideology in the shaping of events." Or this, which Ward would have endorsed heartily: "Christian historians and thinkers have moved beyond abstract theology and ideology into the realms of social, political and economic realities." Finally, a Lutheran church historian describes American religious thought today as still largely unchanged in spite of the efforts of Ward, liberationists, street priests, and the others: "More to the point, western historians [and clergy, too—EPL] have not considered seriously the input of their Marxist colleagues. In almost every instance they return to traditional models in which they rest their case upon ideological categories alone, or incorporate social and economic concerns but only in a clearly ancillary way."[4] With a few exceptions, the United States is still far from confronting this fundamental religious dialogue, preferring instead to forego all reason in a final last tango with Death. Across the world, however, and in the ecumenical churches of America the daring assumption of Ward is each day becoming a basis for Hope and Life.

Notes

1. C. Wright Mills, one of the most stimulating of recent sociologists, introduced this phrase to mean the foresight of a social analyst predicting a change to come, but at the present seen only as an outrage. An example might be to require sterilization of male babies by a draft system as in war time, in order to halt the burgeoning population. Or "collectivism is inevitable," or "In two centuries some of the human population will be living in outer space or in the depths of oceans." "Associating Jesus and Marx" is indubitably an outrageous assumption among large numbers of people, whether living under capitalism or socialism.

2. This debate went on in the *Nation* (Fall 1980–Spring 1981), where a Latin American correspondent tended to sympathize with liberationists more than with worker-farmer unionization. This tendency could be manipulated by the Christian Democratic Party to frustrate the struggle for economic democracy.

3. American Federation of Labor.

4. "Dialogue: Christ and Marx," *Newsweek*, Jan. 16, 1967. Under the heading "Religion" appeared a summary of theologians in Germany, Spain, France, and elsewhere, advancing the need for dialogue. See also "Trilateralism," put out by the CIRCUS (Center for Interreligious

Concerns in the United States), an endorsed ministry of the Metropolitan New York Synod of the Lutheran Church in America. See also the extended statement by the National Conference of Catholic Bishops on Christianity and Marxism. Although the dialogue is growing in the United States, it is arising more slowly.

15
What Needs Now
To Be Done?

How shall [Harry Ward] become dumb or cease
to speak to men unless the children of those
who are now half-devil and half-God shall
prove to be wholly devil—or wholly moron.
—**Vernon L. Parrington**
on Whitman

The Wards' senior years brought new rituals to be fulfilled. Earlier family rites faded into memories and gave place to pathos associated with anniversaries and death's painful punctuations on the pages of life. Daisy always remembered the family birthdays, and until the onset of her last illness, she noted her wedding anniversary by writing an affectionate personal note to Hal, the intimate name used before the children arrived. The Ward letters (11.1) contained notes for their fiftieth and fifty-fifth wedding anniversaries. The following is representative of Daisy's expressions of respect and love for her lifelong mate:

October 15, 1949

My own dear Hal:

It was 54 years ago tonight that you asked me a question, do you remember what it was? Not the usual one, and I couldn't answer it—you had to—and then began a wonderful life for us together. We really have had so many fine experiences together for most of the years. The eight months you were going around the world with Mr. Thompson were difficult but you came back safe in better health and with a fund of understanding of world conditions and problems that I think made it possible for you to be the leader you are. So it was worthwhile.

That is a comfort as we grow older together. Whatever comes, we'll chance it and we can be thankful for our life, our experiences, our children, our friends—living and working together—and our love abides.

Your Daisy

The children, now adults, joined in noting a birthday or an anniversary. Lynd, for example, wrote a birthday note to his father (October 6, 1953), which says how much he believes in his work and life. Only recently had he realized how hard his father's work was: "God bless you . . . but I'm afraid I'm not quite clear about the Deity yet. . . . I only hope I may do a bit, as you have so nobly done yours" (11).

Others outside the circle of the family also remembered anniversaries. Letters were received from Colonel Raymond Robbins, an old friend from Chicago days, who was a food-relief administrator in the New Deal era and an adviser on Soviet affairs for President Franklin Roosevelt, among other useful activities.[1] Telegrams came from the Reverend Richard and Mrs. Morford for the fiftieth and again for the fifty-first occasion. The Reverend Alfred Swan, whose large First Congregational Church adjoined the University of Wisconsin campus, and Aubry Williams, important New Dealer, sent letters. Compliments in these and other letters were always, "You changed my thinking," "I can never forget your inspiration," or "You are a modern prophet."

The rituals when death called at Arcadian Way were brief, simple, and entirely private. Muriel went first, in 1957. Though her loss was a major grief for both elderly parents, the two sons and their wives joined them to follow Ward in his public and now private commitment to life first and death as only an incidental, like a rest in a musical score that gives stress to rhythm and harmony in the full composition. The fire of the crematorium took Muriel's physical remains back into nature; a memorial service recalled her sensitivity toward children and the high regard parents held for her school. Muriel's books written about and for children,[2] as well as her methods, reveal inspiration derived from others, especially Sophia Lyon Fahs, the sturdy defender of Muriel's father during stormy times at Union Seminary.

Muriel's social thought was much like that of her father. Her letters written home in 1938 during her summer trip to the Soviet

Union and Italy reveal youthful expressions of her father's perception of things:

> Some of us went through first class [on the ship *Conte Di Savoia*] for a peek—some snooty people lolling around in luxury. We felt much more comfortable back here. [Third Class] Everything has St. Vitus's dance up here.
>
> In order to save themselves trouble the Italian Lines put all the people bound for Odessa in one party—so we have to trot around after the petty bourgeoise of the 1st and 2nd class. We are always taken care of last which entails annoying delays.
>
> Rome was interesting but even the old ruins symbolize exploitation and cruelty. I was not anxious to remain longer. The inside of St. Peter's gave me such artistic indigestion I doubt if I'll survive. Lord, what a mess.
>
> At my table [on shipboard] is a Turkish girl who has been working as a commercial foreign correspondent in Germany. I have been trying to get news of the situation there from her but she won't talk much. She says Hitler admits 77 executions, but there is no means of checking. . . . The people themselves are desperate but can't agree among themselves and have no arms. If the police and army would join them they might have some hope. She feels the Jewish persecution is racial and not economic. Those whose fathers were in the firing line in the war [1918] have been allowed to retain their positions.
>
> Met a man, Waldman I think, who was deported with Emma Goldman. Asked him questions and everything checks with Dad's book.
>
> Met an Intourist guide who knew "Ray" [Robbins] and who knew "Prof. Ward." Beamed all over. She remembered you and said nothing pleased Ray more than your [Ward's] book [*In Place of Profit*]. (11.1)

Shortly after Muriel's death, Daisy developed a slowly debilitating illness that ineluctably would bring death to her; one ritual of family severance was soon followed by another. Arteriosclerosis of the brain gradually deteriorated her mentality, leading to confusion, wandering, picking up things that didn't belong to her, and the need for constant care. On one freezing night she strolled out to "look for Muriel." Independent testimony given by her children, grandchildren, and friends reports Ward's extraordinary patience and understanding in caring for her. The idea of a nursing home was repugnant to him as well as for her. Only when she was so ill she recognized no one and could not care for herself in any way, did he consent to a nursing home. Muriel's savings from her highly successful children's school were used to ease the costs of her mother's care and later that of her father's also. As Gandhi chose third class on trains in India, in like manner did this family choose the hospital ward (the third class) when assigned to an American hospital.

Daisy deserves an abundance of credit for living successfully with a genius who at times in interpersonal relations was not so democratic as his pragmatic philosophy might have called for. Both he and his closest associate, George Coe, would occasionally lose their tempers, even with one another. When Ward expressed a dash of anger, the family members were ill at ease during its usually short duration. Daisy bore up well in these spitfires, always explaining him to whichever child or grandchild was the current victim of his emotions.

When Gordon was graduated from college in 1925, Daisy perpared him for his father's critical position by writing that in Russia the young man would have lost out, being a member of the "intelligentsia," a professor's son. Intellectuals tend not to understand "the needs of their time and join forces with the workers." This is especially true in the United States, she pointed out. "Your Dad is an outstanding exception and I know you are proud of him." That prophet of single purpose, who was demanding of his children, made these emotional cushions and explanations necessary. Daisy was always there in this capacity with a voice and dignity all her own.

Though her husband's pace was exhausting, she never lagged. The pages of her diaries and notebooks, interspersed with clippings, record many of her interests (11.1). One clipping was an editorial in the *Ladies Home Journal*, written by Dorothy Thompson (for a time the wife of Sinclair Lewis), entitled "War and Revolution." Across it Daisy had written "sound article." Other clippings were about women and the Canadian peace movement. Two issues of the *Peacemaker*, a newsletter, were there, with two pamphlets written by her son, Dr. Gordon Ward, about farmers' cooperatives. One of her diaries is evidence of political alertness;

she kept the voting record of New York and New Jersey senators and congressmen. Daisy wrote a book with her friend Mary Moxcey to aid Sunday School teachers and parents in presenting a more-ethical interpretation of religion to children.[3]

Of the more than sixty years of married life, the first fifty Daisy gave undividedly to the social education and drives of her "dear heart." During the last ten, the roles were necessarily reversed with Ward, in his eighties, guarding and protecting his beloved mate. William Howard Melish conducted the private family funeral service immediately following Daisy's death on November 20, 1960. The flowers came from Ward's garden, then full of multicolored fall chrysanthemums.

Through the long stretch of the Ward's senior years rituals continued, including the summer months at Lonely Lake. Ward's canoe trips with son Gordon, and sometimes others, continued until 1949. Warned by heart attacks to take precautions, he still at age seventy-six went on ten-day to two-week trips, helping to paddle the canoe and using the paddle as a staff when portaging. According to Gordon, he was aware of the limits of his exertion and stayed strictly within those limits. Even then, he carried a sixty-pound pack on his back.

Jim Dombrowski tells of the careful organization that went into all Ward's activities, including the recreation rituals at Lonely Lake. Working hard and playing hard persisted to near the end of his days. One time one of his most loyal disciples, Jack McMichael, rowed in at the Canadian rendezvous unannounced. With him were Mrs. McMichael and their three children. Jack sent word up to the house, "I have several world problems to discuss with you." Ward sent back an abrupt reply, "I can't today, every minute is filled." So the McMichaels paddled back across the lake to the long wooded road that led to the highway and the United States. May dared to ask Ward why he was so busy, and he replied, "I have to pick the peas, shell them, bake bread and lots of other things." Organizing and planning must be done, then the activities must be carried out strictly. This was the only way to appreciate Lonely Lake or to enjoy ten days in the surrounding wilderness with no hitches. He wanted no mistakes to mar the freedom of throwing oneself into the full joy of the wild scenery, the sight, sound, and aroma of "bass broiled over the embers" (11).

Daisy continued to prepare tea and sandwiches on Sunday afternoons and invite the three or four neighboring families. Boulderwood, the Ward cottage, was the unofficial central shrine of these environmentalists. On the fiftieth anniversary of the place, the Wards initiated a square dance where old and young alike "cut the pigeon wing" with music provided by members of their versatile group.

Many have reported Ward's mind, as sharp and analytical as ever at ninety-one years. His garden at Lonely Lake throve under his care, its bounties being announced at the back door of Lynd and May's cottage as he walked in shouting "Hello" with his arms loaded with vegetables. At eighty-six he was following heavyweight boxing and baseball as he had done from youth. He wrote to Lynd on July 8, 1959, about the skill and the effect of the punches and dodges of Floyd Patterson, the world champion. After Daisy died Ward lived alone in his cabin at the lake. Lynd and May suggested that he communicate his state of health to them each morning. In response, he used a megaphone to yell at 7 A.M. "Lynd, Lynd, I'm all right" and continued until Lynd came out on the porch and shouted back "Very good, Dad." After several mornings of this exactly at seven, the family suggested he call at eight o'clock instead. It was said that everybody else in the area could set their watches by the imam imitator of Lonely Lake.

Ward's pension from Union Theological Seminary, combined with his Social Security, added up to a little over $4,000 a year. Then, as always, he pondered the most effective institutions, in order to support those that would not continue charity and reform but would seek to destroy the private-profit system and build a cooperative commonwealth. He chose the following for his limited giving in 1958: the Southern Conference Educational Fund headed by his former student and assistant, James Dombrowski—$50.00; the Methodist Federation for Social Action—$50.00; the reconciliation trips led by his former student, Clarence V. Howell—$50.00. These trips introduced many students at Columbia University to the reality of poverty, cold, and hunger on the streets, in the flophouse, and in the soup-kitchen line. Friends recalled how Ward all his life made such trips wherever he traveled. Fifty dollars went to the support of a free pulpit defended by the Religious Freedom Committee, a pulpit that could criticize the immoralities of industrialism and the market society.

Church attendance was not among the rituals of Ward's life. Granddaughter Robin Ward Savage asked him, "Do you go to church?" "No," was the quick response, "I only go when I am giving the sermon." "Why?" she pressed, and that brought the reply, "Because it is often too dull and boring." His dislike for trivia, pomp, and escapism surfaced in many ways.

Whether in Canada or at his home on the Palisades, whether as a youth writing his sermons for a Methodist Chapel in England or a man of four score and more years writing his thoughts for the *Bulletin* of the Methodist Federation, Ward never tired of offering insightful interpretations of important public concerns. Fourteen books and more than two hundred articles were written during his lifetime, of which *Our Economic Morality* (156) and *Which Way Religion?* (167) were read widely (see the Bibliography). The latter was chosen as the best for that year by the Religious Book Club. However, these expositions, tightly argued as they were, were not always understood. When he wrote about the new social order in Russia, his views were as twisted by some readers as was the body of the Elephant Man. Therefore, there were many who failed to read his last published book *Democracy and Social Change* (201) which some today consider his best.

By and large reaction to his works was affected by the public's pervasive anticommunism, and they either were not read or were aborted by publishers. The Communist *New Masses* could usually print his articles, but that was not to Ward's complete satisfaction. He wanted to reach a larger circle of people, especially church people who would seldom, if ever, see a copy of *New Masses*, let alone read it. Sometimes he tried to answer an article, such as one in the *Reader's Digest* (February 1943) by the president of the U.S. Chamber of Commerce urging Americans to uphold capitalism, but his effort was rejected. In the forties, when he wrote the *Christian Century*—which in the twenties under editor Charles Clayton Morrison had been responsive to him—he was repeatedly denied attention by Paul Hutchinson, Morrison's successor. In fact, this journal of opinion was closed to him from

1945 to 1955—a journal for which Ward was invited to write in 1921 and had then served almost as an editor for (letter from Hutchinson to Ward, December 3 and 30, 1921) (11). Comments on rejection slips said that he had attacked the *Christian Century* by using "slurring remarks," and that he was too controversial.

In 1952 and 1953 another spate of letters between editor Hutchinson and his eighty-year-old former contributor was exchanged. "Blacklisted" was the word for his condition, Ward said, after receiving still another denial of an article on the international crisis, but he was persistent in spite of negative replies. In effect, he said he would like to raise questions in the journal about religion and the profit motive, since the topic has been abandoned by the Methodist general conference. Moreover, Ward told Hutchinson that since Charles Hopkins's articles defended "liberal, reformed capitalism," he would like to present a contrasting view. Not even would the editor allow Ward to answer an attack on the *Christian Century* for its opposition to released school time for religious education. Again Hutchinson claimed Ward's international policy was too controversial (Hutchinson to Ward, Mar. 11, 1953) (11).

"What kind of article, in what field, would you accept from me?" asked the beleaguered Ward, surrounded as he was by the hysteria of McCarthyism. Could he not at least challenge "some of the lies" appearing in this, one of his favorite journals, and perhaps openly debate some of its writers? Ward was hopeful the adamant editor might respond to one of the following topics: "Methodists and the Profit Motive," "What Is Happening to the Protestant Conscience?" "How Much Is Left of the Bill of Rights?" "A Report on Germ Warfare," and "Is Peaceful Co-existence Possible?" There were others in the list, but none could break through the harsh suppression of Ward's freedom to speak and publish. Instead, all subsequent exchange of letters—briefly summarized—went with Hutchinson's answer on March 14, 1953, insisting that as editor he must not be partisan. March 17 Ward again advised the presentation of both sides, and the editor stung him by answering that he would keep all in mind and when he thought "you could speak effectively to our readers I will get in touch with you."

The concerns that shook the fragile frame of the prophet of the Palisades in his last decade were in the list of topics sent to the *Christian Century*. He hoped that he might warn of the unethical and immoral growth of nuclear violence, war, unemployment, profiteering, dishonesty, and all manner of social diseases in human relations. It was a time when, as Rauschenbusch said, one could hear "human virtue cracking and crumbling all around." Such pathologies Ward attributed to three primary trends that worried him to the very center of his thin body:

- The Methodists turned against the condemning of the private profit motive.

- Protestantism's decay as capitalist society steadily declined in serving the needs of mankind. What will happen to religion?

- The undermining of the incomparable Bill of Rights: a precious social discovery for the growth of the human self (11).[4]

Those whose egos flare up at the end of their days, inspiring them to get biographies written of themselves or write autobiographies, find one way at least to "rage against the coming of the night." For Ward it was different. Why take the precious time of the human phase of ongoing life for mourning, for extended funerals, for rage? Individualism is an illusion which the rich and powerful seek to preserve by steel and stone, and always fail. Individualistic religions, economics, or laws can immortalize no one. Life as process can be compared to the tossing waves of the sea. Droplets like "selves" arise for a fraction of time from the crests, respond to the surroundings of stars, and flow up the rocks and the beaches of the coastline carrying moisture to feed life, soaking up oxygen to feed the deeps. Why praise oneself with an autobiography of the tiny, evanescent self, which is, in fact, composed of many blended selves as Life proceeds?

At Ward's ninetieth-birthday celebration in 1963 a large proportion of letters of eulogy came from working men and women, especially considering that labor-union officers often signed for membership action. Some well-wishers included:

- Harry Bridges for the International Longshoremen's and Warehousemen's Union
- Tom Scribner, editor, the *Lumberjack News* (brother of Grace Scribner)
- Alexander Hoffman for the Cleaners' and Dyers' Union, Local 239 (special praise to Ward for his leadership of the American League Against War and Fascism)
- Samuel Burt for the Dressers' and Dyers' Joint Board, CIO (Our 5,000 members hail your fight for Peace and Freedom)
- T. A. Jackson for the Dining Car Employees, Local 379
- Benjamin Gudes for the Retail Drug Store Employees
- Conrad Kay for the Meat Cutters Union, Local 623
- Morris Munster for the United Furniture Workers of America
- George Starr for the International Workers Order
- Frank Dutto for the Bakers' Union, Local 87
- Abe Silverberg for the Retail Employees Union, Local 830
- Armando Ramirez for the United Cigar Workers Union, Local 273
- Rose Russell, Teachers Union of the City of New York (Ward's own union)

The longshoremen sent a check for thirty-five dollars with this note from their leader, Harry Bridges:

> Of all the fighters for peace and freedom I can think of no greater contribution than Dr. Harry F. Ward. All the elements necessary to the building of a successful trade union—understanding, militance, vigilance, wisdom and the spirit of unity—were embodied in him and applied to the larger community. We have seen over many years those who run from their announced principles when going got tough, but never Dr. Ward. I am proud to have been associated with him. (11)

Greetings came from those who were directly associated with labor, but were not workers: the writer Leo Huberman; Norman Thomas (who mentioned differences in viewpoint, but acknowledged "the friendship and instruction" derived from his teacher);

Anna Louis Strong, his good friend of many years, from Beijing, China; John de J. Pemberton, executive director of the ACLU ("congratulations"); Elizabeth Gurley Flynn; and Anna Rochester. The latter started in the field of religious education, but turned to writing fact books for the progressive labor movement. She contributed the following anecdote to Ward's "Birthday Folders" (11):

> Thinking of Dr. Ward and his widespread influence during these many years, I remember a story about him that Mother Ella Reeve Bloor used to tell. On her speaking tours across the country, she would often find some young clergyman willing to be chairman of a local meeting for a communist speaker. After the meeting she would say to him: "You went to Union Theological Seminary in New York. And you studied under Prof. Harry Ward." The young minister would answer: "Why, yes. But how did you know that?" And she would say, "I know because of what you are doing now."

"Gurley," as her friends addressed her, wrote a succinct summary of Ward's life:

> It is an honor to greet Dr. Harry F. Ward, dear old friend, co-worker for many years, valiant anti-fascist and fighter for human rights, peace and freedom. Young in spirit, rich in experience, he has dedicated his eloquent voice and pen to these causes all his life. My introduction to Harry F. Ward was in the splendid amnesty campaign of the 20's, for hundreds in prison after World War I—religious pacifists, socialists, IWWs and others. As co-members of the American Civil Liberties in its earlier years, we participated in the defense of the victims of the Palmer raids, for freedom for Tom Mooney and Sacco and Vanzetti. He was fearless in defense of communists and was ever a friend of the Soviet Union. He has spoken out in defiance of McCarthyism and for the victims of the Smith and McCarran Acts. He has inspired thousands to think and to act for civil rights and liberties. Long life and good health to a great American, Harry F. Ward, with deep affection.

The ninetieth-birthday celebration aroused commendatory statements from humanitarians who were active in defense of human and civil rights in other countries. Space permits only a few representative ones to be included.

The Czechoslovak Unitarian Association sent greetings. The Canadian Peace Congress wrote this timely statement: "Mankind owes much to this man who has for so many years been an inspiration to those of us who strive to see that our children will inherit not a radioactive earth, but one where all can enjoy its riches." The World Council of Peace in London cabled, "You must rejoice at great growth in strength and unity of worldwide movement for disarmament and peace to whose development you have contributed so much."[5]

H. E. Brunner, the Swiss theologian who with Karl Barth advocated a neoorthodoxy that swept over Europe, came into the United States and almost saturated Union Theological Seminary. Although his Thomistic theology somewhat blunted the religious dynamism of Ward, Brunner nonetheless approved much of the teaching of America's great Christian Ethics professor and asked to have the *Social Questions Bulletin* mailed regularly "in exchange for our socialist Swiss weekly." His letter contained this high compliment:

> There has never been any doubt in me since I came to know UTS and you, that you were the man who had to give that which the world is longing for more than any other. In you I found that radicalism which springs from the depths of God-experience and means God; the faith which is old-fashioned enough to make God real and radical enough to believe in a new world. There are only a few other Americans with whom I found that spirit of the kingdom. . . .[6]

An interesting international recognition in 1931 was recalled at Ward's birthday conclave. With other "holders of academic positions" in Europe and America, he was invited to sign a petition addressed to the Swedish Academy of Letters requesting the consideration of Upton Sinclair as a candidate for the Nobel Prize for literature. Among the other signers were such prominent persons as John Dewey of Columbia University, Albert Einstein of the University of Berlin, Harold Laski of the University of London, Edwin Markham of the American Academy of Arts and

Letters, William McDougall of the University of Oxford, Bertrand Russell of Cambridge University, and Bernard Shaw.[7]

The list of admirers living abroad who hailed this ninety-year-old on his birthday included Radhakrishnan, the philosopher and first president of India, and Bertrand Russell, himself ninety-one, who wrote:

> His [Ward's] efforts are part of the record of individual courage on behalf of things which powerful people and prevalent sentiment abhor: compassion, insistence upon the recognition of individual rights irrespective of the person concerned, and an intense hope that the intelligence of men may be put towards their welfare rather than the pain of others.

This eulogy came from the philosopher who wrote the provocative booklet entitled *Why I Am Not A Christian* in 1927.

Telegrams, notes, and letters hailing Ward, sent by Americans from all walks of life, were the most numerous of all, although the red scare caused fewer plaudits than might have otherwise been left in the Ward birthday file. The fanaticism and fury of the times brought suicide to some, killed the basic human ability to make moral decisions in others, and turned still others into physical wrecks or mentally ill cowards who lied to the press and the courts. Many feared writing one good word as tribute. Others who did express themselves, even in 1963, had already been maligned and pushed toward oblivion in history, the fate suffered so severely by Ward himself.

The words of praise by those willing to stand up, to *pro testare*, were more valuable because of the fearful conditions surrounding them. Dean Walter G. Muelder of the Boston University School of Theology paid tribute to the once-young clergyman from the stockyards district of Chicago who had sketched the Social Creed in 1907. He wrote:

> The subject which has been chosen for the occasion of this Celebration "What Needs To Be Done" is characteristic of your whole prophetic ministry. Because you have not chosen to think and act at the level of mere idealism and on an abstract principle but have always wrestled with the concrete unity of theory and

practice, many have disagreed with you and many have been strongly opposed to the policies which you have recommended. But the very concreteness of your witness has given courage to the fainthearted and has contemporary relevance to the eternal Gospel. (11)

Winifred Chappell (for so many years secretary of the Methodist Federation in association with Ward), a woman of intelligence and fortitude who is being slowly elevated to a status of importance in women's history, honored the man with these words: "It is amazing what just a couple of lines from you can do in the way of brushing cobwebs out of my mind and adjusting my vision toward reality. It's one of the things I admire most, the clarity and absolute intellectual honesty which comes out in everything you write" (328).

The fight that limited the extent of Ward's positive recognition was his defense, to the end, of the world's first Marxian socialist state. The artist Rockwell Kent, for a number of years president of the National Council of American-Soviet Friendship to which Ward contributed articles and travel time,[8] with his wife Sally was among the conveners of the birthday party and wrote in a letter of invitation: "How correctly and faithfully through the years has he interpreted the development of the new socialist society in the Soviet Union with the aim of bringing about understanding and friendship between the peoples of the two countries" (11).

Many contemporaries know the name of David Dellinger, one of the most militant among the young leaders in resisting the draft and the Vietnam War. His father, a student at Boston University School of Theology when Ward was there, was lastingly impressed. David wrote that Professor Ward must be given "most of the credit for getting us started on our progressive course."[9]

D. N. Pritt, distinguished Queen's Counsel from England— internationally known for his work in civil liberties around the world, was the chief speaker at the birthday occasion. After songs by the Harlem Opera Singers, the black leader W.E.B. DuBois gave a second address. Then the honored man of the evening stood straight for his age and spoke for more than an hour! The topic, as one might expect, was "What Needs Now To Be Done?"

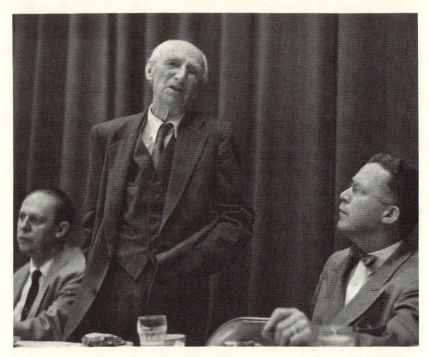

Figure 15.1 *Harry Ward speaking at his ninetieth-birthday celebration, October 15, 1963, with D. N. Pritt* **(left)** *and William Howard
Melish* **(right).** *(Photo by Mildred Grossmer.)*

Later William and Dorothy (Chertak) Manealoff, who aided
Ward's causes with money and Ward with hospitality at their
Central Park South apartment, offered six well-chosen words to
characterize the man. "Dr. Ward was a rare combination of theory,
spirit, practice, dedication, modesty and total selflessness." Although such nouns may hide a multitude of sins, still Ward's
virtues-in-action gave these friends and all who had worked
with him a firm confidence and ready freedom to use the words.

The last recognition given came from Dr. Herbert Aptheker,
director of the American Institute for Marxist Studies, who invited
Ward to become its first honorary chairman. A festschrift for
him, edited by Aptheker and Robert Cohen, was almost complete
when, as happened with the addition of the Marxist to the Union
Theological Seminary faculty, Ward was no longer alive to ac-

knowledge it. Aptheker's book *Marxism and Christianity* (265) became instead a memorial tribute.

"What is the task before us? What needs now to be done?" asked Ward in his last published book, *Democracy and Social Change* (201). "The present duty is to proceed with the mobilization of the democratic forces and trust the people. This is the essence of democracy—faith in the capacities of the people. It is time to act upon it, remembering, through all defeats, that the future belongs to the forces which seek to push life forward. The forces of death may win some battles, but they are doomed to defeat in the end." Is this an idealist or a utopian writing? It is rather an ethicist who knows the source for ethics to be in a developing, perfecting process that of necessity must include both success and failure. It is in the struggle against life-destroying forces "that we come into and keep in touch with ultimate reality." Vital religion is knowing that we personally cannot win in our day. Nevertheless, we must continue to struggle for what is for us unobtainable. In so doing we are vitalized by creative forces that continually renew life. This in essence was the faith of Ward.

* * *

Two years before his death this prophet was bedridden and needed almost constant care day and night. His aides, and Daisy's too before her death, were black women, long employed, who always ate at the family table.[10] Ward resented firmly the slightest talk of his going to a nursing home. His mind was alert and clear to the end, so he wished to stay home where he could be among young people, near his garden and roses, and the Wards "saw to it that he did." Muriel's small fund helped her father in his illness as it had her mother. He would have nothing to do with either medical sedatives or social soporifics. Methodist Bishop Lloyd Wicke recalled almost a motto for Ward, "No nonsense here." Pain and death were real. Life must be dealt with in full realism, no nonsense even in the last of his family rituals.

Found in Ward's papers, given to Union Theological Seminary (11), was a small, sealed envelope that had not been opened. On the outside was typed "IN CASE." Hoping not to violate privacy, it was opened and these straightforward requests were read:

In Case of Fatal Accident

Cremation desired. Everything as simple and inexpensive as possible.

No flowers except one or two red roses on coffin.

No "viewing of remains."

No lying eulogy—especially to the Lord in an all worship Memorial Service at Union.

As to the ashes I've always wanted what Coe did and got; except that I've long had a fancy to let the N.W. wind take them where it will from on top of the bluff between our camp and Lynd's, maybe where I finished writing *Our Economic Morality*. If the wind were strong enough they might get out to the lake. But in this matter, as in the others, except the first, I think the living should do what will give them the most pleasure, I mean satisfaction.

This private request underlines a life-style in a brief expression.

Ward's wishes were in large part accomplished without the family reading his terse, typed note. They did not need to. All of them—daughters-in-law, grandchildren, neighbors, and close friends—knew him well. Accordingly, his strictly private funeral cost $425.55. Of this amount $315.00 went to the funeral home. Sixty dollars went for the crematory, another $40.55 covered "death notices," and $10.00 was for "transcripts of death."

Lee H. Ball, who might with respect be called Ward's man Friday, was invited to the funeral home on December 12, 1966, to conduct a brief service. There were red roses on the coffin and the quiet group "to hail Dad and farewell" was the immediate family only.

Because the sealed note was not read, the one request of no memorial service at Union was not followed. Such a service was arranged on January 4, 1967. The faithful Lee Ball planned the service, and that should have helped to quiet the questioning spirit of Ward about the occasion. Bishop Welch, who knew from the beginning the true author of the Social Creed of the Churches but waited for half a century before publishing the fact in his autobiography, gave the invocation. Howard Melish, like Ball one of Ward's closest associates and the one who had enabled Angela Davis to get an education, read from the Scriptures. Three clergymen gave addresses, but only the third, Richard Morford, had known Ward well. A young student at the seminary, John Collins, read from the writings of a teacher he had discovered, but had never met. Today Collins leads Clergy and Laity Concerned (CALC), a type of people's front of Catholics, Jews, and Protestants clearly in Ward's tradition. Ward would have respected the men who took part in his memorial service. Their praise was neither vapid nor lying.

James Memorial Chapel, seating approximately five hundred people, was not filled. Some still shook with the fear of guilt by association with the prophet's ideas or with the remaining members of his Gideon's army. Others reported, "We have never heard much about him." Even his seminary had not arranged this act of recognition.

Ward's short request "In Case of Fatal Accident" proved to be strikingly similar to the "Last Will" of Joe Hill, a leader who was a folk hero of Ward and his family. According to tradition, Hill wrote his wishes in his cell on Nov. 18, 1915, on the eve of his execution. His body, too, was cremated, and his ashes were distributed to Industrial Workers of the World delegates from all over the world at a memorial meeting for him in West Side Park, Chicago. Win Stracke, a folk singer who lived in the "vibrant" city, in 1947 sent Ward a copy of the labor leader's alleged last "will," written in poetic style:

My will is easy to decide
For there is nothing to divide
My kin don't need to fuss and moan
"Moss does not cling to rolling stone."
My body? Ah if I could choose
I would to ashes it reduce
And let the merry breezes blow
My dust to where some flowers grow
Perhaps some fading flower there

Would come to Life and bloom again
This is my last and final will
Good luck to all of you, Joe Hill. (11)

These lines, taken as doggerel or as social document depending on viewpoints, touched the deepest sentiments and convictions of Harry Ward. Labor was the "vehicle" of ethics as Ward understood and wrote in *The Labor Movement* (64). Granted this, his book *Our Economic Morality* (156) dealing with production, exploitation, and profit relates the substance of the two books as inseparable Siamese twins.

By a strange coincidence, on the night of Ward's death, Lonely Lake had the worst storm in memory. A blizzard of wind and snow smashed at the dwellings and the shore and uprooted huge trees. If a call can come down from the North by storm or—as he wrote in his poem—on "the whirr of the wild-goose wing" and if the call can be heard in "the calm and gentle converse of the trees," it is not quite so strange that Lonely Lake might have shouted to its first summer settler, his body agonized with pain on that cold December night, to "come away." The next storm on the lake swept his ashes over the earth and the waters and into the turbulence of the sky.

One of the last letters Ward wrote to his great companion, Coe,[11] closed with a prescient statement that seems to contain the essence of the man: "Our labor and economic policy at home is weak and dangerous, our foreign policy a compound of ignorance, silliness and wickedness. So we are in a beautiful mess and the fighting is going to be good all along the line."

Notes

1. Most social or labor historians know of Margaret and Mary Drier, the sisters who founded and led the Women's Trade Union League. Margaret gave thirty-eight years of her life to it. Mary married Raymond Robbins. All three were close friends of the Wards, close enough to join a relative few who addressed them as "Harry" and "Daisy." They exchanged books and flower bulbs and all of them admired Lenin and defended the Soviet Union.

2. Muriel's writings include *The Little Pond* (1948), a children's book; *On The Line*, a small drama; and a book on children's literature, *Young*

Minds Need Something to Grow On. Her collection of children's books was given as "The Muriel Ward Memorial" to the library of the Department of Education, State of New Jersey.

3. Daisy K. Ward and Mary E. Moxcey *Parents and Their Children: An Introductory Manual for Parents' Classes* (New York: Methodist Book Concern, 1922).

4. These *Christian Century* letters were in a folder so marked. All the major events of Ward's life were, in general, classified in file folders in his papers.

5. These encomia are all in folder marked "90th Birthday" in Ward Papers (11).

6. So far as is known Dr. Brunner never retreated from this position which he wrote to Ward in June of 1920, anachronistic though it seems here. "God-experience" or God in and of experience was central for the religious pragmatism of Ward's entire life.

7. Shaw wrote a witty and cogent letter to the secretary of the Swedish Academy when he mailed the petition. (See Upton Sinclair, *My Lifetime in Letters* (Columbia: University of Missouri Press, 1960), pp. 58–62.

8. On a trip to the People's Republic of China in 1980 it was informing to learn of the vast respect for Kent in China. An art-institute director in Guangzhou thought he was America's most outstanding artist of this century.

9. J. C. Coleman to Ward, Jan. 9, 1941, Ward papers, "Democracy and Social Change" file (11).

10. From one of many interviews with the Ward children and grandchildren. This one was Jan. 8, 1981.

11. Jan. 6, 1946 (6).

Appendix A:
"Why I Have Found
Life Worth Living"

Author's note: Ward at age fifty-five (and he lived to be ninety-three) wrote the following essay in the *Christian Century* (March 1, 1928). Western culture has changed, but the need to understand one's beginnings and how to resolve the eternal question of how to relate to the larger universe—nature and human nature—seems as necessary and as fundamental in the last decades of this century as it was in the first. Ward approaches the question as a man, an intellectual *cum* activist, but his process of inquiry, his experience and conclusions bear consideration by women, persons in any occupation or status, or by the young and those growing older.

*   *   *

WHY I HAVE FOUND LIFE WORTH LIVING

Offhand I said: "I can answer that question in two words." But concerning them nothing will be written. Without some reticences life does lose its flavor. And those of the younger generation who are rebelling against the possessive element in the family must make the worst of it, until they get their eyes open wide enough to see the relationship between "mine" and "ours" in the affections as well as in property.

But the next second I knew that I must add two more words—"the job." As long as a man has a job that absorbs him, that obliterates all concern for self, this question of the worthwhileness of life does not exist. Go ask it of the artist in the hour of creative activity! Or of the soldier in the day of battle for freedom! Or of the craftsman finishing his product! Or of the lover proving in service his devotion to the beloved! Our bit of life that we call the self, is realized to the full in those times when it goes out in some contribution to the rest of life from which it came and by which it is sustained. We become persons more by what we put back into the stream of life than by what it pours into us. That is why the family does so much for us, and why life will be so much more worthwhile for everybody when the rest of its institutions are organized on the family principle giving and sharing, instead of getting and ruling.

Living and Questioning

It is also true that there is no questioning of life while it is giving us its best, while we are lost in the ecstasy of music, the beauty of earth and sea and sky, the rapture of visions of the world that yet shall be. Nor do its disasters give us doubt concerning our fragment of existence as long as we are in action against them, to mitigate or to prevent. Not even the inscrutability of life concerning its outcome causes us to query the worth of our span of it so long as we are wrestling with the problem. While we are actively living, life is obviously worth while. Only when we stop to question do we discover that it may not be. In this western world, where an industrial society is aging prematurely because it has wasted so much of its vital substance in riotous, brawling living, pessimism once again seems to have the better of the philosophical argument, and skepticism clearly has the field.

Yet is it not enough to say that we must go on working without thinking. Reflection too is part of living. The job that absorbs us, the pleasures that detach us, must stand the test of analysis. The "activism" of our cool-climate temperament must justify itself. When the younger generation heard me say: "It's the job that makes life worthwhile," it promptly answered: "Yes; but what kind of a job?" Heavy on youth is this tragedy of our present way of organizing life. It deprives them of the chance to be persons in the activity at which they must pass most of their time, and thus incites them to be possessors rather than creators. Hence if a man is to get satisfaction out of looking at his job, whatever else it does, his reflection must help to make a world in which all others too can know that they are putting more into the stream of life than they take out.

Happiness and Courage

On these terms one finds the answer to that part of the question before us which asks about "the springs of happiness and courage." What concern have we with happiness in a world that organizes and trains for war, holds weaker peoples for tribute, drafts super-navy programs, officially lynches Sacco and Vanzetti, shoots and clubs workers while half starving their families, and puts their defenders in jail for asserting in orderly fashion the constitutional right of free speech. In such a world happiness, as that world counts it, is only for those who have good health, plenty of money, minds that never question and no conscience. As for peace that underlies pain, the joy that shines through suffering, is it not known that they cannot be found by seeking? Only as one's job is a part of the lessening of misery and ignorance, of the search for freedom, justice, and fellowship, does he find the springs of such happiness as is possible in this disordered world. And these springs of happiness he finds welling up around him, unsought and unbidden, in the nobility of common folk and the "dear love of comrades," a happiness which is replenished constantly from the inexhaustible resources of the unseen world.

But always there is the issue of health, to make bright or gloomy the day, easy or hard, and sometimes good or bad, the work. The curse of poor health is that it turns too much of your attention in upon yourself. Also it asks for too much sympathy or gets too much consideration. The only remedy is in work. And here we intellectuals have an advantage. We can refuse to let pain disable us altogether. And as for courage, what is it but doing what has to be done whether you are fit or not, and even though the rest quit? But it is good for a man to find out early in life how many will be missing from roll call on the day of battle. Then he will discover in time that the few who will stand are sufficient. And in ordinary days when the road gets lonesome he will find the trees more friendly, and even those far-off stars. And when many evil things are said of him falsely, with time too short to grow the hide of a rhinoceros, and without grace enough to "rejoice and be exceeding glad," he suddenly finds himself in better company than he deserves. Then is his courage reinforced by contagion from the greater souls who have journeyed in the same direction.

Dignity out of Suffering

Also there is a kind of virtue which passes into one from the humble people who in harsh circumstances manage to live with dignity. From some of these, thrust up into distinction of stature by tragic events and terrible forces, I have received more than from any whom these times call their great ones. In my younger days there was the leader of a big strike of polyglot wage-earners. Incorruptible he was. And he disappeared into the darkness, denied a living by those who could not buy him and beaten out of his senses by those in his own ranks who could not cow him. And there have just died in Massachusetts a worker in shoes and a peddler of fish. . . .

What Kind of a Job?

But, the younger generation reminds me, "What kind of a job is it that discovers the resources of life?" Well, each must find his own; but, as for me, I belong to a generation of uplifters and converters; without apology. Some went out to evangelize the world in one generation. Some became muck-raking journalists. Some went into the young settlement movement. And some made American socialism. They said: "Why waste your time with the church?" But before I went to college I had read a book which showed me with a great light that it was the function of religion to transform human society. So I said: "Here is machinery and power dedicated to the achievement of the highest life for man. I will try to use it." And they said: "You will get kicked out." But I replied: "If so, then it will be time to work elsewhere. Meantime this is my place."

The man who wrote the book later made some money, and in his old age complained that some young preachers to whom he had spoken did not seem to recognize that he was a liberal. I have seen the settlement movement stereotyped; the socialist party blown to pieces by the war and the Russian revolution; the missionaries alter their slogan to "the Christianization of the world" or "the sharing of experience"; the churches formally adopt the social service movement without understanding the revolutionary nature of the religion of Jesus; and I am more convinced than ever that this religion of Jesus can become the transforming force in all human affairs. Also that we must make every kind of a job religious by making it serve some common need and aid in the development of man.

It was the need of people that called my generation. We were not after self-expression or self-realization. I remember how I wrote it down one day in college—our obligation to help those who had not our opportunities. From people we got back to conditions. Dirt, disease, ignorance, injustice, oppression—these challenged us; and we became reformers. Then beneath conditions we dug down to causes and became—well, we must leave that to the profit-takers and superpatriots. Their quarrel is not with us but with the religion of Jesus. And our concern is not with them but with his judgment: "Inasmuch as ye did it not. . . ."

The Two Cities

So this was our Pilgrim's Progress and it led not away from but into the City of Destruction, which is to be made over into the City of

God. And while we lost some burdens we gained others. Those who saw that this world was the subject of redemption did not always forget that the world is made up of people. Certainly not if they served an apprenticeship with Jane Addams, Mary McDowell and Graham Taylor. But life is not healthy and the job is not best done if one takes too much responsibility for others, especially if one is more anxious to get them to accept one's religion or program than to get them to discover the truth or to tackle the job. One whose business is teaching and preaching, discovers that the less he is burdened about converts and majorities the more he is burdened about the truth, the heavier is his concern with righteousness, and with getting both truth and righteousness lived out in action. Since life is change it is not enough to get people to see. They must also move, and in the direction that the facts require. But one needs ever to remind oneself that people will always move in different companies and at varying rates of speed. After putting in some time in securing cooperative effort, and expecting to put in more, I nevertheless find myself in as much revolt against an over-valuation of harmony as the harmony seekers are against an over-stimulation of the desire to convert. The more necessary it is for us to think and act together, the more imperative it is that we should be able and willing to go it alone when the others are not ready. If we have hit the right trail, they will come after.

Hence such answer as my experience enables me to give to the younger generation asking what kind of a job makes life worth living boils down to this. It must be a job that helps to make life more worthwhile for everybody else. It must continually reduce the part of self-interest in life by increasing the consciousness of meeting some definite common need. A man must know that by improving the function of such a job he is working through his institutional segment of life to reduce the total of misery, evil or ignorance that is in the world. Then he will discover some connection with the creative and redemptive forces of the universe that are working for the transformation of life. Also I have found that the best safeguard against the limitations and vices of professionalism is to take some part, outside one's vocation, in the fight against injustice and tyranny.

Give Me a Garden!

But the more one interprets life in terms of work the more necessary it is to find some play that will keep one fit for work. There are the arts, whose contribution of release and invigoration is indispensable. But what the brain worker needs most is the outdoors, and what is required by those who are motivated by sympathy, and impelled to challenge intrenched evils, is the touch of hardness that comes from some contest with nature or with other men. I have seen muscular Christianity replace a flaccid, neurotic pietism, and now I hear the college highbrows complain that it is the athletic type which falls for an ignorant, sentimental religion and the R. O. T. C. bunk. Here we can learn from the Greeks. I have done a bit in my day with about all athletic games and outdoor sports and have got a good deal from all of them. But for continuing recreation through all periods of life give me a garden. I remember comparing with Gandhi for a moment the comparative joys and values of spinning and working with the soil. Is it merely a conceit that healing and vigor pass directly from mother earth into those who labor with her to produce things of use and beauty? Earth-bound we need not be; but earth-nourished we surely are.

Those upon whom the crowd pulls need, on occasion, to get far away from it. And for complete release from the pressure and the artificialities of modern life there is nothing like a journey into the far places of the forest or the mountains—on your own. Your way, your food, your fire, your bed is up to you, with just enough spice of danger. You look up at the stars with a strange sense of freedom. It is between you and them; and you are content. And when you come back you can look at yourself and your job from the outside. And if you cannot find a way to do that, you can neither laugh at yourself nor know your job.

I may as well confess that I have never yet come out of the wilds without regret, and I have wondered if more time would cure that; and how long I could be content to grow roses—along with a few things to eat—and let the world go by; or to wander round the earth just "for to admire and for to see," and also to understand. Heirs of two traditions—the Hebraic and the Hellenic, children of both the renaissance and the reformation, we are necessarily divided within ourselves. And we will be so divided until, through some intelligent and just scheme for society, we provide for all a sufficiency of both the proletarian and leisure class necessities. Meantime, I am not ungrateful to my peasant forefathers, nor to the tradition of duty and self-discipline, for the little blue imp who is most of the time on my shoulder, whispering: "Get on with the job." He may be a spoil sport at times, but it remains to be seen whether his yellow playmate of the cult of self-expression will help us to make a better fist of it when the task is unpleasant, adversaries many and seductions abundant.

Winning but Never Won

I suppose the best test of whether one has deceived oneself about this business of living is to ask what one hates most to leave behind on the day of the inevitable rendezvous with death. First, those who are life of our life! But by watching how time heals and replaces one is cured of too much possessiveness in the affections. Then, the job not done! Ah, there, "I long have had a quarrel set with Time because he robbed me—I have known no truce with Time nor Time's accomplice Death." I have found life not too meager but too rich in opportunity. It needs eternity to justify itself. But one must not take oneself too seriously. Always there are other workers, and the job does not go unfinished. What gives me pause is to discover that what I could lose with least grace is the capacity to know how the human struggle is getting on. If death means that. . . . Does this indicate that the essence of life, its real activity, is in the mind? Or that I have been too long trying to understand and interpret this magnificent game of life, and not playing it enough? Or merely that, after all, one cannot be cured of the desire to see some results of his labors? But then I ask: "Why do I want to know?" And I think it is not merely for the satisfaction of curiosity, or results, but also for the challenge to action. To understand with no chance to take a hand would be worse than oblivion. If intelligence is to direct life it cannot remain above the battle.

So those of us who are working to get life changed intelligently and in the direction of ideals, instead of blindly and brutally, are left with only the future. And with no knowledge at the last, but only faith. And is not that enough? To those who have found and do follow the perennial ideals of the race, the future is more than escape from the present defeat that is ever their lot. It belongs to us, not to the majority who have resisted change. And if there is no final victory, but evermore the battle that is sometimes winning but never won, always losing and never lost? That is not the ultimate test? What if the mind has tricked us after all, and we have guessed and chosen wrong about the direction of progress? Then—and here is where the papacy of the intellect is overthrown—would it not be worth while to have sought the highest that we could see, to have battled side by side with those who were the weaker?

How much of the final conquest of life is in that line of Cyrano: "But I have never fought with hope to win"? Does God know whether he can win? Or that life would be worthwhile for him if he did? Isn't it more worthwhile to be helping that kind of a God and to have him helping us, than one who has the game of life all fixed before it begins?

A war in which there is no discharge and no certainty of winning?

A job never completed and often, just when it is going forward, botched by others!

If that is good enough for God, it ought to be good enough for us.

Appendix B:
"Stay In!"

Author's note: "Stay In" is an undated essay possibly written in response to the criticism Union Theological Seminary was receiving because many graduates were going into social work, union organizing, and other social change–related occupations. It does represent Ward's reasons for not going outside the church to fulfill his Christian Ethic principles.

*   *   *

STAY IN!!

"I am through with the church. It is on the wrong track."

This was the word of a Socialist leader, an active church member. Now he says he will stay and help us.

"One day I think I will stay in the church, the next I think I cannot possibly do it. I don't know how it will come out."

This was the word of a younger preacher who also is a Socialist.

There are many others feeling and saying the same things, social workers who are not Socialists.

Many young people who are getting the vision of social Christianity will come to such a place.

A word with you!

When that hour comes, it may be worth remembering.

Stay In! There is Good Precedent!

Jesus did. He drove out the money changers and called the rulers of the synagogue whited sepulchers, but he used the synagogue and the temple and took part in their services.

Wesley did. He organized a movement within the church that after his death broke away from it, but he himself refused to withdraw.

When the church puts you out, it will be time enough to conclude that the church no longer desires to know the truth and to do the right.

Stay In! Others Wish They Had!

There are two Socialist leaders, former preachers, and a social evangelist of national reputation who wish today that they could proclaim social Christianity from the vantage ground of church organization. They have changed, and the church is changing, since they left.

You will have more company than they had. The pioneering has been done.

Stay In! And Use the Church!

The radical wing of the labor movement continually disputes over tactics. One group says "Bore from within"; the other, "Smash from without."

Those who would proclaim the full message of Jesus have a right to use the machinery of the church to that end. They may justly work from within.

Just before he died, Keir Hardie, the great Socialist leader of England said, "I have spent many years in organizing the working class politically. If I had it to do over again, I think I would give up everything, friends and home if necessary, in order to go forth and proclaim the full message of Jesus."

Where else will you find so large an opportunity to do this as through the educational machinery of the church, with its hold upon future generations.

Stay In! It is a Good Place!

Where else will you find so many folks who want to do right. If you have a vision, show it to them.

You will find just as large a percentage of mean and narrow folk in any other group devoted to social propaganda as you will in the church. Human nature assays about the same anywhere you find it.

Stay In! And—Keep Good Natured!

Remember that negative criticism never gets far. Instead of telling the church what it has not done, show it what there is to do. There are some folks who will still think you are destroying the ark, but they can be laughed at.

Don't expect to change the church over night. A lot of forces have been leading it away from the social meaning of the gospel, for a long time.

Don't expect to change the world in a day. Take the advice of Rauschenbusch and be willing to leave some things to God and our grandchildren.

Learn to think as the geologists in aeons not centuries!

Remember that the long-suffering of the Lord is *our* salvation!

It is also good to see that the world moves in the direction of the social idea of Jesus.

Those who are sure they are seeking his goals may know that tomorrow belongs to them.

Appendix C: Letter to Dean Wicks

Author's note: The precise request that Dean Robert Wicks made, which prompted the following letter from Ward, is not in the Ward papers. Dr. Ward was eighty-two years old when he wrote this concise "rough and hasty attempt" to summarize the development of church-labor relations from John Wesley to 1956. It is an example of his clear mind and his ability to state objectively issues, because he follows his own teaching of considering all sources and facts (an axiom for him). It reveals his wide knowledge of the history of Methodism and the need of history for observation and guidance. (Note the second to last paragraph.) Ward received many requests for this kind of guidance and this is an appropriate example.

*   *   *

March 6, '56

Dear Dean Wicks,

Because of engagements in the city Sunday and Monday this is my first opportunity to sit down and try to answer your request, though I have been thinking and doing somewhat about it.

Assuming your purpose to be a summary sketch the best brief assessment of the contribution of Wesley to the social development of England that I know is an article by Dr. Chas. Little, then President of Garrett, in a symposium put out by the M.F.S.S. in 1910. I can loan you this if desired. An article in the Bliss *Encyclopedia of Social Reform* (Funk and Wagnalls 1897) on Methodism and Social Reform stresses the philanthropic work of Methodist missions both in England and here. Eric North has a book on Early Methodist Philanthropy

(Methodist Book Concern 1914). I was in touch with the Wesleyan Methodist Union for Social Service for some twenty years. They concentrated to begin with on the social teaching of the Bible and so far as I know did not print anything on social and economic thought beyond that. If this interests you, again I can loan. Because I have not heard of anything done by or on British Methodism and recent developments since I left the seminary I have asked Prof. Handy of Church History to check on this point. If he finds anything he will send you the word direct. Should you wish to enquire from England the address of the Union should still be Central Buildings, Westminister, S.W.

As you know the major impact of Methodism here upon social and economic thought prior to the stirrings of the social conscience in the last decade of the 19th Century was over the liquor and slavery issues. On the former Prof. Albion R. King of the Department of Philosophy of Cornell College in Iowa (the town slips my mind) has been doing some research. I remember in the days of the Anti-Saloon League, several Methodist ministers of Mid-West annual conferences were on the supernumerary list for a time to serve as League Secretaries, in the effort to get prohibition.

On the slavery question Wade Crawford Barclay has done a splendid job in his Vol. 2 of the *History of Methodism* on Methodism and Social Reform, and as you may recall he prefaced it with some general remarks about social relations. He tells me that in his Vol. 3 he says something about the awakening of the Methodist social conscience in the eighteen nineties. If this would be of interest to you he will send galley proofs.

The pattern for the development of social and economic thought in the Methodist Episcopal Church was made in the decade between 1907 and World War I. It was woven by the relations between the M.F.S.S. and the General Conference, the educational system of the Church and its Home and Foreign Missions. Whatever kinship with this there was in the Church South was personal and was gathered into the Federation by individual members. This was the reason for the word Federation. The central motif of the pattern is made clear in the first draft of the so-called Social Creed of Methodism which immediately grew into the Social Creed of the Churches. The original pronouncements set forth concrete standards in industrial relations for which the church stands, with an opening and closing general principle, and by these other standards were later worked through the entire life of society. To these were added more inclusive pronouncements by the General Conference and the Council of Bishops. The Federation was instrumental in securing these, along with the various official agencies concerned, by its presentation of Memorials to the General Conference and discussions of them in the Committee on the State of the Church; in the Council of Bishops through its chairmen and several members. Also in this period it had some Gen. Conf. commissions.

This general story, and the various pronouncements, for the formative decade 1907–1917, is told in "A Year Book of the Church and Social Service in the U.S." issued in 1916. Again I can loan a copy if you would like it.

If this Handbook had been continued you would have what you want. As it is if you want it in detail you will need to have someone go through the General Conference and Bishops Council records, also through the general trend of our religious education.

The general course can be seen in the development of the M.F.S.S., and now the M.F.S.A. as portrayed in its Social Questions Bulletin, a copy of which I am sending under another cover. To begin with there were three strains united in the organization: interest in community service by the church; interest in social justice for the wage workers and poorer farmers; interest in Christian socialism with no political connections. (This latter has a bearing on the question of infiltration of religion by communism. The Social Crusade of that period, a midwest movement, was led by some Methodist ministers. One of them, J. Stitt Wilson later left the church and served two terms as Socialist mayor of Berkeley, Calif. seat of the University of California. The Christian socialist movement became strong enough to have a national paper, politically independent—and a Methodist minister was its editor. The whole Debs movement had this strain in it, and some of it went over into the Communist Party. It is that which remained in our church, seeking to express there the ethical imperatives of our gospel, which the witch hunters are attacking.)

The general development in the church runs from social service, to social justice, to social regeneration. In the first period the main task was to develop social consciousness and the social conscience in the church, to socialize its evangelism, its education, its missions, its preaching. Because the social struggle of the period was the right of the wage worker to organize against the increasing organization of industry and finance that was the main objective of the cry for social justice which the church was re-discovering in Jesus and the 8th Century prophets. This interest reached its highest and broadest expression in the study of the steel strike which Bishop McConnell headed. Meantime the continuance of poverty, preventible ignorance and disease and the increasing trend towards war are raising the question of the nature of the social-economic order. So the peace movement appears and becomes official. Then the 1929 economic breakdown compels examination of the need for a change in the nature of the economic process and what Jesus had to say about this. So the Federation decides to reject the method of the struggle for profit etc. etc., and the General Conference of 1932 declares that "The present industrial order is un-christian, unethical and anti-social because it is largely based on the profit motive which is a direct appeal to selfishness." Then the development and use of thermo-nuclear weapons makes it clear that war is no longer war but collective suicide and the Federation decides to stand "for the complete abolition of war," while leaders of our official peace movement personally take the same position.

Thus the development of social and economic thought and action in the church is a progressive application of the religion of Jesus to the moving panorama of history. This of course has been checked by our union with the Church South which did not go through this development, and then by the combined forces of political and economic reaction which are seeking to stop the course of human progress.

So the vital question is, do we go further backward at the approaching General Conference or will the beginning of a turn in the tide that is now manifest register itself there.

This is a rough and hasty attempt to answer your appeal. If I can be of any service as you proceed please let me know.

Faithfully yours,
Harry F. Ward

Bibliography

PRIMARY SOURCES

Manuscripts and Papers

1. American Civil Liberties Union, collection, Princeton University Library. This collection includes many Baldwin letters.
2. American League Against War and Fascism (later American League for Peace and Democracy), papers in Peace Collection, Swarthmore College Library.
3. American League Against War and Fascism, collection, New York Public Library.
4. Amlie, Thomas, papers, State Historical Society of Wisconsin Library.
5. Brightman, Edgar, papers, Boston School of Theology Library.
6. Coe, George Albert, papers, Yale Divinity School Library.
7. Coffin, Henry Sloane, papers, Union Theological Seminary Library.
8. Methodist Federation for Social Service (later Social Action), collection, Drew Theological Seminary Library.
9. Rice, William Gorham, papers, State Historical Society of Wisconsin Library.
10. Spanish Refugee Relief Campaign Records, 1935–1940, Columbia University Library.
11. Ward, Harry F., papers, Union Theological Seminary Library. 11.1 These include Daisy Ward's papers from the beginning of courtship to the end of her life. 11.2. The Religious Freedom Committee Papers are also a part of the Harry F. Ward Collection.

Interviews (Between 1972–1980)

12. Aptheker, Herbert, historian, American Institute for Marxist Studies.
13. Baldwin, Roger, director, American Civil Liberties Union.
14. Ball, Lee H., and wife, Mae, executive secretary, Methodist Federation for Social Action.
15. Beach, Robert, librarian, treasurer of Methodist Federation for Social Action.

16. Bonbright, James C., professor of economics, Columbia University.
17. Chertak, Dorothy (Mrs. William Manealoff), close friend and financial supporter of Ward.
18. Collins, John, director, Clergy and Laity Concerned.
19. Dombrowski, James, principal founder, Southern Conference for Human Welfare.
20. Frenyear, Marion (student of Ward), a pioneer woman minister.
21. Horton, Myles (student of Ward), a principal founder of Highlander Folk School.
22. Lamont, Corliss, philosopher, Columbia University.
23. McConnell, Dorothy, daughter of Bishop Francis McConnell, retired.
24. McMichael, Jack R., executive secretary, Methodist Federation for Social Action.
25. Manealoff, William, businessman, a supporter of Ward.
26. Morford, Richard, executive director, American-Soviet Friendship Council.
27. Muelder, Walter G., former dean, Boston University School of Theology.
28. Nearing, Scott, and wife, Helen, economists and writers, retired.
29. Pasternak, Morris, militant unionist and friend of Willard Uphaus.
30. Peet, Edward L., clergyman, former president of the Methodist Federation for Social Action.
31. Reitman, Alan, associate director, American Civil Liberties Union.
32. Russell, Maude, editor, *Far Eastern Reporter*.
33. Swan, Alfred W., clergyman, First Congregational Church, Madison, Wisconsin.
34. Thomas, Norman, leader, Socialist Party.
35. Thomson, Alan, director, American-Soviet Friendship Council.

Pamphlets

36. American League Against War and Fascism. *Proceedings of the First Congress.* New York, 1933.
37. _____ . *Proceedings of the Youth Congress, Second U.S. Congress Against War and Fascism* (Chicago, Sept. 28–30). New York, 1934.
38. _____ . *Proceedings of the Third U.S. Congress vs. War and Fascism* (Cleveland, Jan. 3–5). New York, 1936.
39. American League for Peace and Democracy. *Proceedings of the People's Congress for Democracy & Peace, Fourth Conference* (Pittsburgh, Nov. 26–28). New York, 1937.
40. _____ . *Seven and a Half Million Speak for Peace, Fifth Conference, American Congress for Peace and Democracy.* New York, 1939.

41. "Congress and Religious Freedom." New York: Religious Freedom Committee, n.d.
42. " 'Free Speech' in Western Pennsylvania." New York: Amer. Civil Lib. Union, No. 7, 1923.
43. Matthews, Joseph B. "The 'United Front' Exposed. The Prepared Statement of Mr. J. B. Matthews, a 'fellow traveler' before the Congressional Committee Investigating Un-American Activities." New York: League for Constitutional Government, 1938.
44. *New American* for March 15, 1936 to March 15, 1939, files, New York Public Library.
45. Rubinstein, Annette T. (ed.). "The Harry F. Ward Sampler." Methodist Federation for Social Action, 1963. 30 p.
46. "Voices for Freedom." New York: Civil Rights Congress, 1951.

Recording

47. Ward, Harry F. "Does This Nation Want the Bill of Rights or a Police State." Amerecord Record for Religious Freedom Committee, 1952.

Books and Articles by Harry F. Ward

An almost definitive bibliography of 20 books and 192 articles has been prepared by Herbert Aptheker and Robert Cohen and published in a memorial volume for Ward entitled *Marxism and Christianity* (New York: Humanities Press, 1968). The titles are included here in chronological order with additions, marked with an asterisk, that I found in my research.

48. "The Turk Must Go." *Northern Oratorical League of Northwestern University*, 1896.
49. *"How To Make Chicago a Better City." *Chicago American.* 1903.
50. "Palestine for the Jews." *World Today* 17 (September 1909):1062–1069.
51. Ed. *Social Ministry: An Introduction to the Study and Practice of Social Service.* For the Methodist Federation for Social Service (New York: Eaton and Mains; Cincinnati: Jennings & Graham, 1910). 326 p.
52. "The Religion of Kipling." *Methodist Review* 9 (October 1910):318–324.
53. "Muscatine." *Survey* 28 (June 1, 1912):362–363.
54. *The Social Creed of the Churches* (New York: Eaton and Mains, 1914). (Reprinted, 1915, Abingdon Press, N.Y.). 169 p.
55. *Social Service for Young People, What Is It?* (Boston: Social Service Department of the Congregational Churches, 1914). 48 p.
56. Ed. *A Yearbook of the Church and Social Service in the United States,* Vol. 1 (New York: Fleming H. Revell, 1914). 328 p.

57. *Social Evangelism* (New York: Missionary Education Movement of the U.S. and Canada, 1915). 145 p.

58. *Poverty and Wealth from the Viewpoint of the Kingdom of God* (New York: Methodist Book Center, 1915). 135 p.

59. "The Church and Social Service, A Selected List (of Readings)." General Theological Library. Bulletin 8, no. 1 (October 1915):9–13.

60. Ed. *A Yearbook of the Church and Social Service in the United States,* Vol. 2 (New York: Fleming H. Revell, 1916). 318 p.

61. *The Living Wage: A Religious Necessity* (Philadelphia: American Baptist Publishing Society, 1916). 24 p.

62. "Establishing World-Wide Social Justice." *World Outlook* 2 (May 1916):3–4.

63. In collaboration with Sidney A. Weston. *The Bible and Social Living,* edited by Henry H. Meyer (New York: Methodist Book Concern, 1917). 196 p.

64. *The Labor Movement, from the Standpoint of Religious Values* (New York: Sturgis & Walton, 1917). 207 p.

65. *Social Duties in War Times* (New York: Association Press, 1917). 168 p.

66. With Henry A. Atkinson. *What Every Church Should Know About Its Community* (New York: Federal Council of the Churches of Christ in America, 1917) (Rewritten by S. M. Harrison & W. M. Tippy). 27 p.

67. *Foreign Missions and Social Service* (New York: Board of Foreign Missions of the Methodist Episcopal Church) 8 p. September, 103, 96–100. 1917.

68. With Richard H. Edward. *Christianizing Community Life.* For Council of North American Student Movements (New York: Association Press, 1918). 180 p.

69. *The Christian Demand for Social Reconstruction* (Philadelphia: W. H. Jenkins, 1918). 126 p.

70. *The Gospel for a Working World* (New York: Missionary Education Movement of the U.S. and Canada, 1918). 260 p.

71. *The Religion of Democracy* (Boston: The Murray Press, 1918). 12 p.

72. "The Present Task of Christian Ethics." Union Theological Inaugural Exercises (1918):18–27.

73. *The New Social Order: Principles and Programs* (New York: Macmillan, 1919). 393 p.

74. *The Opportunity for Religion in the Present World Situation* (New York: The Womans Press, 1919). 66 p.

75. *Social Unrest in the United States* (New York: Methodist Federation for Social Service, 1919). 15 p.

76. "Capital and Labor after the War." *World Outlook* 5 (January 1919):10.
77. "The Russian Question." *Social Service Bulletin* (Methodist Federation for Social Service) (January-February 1919):1–4.
78. "Labor and the New Social Order." *Homiletic Review* 77 (March 1919):222–230.
79. *"Always the Poor." *Epworth Herald.* Mar. 2, 1919. p. 3.
80. "A Statement by Prof. Harry F. Ward." *Christian Advocate* 94, no. 14 (April 3, 1919):434.
81. "The Kaiser and Others: The Treatment of International Offenders in the Light of Penal Reform." *World Tomorrow* 2 (November 1919):298–303.
82. "Bolshevism and the Methodist Church: An Account of the Controversy Precipitated by Prof. Ward." *Current Opinion* 66 (June 1919):380–381.
83. G. Taylor. "The Bolshevism of Prof. Ward." *Survey* 41 (March 29, 1919):920–921.
84. "The Social Revolution and Religion." *Christian Century* 37, no. 14 (April 1, 1920):10–13.
85. "Why I Believe in Giving Justice." *Bible World* 65 (July 1920):348–351.
86. "Some Studies in Christian Fellowship." *Churchman* 15 (December 12, 1920):12–18.
87. "The Bible and the Proletarian Movement." *Journal of Religion* 1, no. 3 (May 1921):271–281.
88. "The Competitive System and the Mind of Jesus." *Christian Century* 38, no. 23 (June 9, 1921):9–12.
89. "The Moral Valuation of our Economic Order." *Journal of Religion* 1, no. 4 (July 1921):416–417.
90. "Christianity in the Modern World." *The Nation* 113 (July 13, 1921):47–49.
91. "The Open Shop Drive." *Christian Work* 111 (July 30, 1921):142–143.
92. "Can the Church Stand Fire?" *The Nation* 113 (August 24, 1921): 195–198.
93. "Which Way Will Methodism Go?" *Methodist Review* 104 (September-October 1921):685–696.
94. "Dies Turns Philosopher." *Christian Century* 34, no. 7 (February 16, 1922):204–206.
95. "West Virginia and the Church." *Churchman* 125, no. 10 (March 11, 1922):14–15.
96. "The Challenge of West Virginia to the Churches." *Christian Work* 112, no. 11 (March 18, 1922):339–340.
97. "The Function of the Church in Industry." *Annals of the American Academy of Political and Social Science* 103 (September 1922):96–100.

98. "Social Science and Religion." *Journal of Religion* 2 (September 1922):476–489.
99. *Repression of Civil Liberties in the United States (1918–1923)* (Chicago: American Sociological Society, 1923). 24 p.
100. "What the Church is Doing for the Workingman: The Challenge of Religion." *Locomotive Engineers Journal* 21 (January 1923):14–17.
101. "Our Political Secret Service." *Christian Century* 40 (April 26, 1923):525–527.
102. "Review of *The Decay of Capitalist Civilization* by Sidney and Beatrice Webb." *New Student* 2, no. 18 (June 2, 1923):8.
103. "Can the Church Influence Public Opinion?" *The Nation* 116 (June 27, 1923):739–740.
104. "Is the Profit Motive an Economic Necessity?" *Christian Century* 40 (June 28, 1923):810–813.
105. "American Christianity and Social Idealism." *American Review* 1, no. 4 (July-August 1923):434–441.
106. "Is Profit Christian?" *Christian Century* 40 (December 27, 1923): 1681–1684.
107. *The Profit Motive: Is It Indispensable to Industry?* (New York: League for Industrial Democracy, 1924). 44 p.
108. "Amnesty and the Civil Liberties Union." (Letter to the editor). *The Nation* 118 (March 26, 1924):3064.
109. "How Can Civilization Be Saved?" *Christian Century* 41 (September 11, 1924):1176–1178.
110. "Professor Harry F. Ward in India: An Interview." *Christian Century* 41 (November 13, 1924):1481.
111. *Ethical Aspects of Industrialism* (Peking: Peking Leader Press, 1925). 88 p. A series of lectures delivered at the National University, Peking.
112. "The Future of the Intellectual Class." *Calcutta Review* 14, no. 2 (February 1925):227–243.
113. "Will Religion Survive in Russia?" *Christian Century* 42 (February 12, 1925):215–218.
114. "Civil Liberties in Russia." *The Nation* 120 (March 4, 1925):234–237.
115. "Lenin and Gandhi." *World Tomorrow* 8, no. 4 (April 1925):111–112.
116. "The New Situation in India." *The Nation* 120 (April 29, 1925): 489–490.
117. "Gandhi and the Future of India." *Christian Century* 42 (June 4, 1925):727–729.
118. "Will Russia Return to Capitalism?" *The Nation* 121 (July 8, 1925): 64–67.
119. "Chinese Christians and the Shooting in Shanghai." *Christian Century* 42 (July 16, 1925):918–920.

120. "The Meaning of Shanghai." *The Nation* 121 (July 22, 1925):108–109.
121. "China Learns from the West." *Christian Century* 42 (July 30, 1925):973–975.
122. "What the Chinese Want." *New Republic* 44 (August 26, 1925):9–11.
123. "Strike! The Students of China Fight for their Country's Freedom." *New Student* 5, no. 1 (October 3, 1925):13–15.
124. "Race Contacts in the World Today." *World Tomorrow* 8 (November 1925):327–329.
125. "The White Boomerang in China: The Patronizing Superiority of the West that is Firing China to End 'Special Privilege.'" *Asia* 25 (November 1925):936–940, 1004–1012.
126. "The Morality of Capitalism." *Kirisutokyo Kenkyu* (Studies in the Christian Religion) 3, no. 1 (November 1925):125–140. (Text in Japanese.)
127. "War Talk in China." *Christian Century* 42 (November 19, 1925): 1438–1440.
128. "The Future of Religion." *World Tomorrow* 8 (December 1925): 372–374.
129. "Meaning of Upheaval in China." *Religious Education* 20 (December 1925):426–429.
130. *The New Social Order: Principles and Programs* (New York: Macmillan, 1926). 384 p.
131. *Creative Ideas in the Orient* (Bloomington, Ill.: Public School Publishing Co., 1926). This is reprinted from *American Review* 4 (December 1926):520–527.
132. "Can China Be Stabilized?" *Christian Century* 43 (January 14, 1926): 46–48.
133. "The Political Puzzle in China." *American Review* 4 (March 1926): 167–176.
134. "Free Speech in China." *The Nation* 122 (March 10, 1926):253–255.
135. "China's Industrial Battlefront." *Christian Century* 43 (March 18, 1926):611–613.
136. "The Place of Religion in the Industrialization of China." *Chinese Students' Monthly* 21, no. 6 (April 1926):12–14.
137. "China's Anti-Christian Movement." *Christian Century* 43 (April 15, 1926):474–476.
138. "The Student Crisis in China and Political Consequences." *Chinese Students' Monthly* 21, no. 7 (May 1926):50–52.
139. "China's Anti-Christian Temper." *Christian Century* 43 (May 13, 1926):611–613.
140. "Plight of the Japanese Preacher." *Christian Century* 43 (August 19, 1926):1034–1036.

141. Will China Turn to Force?" *Christian Century* 43 (October 1, 1926):1231–1233.
142. "The Kingdom of Gold." *World Tomorrow* 9 (December 1926): 246–248.
143. "Growth of the Soul." *Christian Century* 44 (February 24, 1927): 239–241.
144. "Why Violence?" *World Tomorrow* 10 (March 1927):111–114.
145. "Are We Slipping into a Chinese War?" *Christian Century* 44 (May 12, 1927):585–587.
146. "Free Speech for the Army." *New Republic* 51 (July 13, 1927): 194–196.
147. "Anglo-American Relations in China." *Christian Century* 44 (September 1, 1927):1016–1018.
148. "China Tests Our Religion." *Nation* 125 (September 21, 1927): 283–285.
149. "Progress or Decadence." In Kirby Page, ed., *Recent Gains in American Civilization* (New York: Harcourt, Brace, 1928), pp. 277–305; being a reprint of article with same title in *World Tomorrow* 11 (November 1928):463–466, with some additions.
150. "The Challenge of the Chinese Revolution." *China Outlook* 1, no. 4 (March 1, 1928):4–5.
151. "Why I Have Found Life Worth Living." *Christian Century* 45 (March 1, 1928):281–283.
152. "Twenty Years of the Social Creed." *Christian Century* 45 (April 19, 1928):502–504.
153. "A Social Strategy for Religion." *Christian Century* 45 (May 3, 1928):566–568.
154. "The Ministry." *Survey* 60 (June 1, 1928):289–290.
155. "The Function of Faith in Modern Life." *Christian* 4 (July 12, 1928): 532–533.
156. *Our Economic Morality and the Ethic of Jesus* (New York: Macmillan, 1929). 338 p.
157. With Harry Emerson Fosdick and others. *What Religion Means to Me* (Garden City, N.Y.: Doubleday, 1929). 88 p.
158. "Perils of Competition for Private Gains." *World Tomorrow* 12 (January 1929):21–24.
159. "Who Commands the Officer's Reserves?" *Nation* 128 (January 2, 1929):8–10.
160. "Religion and Justice." *Christian Century* 46 (February 7, 1929): 194–196.
161. "The Rauschenbusch Memorial." *Religious Education* 24 (April 1929):297–298.

162. "Religion and Political Corruption." *Christian Century* 46 (June 12, 1929):772–774.
163. "Strategy for a New Economic Order." *World Tomorrow* 12 (August 1929):328–331.
164. *"Civil Liberty for Teachers." *American Teacher* 15 (October 1930): 3–4.
165. "Is Jesus Superfluous?" *Journal of Religion* 10 (October 1930): 471–486.
166. "Stagger Incomes Instead of Jobs." *Christian Century* 47 (November 12, 1930):1385–1386.
167. *Which Way Religion?* (New York: Macmillan, 1931). 221 p.
168. "Jesus' Significance in our Modern Age." *World Tomorrow* 14 (January 1931):15–17.
169. "The Challenge of Unemployment Relief." *Religious Education* 26 (March 1931):200–205.
170. "The Handwriting on the Wall." *Christian Century* 48 (March 4, 1931):304–306.
171. "Religion Confronts a New World." *Christian Century* 49 (February 3, 1932):146–148.
172. "Working for Themselves." *Christian* 8 (May 21, 1932):445.
173. "Pioneers Among the Soviets." *Nation* 134 (June 22, 1932): 696–697.
174. "Soviet Russia, Land of Youth." *Nation* 135 (August 3, 1932): 103–104.
175. "Religion and Anti-Religion in Russia." *Christian* 8 (September 3, 1932):649–651.
176. *In Place of Profit: Social Incentives in the Soviet Union* (New York and London: Scribner's, 1933). 476 p.
177. "Preaching and the Industrial Order." In *Preaching and the Social Crisis*, edited by G. B. Oxnam (New York: Abingdon Press, 1933), pp. 44–62.
178. *Fighting to Live* (New York: American League Against War & Fascism, 1934). 15 p.
179. "Methodists Assail Roosevelt." *Literary Digest* 109 (February 16, 1935):17.
180. "Religion and the Economic Crisis." *Friends Intelligencer* 42, no. 14 (April 6, 1935):213–214. (Abstract of address at Philadelphia Yearly Meeting.)
181. "The Supreme Court and the Aftermath of N.R.A." *Fight Against War & Fascism* 2, no. 9 (July 1935):3.
182. "The Development of Fascism in the United States." *Annals, American Academy* 180 (July 1935):55–61.

183. "The Development of Fascism in the U.S." *Christian Leader* 38 (October 19, 1935):1324–1327.
184. "Judgment Day for Pacifists." *Christian Century* 52 (December 18, 1935):1620–1622.
185. "Christians and Communists." *Christian Century* 52 (December 25, 1935):1651–1653.
186. *The Development of Fascism in the United States* (New York: American League Against War & Fascism, 1936). 7 p.
187. *Spain's Democracy Talks to America: An Interview* (with A. A. MacLeod) (New York: American League Against War & Fascism, 1936). 18 p. Anna Louise Strong took the notes and compiled the material for this publication; it also was published in Toronto.
188. "Ethiopia." *Fight Against War & Fascism* 3 (February 1936):7.
189. "Liberalism at the Crisis." *Christian Century* 53 (March 25, 1936): 463–465.
190. "Greetings on 25th Anniversary." *New Masses* 21 (December 22, 1936):22.
191. *The Fascist International* (New York: American League Against War & Fascism, 1937). 16 p.
192. *Concerted Action for Peace* (New York: American League for Peace & Democracy, 1938). 12 p.
193. *"For Peace and Democracy." *American Teacher* 22 (May 1938): 20–29.
194. *The Neutrality Issue* (New York: American League for Peace & Democracy, 1938). 8 p.
195. "Appeal to Members of the Methodist Federation for Social Service to Boycott Japanese Goods." *Congressional Digest* 17 (April 1938):117.
196. "The Morals of Reaction." *Christian Century* 55 (November 16, 1938):1395–1396.
197. "Introduction." In *Russia Without Illusions*, by Pat Sloan (New York: Modern Age Books, 1939), pp. vii–x.
198. "Non-Cooperation and Conference." *Christian Century* 56 (April 12, 1939):474–476.
199. "The International Situation and America's Relation to It." *Radical Religion* 4 (Summer 1939):22–27.
200. "The Dies Committee and Civil Liberties." *Union Review* 1, no. 1 (December 1939):9–11.
201. *Democracy and Social Change* (New York: Modern Age Books, 1940). 229 p. (Dr. Ward's views and actions provoked expressions of administrative displeasure this year from Union Theological Seminary; the next three entries are reactions to this: Aptheker.)
202. "Union Seminary's Ward." *Time* 35 (February 5, 1940):38.

203. "Valiant Churchman Takes a Well-Earned Rest." *Christian Century* 57 (February 14, 1940):205.
204. "Rebuff to Reaction (Dr. Henry Sloane Coffin rebuffs efforts to remove Dr. Ward from Union)." *New Masses* 35 (June 18, 1940):16.
205. "Star Chambers for Teachers (on the Rapp-Coudert investigation of New York Schools)." *New Masses* 38 (December 24, 1940):11.
206. "As Seen by a Churchman and Scientist." *Soviet Russia Today* (January 1941):16.
207. "30th Anniversary Greetings." *New Masses* 38 (February 18, 1941):26.
208. "Debs, Bourne and Reed." *New Masses* 38 (March 4, 1941):13. (Text of address at 30th anniversary meeting.)
209. "Why Earl Browder Should Be Free." *New Masses* 39 (March 25, 1941):17.
210. "The Crime of Thinking." *New Masses* 39 (April 22, 1941):24. (Concerning witch-hunt in N.Y.C. schools.)
211. "Christianity, an Ethical Religion." *Union Review* 2 (May 1941):7–9.
212. "The Communist Party and the Ballot." *Bill of Rights Review* 1 (Summer 1941):286–292.
213. "Two Democracies: Soviet and American." *New Masses* 41 (November 11, 1941):8.
214. *"School's Out for Geo. A. Coe." *Religious Education* 22 (April 1927):419–447.
215. In 1941 Dr. Ward left Union Theological Seminary; a characteristic story was "25 Years of Social Gospel: Prof. Ward of Union Retires." *Newsweek* 17 (June 30, 1941):46.
216. "Protestants and the Anti-Soviet Front." *Protestant* 4, no. 3 (December 1941-January 1942):62–69.
217. "Religion and Economics: A Bibliography." General Theological Library. Bulletin. 44, no. 2 (February 1942). 8 p.
218. "The Anti-Soviet Front and its Objectives." *Protestant* 4, no. 5 (April-May 1942):35–42.
219. "Is Russia Forsaking Communism?" *Christian Century* 59 (October 28, 1942):1314–1316.
220. "Review of *Victory and After* by Earl Browder." *New Masses* 45, no. 11 (December 15, 1942):23–27.
221. "It is Time To Fight." *Protestant* 5, no. 1 (December 1942-January 1943):56–61.
222. "The Future of the Profit Motive." *Christian Century* 60 (March 31, 1943):389–390.
223. "Pulpits in War." *New Masses* 47, no. 11 (June 15, 1943):15–17.

224. "Reader's Digest Capitalism." *Protestant* 4, no. 10 (June-July 1943):26–31.
225. "The Moral Equivalent of War." *Christian Century* 60 (July 14, 1943):817–819.
226. "Soviet Morals and Morality." *New Masses* 49 (November 9, 1943):17–18.
227. *The Soviet Spirit* (New York: International Publishers, 1944). 160 p.
228. "Fascist Trends in American Churches." *Christian Century* 61 (April 19, 1944):490–492.
229. "Official Protestantism and Soviet Aims." *Protestant* 5, no. 8 (May 1944):37–41.
230. "So You Are Going to Russia." *Motive* 4, no. 5 (May 1944):17–19.
231. "Vatican Fascism." *Christian Century* 61 (June 12, 1944):693–695.
232. "The Soviet Personality." *New Masses* 53, no. 7 (November 14, 1944):13–16.
233. "Black Markets." *New Masses* 54, no. 13 (March 27, 1945):22.
234. "What Is Soviet Democracy?" *New Masses* 57, no. 7 (November 13, 1945):6–8.
235. "Whose State Capitalism?" *Protestant* 6, no. 11 (February 1946): 32–39.
236. *Soviet Democracy* (New York: Soviet Russia Today, 1947). 48 p.
237. "Our Relations to Russia." *Witness* 30, no. 11 (February 27, 1947):8–10.
238. "Method in Madness." *New Masses* 65, no. 7 (November 11, 1947):3–6.
239. "Faith, Phrases and Facts." *Zion's Herald* 125, no. 51 (December 17, 1947):1203–1205, 1222–1223.
240. "Organized Religion, the State and the Economic Order." *Annals, American Academy* 256 (March 1948):72–83.
241. "War and Peace: The Basic Moral Issue." *Soviet Russia Today* 18, no. 11 (November 1950):8–9, 26.
242. "The Necessity for Peaceful Co-Existence." *Soviet Russia Today* 18, no. 12 (December 1950):14–15, 27–28.
243. "Soviet Deeds Back Soviet Words on Peace." *Soviet Russia Today* 18, no. 13 (January 1951):16–17, 34–35.
244. "Concerning Aggression." *Zion's Herald* 129 (May 23, 1951): 798–802.
245. "Why I Believe in Justice." *Bible World* 54 (July 20, 1951):348–351.
246. "The Case of Dr. DuBois." *Jewish Life* 5, no. 9 (July 1951):23–25.
247. "The U.S.S.R.: A Reliable Partner in Peace." In *Thirty-Five Years of the Soviet State* (New York: National Council of American-Soviet Friendship, 1952), p. 11–24.

248. "Judgment Has Begun." *Protestant* 9, no. 1 (January-March 1952): 1–16.
249. "We Were Friends." *Religious Education* 47 (March 1952):88–91.
250. "Professor Ward's Denial." *Christian Century* 70 (August 19, 1953):943. (A letter to editor, denying truthfulness of testimony concerning him offered to the House Un-American Activities Committee.)
251. "Congress and Religion." *Social Questions Bulletin* 46, no. 3 (March 1956):10–11.
252. "MFSA vs. Congress: The Issues." *Social Questions Bulletin* 46, no. 6 (Summer 1956):1–22.
253. "The Federation and Congress." *Social Questions Bulletin* 47, no. 8 (November 1957):34–36.
254. "The Soviet Contribution to Mankind's Future." *New World Review* 26, no. 10 (November 1958):37–42.
255. *The Story of American-Soviet Relations, 1917–1958* (New York: National Council of American-Soviet Friendship, 1959). 95 p.
256. "Crisis in Cuba." *Social Questions Bulletin* 50, no. 7 (September 1960):29–31.
257. "What Destiny—If Man Destroys Himself." World Fellowship of Faiths. (Unpublished.) 1962.
258. *The Harry F. Ward Sampler: A Selection from His Writings, 1914–1963.* Edited by Annette T. Rubinstein (Ardsley, N.Y.: Methodist Federation for Social Action, 1963). 30 p. (Brief excerpts are offered from: *The Church and Social Service* (1914), *The New Social Order* (1919), *Our Economic Morality and the Ethic of Jesus* (1929), *In Place of Profit* (1933), and *Democracy and Social Change* (1940).
259. "What Needs Now To Be Done." *Social Questions Bulletin* 54, no. 3 (March 1964):17–19.
260. *"Backfire." *The Witness* (Episcopal Church) (April 4, 1963):18.
261. *"Jesus and Marx"—Ward's last book—remains unpublished. Copies are held by the family and Eugene P. Link.

SECONDARY SOURCES

Books (Selected)

262. Abbe, George. *The Non-Conformist: The Autobiography of a Conscience.* Boston: Branden Press, 1966.
263. Adams, Frank. *Unearthing Seeds of Fire: The Idea of Highlander.* Winston-Salem, N.C.: John F. Blair, 1975.

264. Allen, Ted, and Gordon, Sydney. *The Scalpel, the Sword: The Story of Dr. Norman Bethune.* Toronto: McClelland and Stewart, 1971.
265. Aptheker, Herbert, and Cohen, Robert (eds.). *Marxism and Christianity.* New York: Humanities Press, 1968.
266. Brightman, Edgar S. *A Philosophy of Ideals.* New York: H. Holt and Co., 1928.
267. Buche, Emory S. (ed.). *The History of American Methodism.* Nashville, Tenn.: Abingdon Press, 1964.
268. Carter, Paul A. *The Decline and Revival of the Social Gospel: Social and Political Liberalism in American Protestant Churches, 1920-1940.* Ithaca, N.Y.: Cornell Press, 1954.
269. Cavert, Samuel McCrea. *Church Cooperation and Unity in America.* New York: Association Press, 1954.
270. _____. *The American Churches in the Ecumenical Movement 1900-1968.* New York: Association Press, 1968.
271. Cockburn, Claude. *The Devil's Decade: The Thirties.* London: Sidgwick & Jackson, 1973.
272. Coffin, Henry Sloane. *A Half Century of Union Theological Seminary 1896-1945.* New York: C. Scribner's Sons, 1954.
273. Dombrowski, James. *The Early Days of Christian Socialism in America.* New York: Columbia University Press, 1936.
274. Donner, Frank J. *The Un-Americans.* New York: Ballantine Books, 1961.
275. Dorn, Jacob H. *Washington Gladden: Prophet of the Social Gospel.* Columbus: Ohio State University, 1968.
276. Dunbar, Anthony P. *Against the Grain: Southern Radicals & Prophets, 1929-1959.* Charlottesville: University of Virginia Press, 1981.
277. Ely, Richard T. *Social Aspects of Christianity and Other Essays.* New York: Thomas Y. Crowell, 1889.
278. Freeman, Joseph. *An American Testament.* New York: Octagon Books, 1973.
279. Goff, Tom W. *Marx and Mead.* Boston: Routledge and Kegan Paul, 1980.
280. Grubbs, Frank L. *The Struggle for Labor Loyalty: Gompers, the AF of L and the Pacifists, 1917-1920.* Durham, N.C.: Duke University Press, 1968.
281. Handy, Robert J. *A Christian America: Protestant Hopes and Historical Realities.* New York: Oxford University Press, 1971.
282. Handy, Robert T. (ed.). *The Social Gospel in America 1870-1920.* New York: Oxford University Press, 1966.
283. Holmes, John Haynes. *I Speak for Myself.* New York: Harper & Bros., 1959.

284. Hopkins, Charles Howard. *The Rise of the Social Gospel in American Protestantism, 1865–1915.* New Haven, Conn.: Yale University Press, 1940.
285. Hughley, J. Neal. *Trends in Protestant Social Idealism.* New York: King's Crown Press, 1948.
286. Jacobs, Leo. *Three Types of Practical Ethical Movements of the Past Half Century.* New York: Macmillan Co., 1922.
287. Johnson, Donald O. *The Challenge to American Freedoms: World War I and the Rise of the ACLU.* Lexington: University of Kentucky Press, 1963.
288. Krueger, Thomas A. *And Promises to Keep: The Southern Conference for Human Welfare, 1938–1948.* Nashville, Tenn.: Vanderbilt University Press, 1967.
289. Lacy, Creighton. *Frank Mason North: His Social and Ecumenical Mission.* Nashville, Tenn.: Abingdon Press, 1967.
290. Lamont, Corliss (ed.). *The Trial of Elizabeth Gurley Flynn.* New York: Horizon Press, 1968.
291. Lamson, Peggy. *Roger Baldwin: Founder of the American Civil Liberties Union.* Boston: Houghton Mifflin, 1976.
292. McConnell, Francis J. *By the Way: An Autobiography.* Nashville, Tenn.: Abingdon Press, 1952.
293. McLaughlin, Wm. G., and Bellah, Robert N. (eds.). *Religion in America.* Boston: Houghton Mifflin Co., 1968.
294. McWilliams, Carey. *The Education of Carey McWilliams.* New York: Simon and Schuster, 1979.
295. Marchand, C. Roland. *The American Peace Movement and Social Reform, 1898–1918.* Princeton, N.J.: Princeton University Press, 1972.
296. Markmann, Charles E. *The Noblest Cry.* New York: St. Martin's Press, 1965.
297. Marty, Martin E. *Righteous Empire: The Protestant Experience in America.* New York: Dial Press, 1970.
298. Meyer, Donald B. *The Protestant Search for Political Realism, 1919–1941.* Berkeley: University of California Press, 1960.
299. Miller, Robert Moats. *American Protestantism and Social Issues, 1919–1939.* Chapel Hill: University of North Carolina Press, 1958.
300. _____ . *How Shall They Hear Without a Preacher: The Life of Ernest Fremont Tittle.* Chapel Hill: University of North Carolina Press, 1971.
301. Milner, Lucille B. *Education of An American Liberal.* New York: Horizon Press, 1954.
302. Moxcey, Mary E. *Some Qualities Associated with Success in the Christian Ministry.* New York: Teachers College, 1922.

303. Muelder, Walter C. *Methodism and Society in the Twentieth Century.* Nashville, Tenn.: Abingdon Press, 1961.
304. Friends of Frank Mason North. *Frank Mason North: Dec. 3, 1850–Dec. 17, 1935 (A Memorial Volume).* n.p., 1935.
305. Niebuhr, Reinhold. *Moral Man and Immoral Society.* New York: C. Scribner's Sons, 1932.
306. _____. *Nature and Destiny of Man.* New York: C. Scribner's Sons, 1941.
307. Scribner, Grace. *An American Pilgrimage;* portions of letters of Grace Scribner, selected and arranged by Winifred L. Chappell, foreword by Harry F. Ward, woodcuts by Lynd Ward. New York: Vanguard, 1927.
308. Wearmouth, Robert E. *The Social and Political Influence of Methodism in the Twentieth Century.* London: Epworth Press, 1957.
309. Welch, Herbert. *As I Recall My Past Century.* Nashville, Tenn.: Abingdon Press, 1962.
310. White, Ronald C., and Hopkins, C. Howard. *The Social Gospel: Religion and Reform in Changing America.* Philadelphia: Temple Press, 1976.

Articles

311. Bingham, June. "Theologian in the Making." *Union Seminary Quarterly Review* 16, no. 2 (Jan. 1961):149–162.
312. Craig, Robert. "An Introduction to the Life and Thought of Harry F. Ward." *Union Seminary Quarterly Review* 24, no. 47 (Summer 1969):331–356.
313. Deegan, Mary Jo, and Burger, John S. "George Herbert Mead and Social Reform: His Work and Writings." *Journal of the History of the Behavioral Sciences* 14 (1978):362–373.
314. Gorrell, Donald K. "The Methodist Federation for Social Service and the Social Creed." *Methodist History* 13, no. 2 (Jan. 1975):3–32.
315. Gutman, Herbert G. "Protestantism and the American Labor Movement: The Christian Spirit in the Gilded Age." *American Historical Review* 72, no. 1 (Oct. 1966):74–101.
316. Handy, Robert T. "Christianity and Socialism in America, 1900–1920." *Church History* 21, no. 1 (March 1952):39–54.
317. Link, Eugene P. "Harry F. Ward." *Social Questions Bulletin* (of Methodist Federation) 63, no. 7 (1973):25–28.
318. _____. "Latter Day Christian Rebel." *Mid-America* 56, no. 4. (Oct. 1974):221–230.

319. _____. "*The Mind of Norman Bethune* by Roderick Stewart," reviewed in *American Review of Canadian Studies* 9, no. 1 (Spring 1979):73–75.
320. McClain, George D. et al. *Radical Religion* 5, no. 1 (1980). Entire issue devoted to Ward and the Methodist Federation for Social Action.
321. McDonald, Dwight. "The Defense of Everybody: Profile of Roger Baldwin." *New Yorker* 29, no. 27 (July 11, 1953):31–55 and no. 28 (July 18, 1953):28–58.
322. Myers, C. E. "Should Teachers' Organizations Affiliate With the American Federation of Labor." *School and Society* 10, no. 256 (Nov. 22, 1919):594–597.
323. Rodd, Nora. "Daisy Kendall Ward: American Woman of Our Time." *Social Questions Bulletin* 55, no. 8 (November 1965):57–60.
324. Szasz, Ferenc M. "The Progressive Clergy and the Kingdom of God." *Mid-America* 55, no. 1 (Jan. 1973):3–17.
325. Taylor, Graham. "The Bolshevism of Professor Ward." *Survey* 41, no. 25 (March 29, 1919):920–921.
326. Ward, Daisy K. "Peace in Democracy." *The Woman Shopper* 3, no. 10 (Dec. 1939):3.

Bound Manuscripts

327. Bean, Barton. "Pressure for Freedom." Thesis. Cornell University, 1955.
328. Crist, Miriam. "Winifred L. Chappell." Thesis. Union Theological Seminary, 1979.
329. Egbert, Carl. "The Thought and Career of H. F. Ward." Term paper, Union Theological Seminary, 1961.
330. Hester, Carl E. "The Thought and Career of Harry F. Ward." Typescript, Union Theological Seminary, 1961.
331. Huber, Milton John, Jr. "A History of the Methodist Federation for Social Action." Typescript, Boston University School of Theology, 1949.
332. Laubenstein, Paul F. "A History of Christian Socialism in America." Typescript thesis, Union Theological Seminary, 1925.
333. Mobbs, Arnold L. "Some Aspects of the Contemporaneous Social Christianity in the U.S.A." Thesis. Union Theological Seminary, 1933.

Index

About the Series

The Academy of Independent Scholars was established in 1979 for proven scholars and creative people wishing to stay productive and in the mainstream of society after retiring from careers in the professions, academia, and industry. Through its central office in Boulder, Colorado, and regional branches, the academy furnishes fiscal and logistical support for individual and group projects and publishes works by its members.

The Academy's Retrospections Series represents a special contribution by members who, through long and especially productive lives, have learned much and, therefore, have much to teach. In a sense, Retrospections are "living histories," providing valuable insight into the circumstances and environment responsible for individual contributions to society.

Lloyd E. Slater
Executive Director
Academy of Independent Scholars

DATE DUE

CARR McLEAN, TORONTO FORM #38-297